AF304813

PRIMETIME

Author's Note

Although in most cases names and identifying elements have been altered, all the stories in this book are based on the real experiences of people in midlife.

Contents

Introduction • Welcome to Primetime..................... 3

PART ONE:
DEBUNKING MYTHS and REWRITING the STORY of MIDLIFE

Chapter 1 • The Myth of the Midlife Crisis 27

Chapter 2 • The Myth of Stability: Can People
Really Change in Midlife? 53

Chapter 3 • Mastering Midlife: Balancing
the Gains and Losses........................ 73

PART TWO:
RIDING the WAVES of GAINS and LOSSES

Chapter 4 • Healthy in Midlife........................... 107

Chapter 5 • Time Is on Your Side 135

Chapter 6 • The Age of Generativity:
The Dynamic Social Network 161

CONTENTS

Chapter 7 ◆ Building Resilience When
Life Throws You Curveballs 193

Chapter 8 ◆ Choosing Wisely at
the Crossroads of Life. 219

Chapter 9 ◆ Beyond Midlife: Reaping the Rewards 245

Conclusion ◆ Life Begins Now 275

ACKOWLEDGMENTS 281

NOTES 285

BIBLIOGRAPHY 315

INDEX 343

PRIMETIME

Welcome to Primetime

I t's not quite a full-blown pejorative, but the term *middle* could certainly use a better publicist.

The middle seat in a car or airplane—uncomfortable. The middle child—overshadowed. The Middle Ages—barbaric. The middleman—unnecessary. Being middle of the road—wishy-washy.

Each of these middles has a negative connotation, not to mention in today's world of striving and status, no one wants to be merely "average," which is what being the middle feels like if we're talking about money, fame, success, health, and happiness. It's perhaps no surprise, then, that when we talk about *middle age*, the first word that comes to mind is *crisis*, followed by talk of gray hair, reading glasses, and achy joints, and a whole host of other things we'd much rather avoid.

But here's "the but." By focusing on all those familiar bad middles, it's easy to forget that in plenty of contexts, being in the middle has its advantages. It can even be desirable, a genuine asset. After all, *middle* means central, a pivot point with the option of moving in different directions, up and down or from side to side or even around. The middle is flexible, and it can be an ideal position or location. The middle of the fairway is the golfer's aim. A line drive up the middle of the baseball field is a promising play. Sitting center stage in the middle of the theater or a sports arena offers some of the most desirable seats in the house. The middle child has older siblings to learn from and younger siblings to teach, potentially giving them an advantage in cognitive and social development. But no one seems to focus on that. Unfortunately, this lopsided look at the middle generally aligns with how we feel about middle age—that is, mostly negative.

My research, supported by decades of evidence from other researchers, demonstrates that the assumption that our middle years are our unhappiest and that aging is something to be feared is flat-out wrong. Studies have shown that many people in midlife have a higher well-being and sense of control than those both younger and older. Positive affect (psychology-speak for pleasant feelings) continues to increase and then stabilizes from early adulthood through midlife, while negative affect (unpleasant emotions) declines from early adulthood through midlife. All in all, it seems pretty clear from the research that not everyone is down in the dumps in midlife.

Not only is this middle-phobic perspective wrong, it distorts the experience of what can be considered our most important decades. In midlife our well-being affects so many others and also how we will fare in later life. Having a negative viewpoint of middle age and aging can affect our health. It can even *shave years off our lives.* With a large share of Americans moving through their middle years in 2025—Gen X, ages forty-five to sixty, are smack in the middle of midlife, the oldest of the millennials, ages twenty-nine to forty-four, are just entering it, and the youngest baby boomers, ages sixty-one to sixty-six, are at the tail end—setting the record straight about midlife has never been more important. If we want to live our best lives in the middle years, we have to take a more balanced and uplifting look at this critical time period. There are challenges, yes, but there are also more opportunities and joys than the received wisdom about midlife would have us believe.

In fact, it's not enough to correct the record on the negative bias we have against midlife, it's time to reveal it for what it really is: Primetime.

For those of you who have been conditioned to be wary, if not downright terrified, of midlife, you might be raising an eyebrow right now. Let me explain:

Over thirty years of research has given me a unique view of this time in our lives, one that is both zoomed in and zoomed out. Before you can really understand a single period of time you have to look at the arc of the human lifespan, which is all about seeing the big picture. For instance, we know that human development is the story of growth and decline. Every human goes through times when they are more in control—making gains socially, emotionally, physically, and psychologically—and times when they are more out of control, losing abilities and opportunities that they once had. When researchers map these experiences over the span of an average person's lifetime, this is what it looks like:

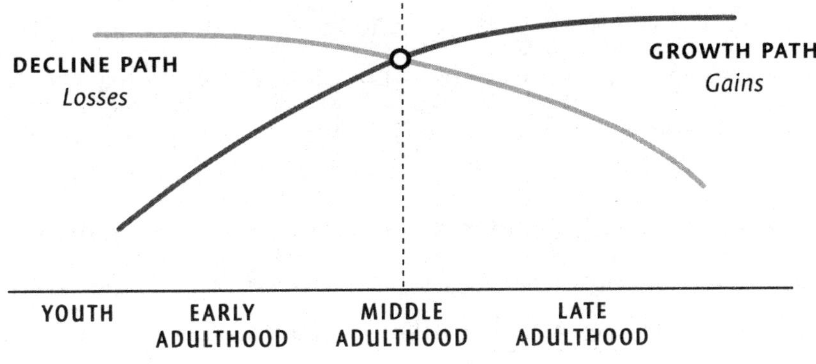

Where the two lines meet—*that* is midlife.

It's the point at which the positives and negatives of aging are just about equal.

If you look at the dark (growth) line in this lifespan figure you see that mid-lifers are still gaining knowledge and experience. They also are growing in terms of emotion regulation, professional accomplishments and productivity, creativity and earnings, new roles in the family, and valuable contributions to the community. All are packaged with the well-earned self-confidence and wisdom gained from experience. We are constantly adding to what we know about ourselves and others, gaining more professional skills, and learning more about our bodies.

The light gray line represents the trajectory of decline over our lives—in speed of processing information, working memory, and functional health. With age we experience losses; our bodies begin to slow down and our immune system weakens. Our responsibilities to others multiply while our time to focus on ourselves diminishes. We may feel that we have less time to accomplish all that we want to. Depression, sleep problems, and financial strain can all surface.

The intersection of these two lines represents Primetime. In other words, the golden moment and opportunity that is midlife.

In midlife we have both knowledge, experience, insight, *and* the capacity to use them. We're still young enough that the major declines in health haven't fully settled in, so instead of finding ourselves hamstrung by limitations, we can explore new opportunities, make a career change, find new love, lean into our creativity, and reinvigorate old relationships. We are more self-aware than ever, and we care much less about what other people think. And while there's no doubt that midlife can bring us temporary lows as new declines settle in (the cranky back, the reading glasses, the hot flashes), the next peak is still right in front of us. Midlife can be much more than popular wisdom would have us believe.

Unfortunately, popular notions of midlife train our focus so tightly on the negative aspects of aging that we miss out on the opportunities for growth. Which means that we don't end up balancing out the losses with wins, wasting the potential of this golden moment when those lines on the graph intersect.

Much of the good, solid information we have about how to leverage our strengths in midlife is not widely known. The aim of this book is to rectify that, and act as an evidence-based guide to the prime of your life. In the chapters ahead I will dispel myths, point out important, hidden truths, and offer actionable tools to help navigate midlife in a balanced way. By the end of the book, I hope you will look at midlife as a time to embrace, grow, and break through.

But before we dive a little deeper into why midlife is pivotal, first we have to answer a burning question.

Midlife by the Numbers

Whenever I go to a party and reveal my research specialty, the first question is wildly predictable: When exactly is middle age?

Whether the person I'm talking to is young or old, there is an almost universal uncertainty about when this critical period of our adult lives begins and ends. There's good reason for this—officially, there is no set age range for midlife. It's generally thought of as the halfway point between youth and old age, but the boundaries feel fuzzy. This is in part because none of us knows how long we're going to live, and also because historical time and circumstance shapes our perception of where we are in the life course. Over the past century "midlife" has been a moving target. In 1900, the average life expectancy was forty-six for men and forty-eight for women. Which means midlife would have been in the twenties.

As of 2025 in the United States the average life expectancy is seventy-nine. But life expectancy is higher in other countries, such as United Kingdom where it is eighty-two, Norway where it is eighty-three, and Japan where it is eighty-five. If we rely on life expectancy as our marker, it suggests the midpoint could begin at different ages—thirty-nine, forty-one, or forty-two—depending on where you live. Life expectancy also varies by sex, with women living on average five or six years longer than men. It also varies by race too, with the highest life expectancy for Asians and Hispanics, followed by Whites and then Blacks and Native Americans.

Of course, these numbers are just rough estimates of what the chronological midpoint of life is. Most people don't typically use this as the way to define midlife—it's much more complex than that. For starters, there are actually many types of age. How old someone is can vary depending on what aspect of life is being considered: biological age, or how your physical health and appearance compare to those who are younger versus those your own age or older; social age, or the roles you occupy like caregiver or mentor; and psychological age, which includes how old you feel. This is why depending on who you ask, the definition of "midlife" can shift dramatically. I've found that many people in their early forties actively resist the idea that they are middle-aged, while many in their late sixties or seventies insist that they are *still* middle-aged. While this is wishful thinking on both ends of the spectrum, it also illustrates how individual markers of midlife can fluctuate over time.

In my research, I typically define midlife broadly as forty to sixty plus or minus ten years, which is to say thirty to seventy. This is the result of many surveys that my colleagues and I have conducted over the last thirty years. When asked when they believe midlife begins and ends, most participants in our surveys say the average ages of midlife are forty to sixty or forty-five to sixty-five. Thus, the heart of midlife is the forties and fifties, even though only a relatively small number live to one hundred, let alone 118 or 120. Yet many people who are in their thirties or sixties and even seventies also consider themselves middle-aged. All told, the number of people who consider themselves "middle-aged" is large. About a quarter of the US population is between forty and fifty-nine.

Adults in midlife typically have more active roles—for instance, parent, adult child, spouse or partner, grandparent, sibling, friend, and coworker—than at any other period of life. Some roles are obligatory, and others are optional, such as service positions in community or religious organizations. However, people of the same chronological age can vary vastly in what life phase they are in with regard to social, family, or work responsibilities. For example, at age fifty, some may have tweens or teens living at home and others may have an empty nest and grandchildren to babysit. In their professional lives, some may find themselves in a mentoring or managerial role at work, while others are striking out on their own as midlife entrepreneurs.

Given the wide variation in the timing of these key milestones and experiences, age is not necessarily the best marker of midlife. Based on my research, I have come to believe that a good way to think of midlife is as a constellation of roles that people are performing in the context of life events and life experiences. In this sense, midlife is when you are in the middle generation, relative to those who are younger or older in the family, at work, or in the community. If we can expand our definition of midlife to include more than just what our age is on paper and recognize that we are serving many important roles for ourselves and others in midlife, it can bring a greater sense of meaning, purpose, and clarity to our experience of the middle years. This new perspective on this time could also go a long way to helping us manage the complicated feelings that we have about it. After all, when exactly middle age occurs chronologically matters far less than how we actually feel about it when we inevitably get there.

The Hinge: Why Midlife Is Important

Regardless of the exact age you believe middle age begins and ends, we know this: Midlife is the hinge point between the first half and the second half of our lives.

Who we were *before* and who we want to become *after* middle age presses in on us from both sides. Midlife is when the bill from adolescence and early adulthood comes due. What that bill looks like varies wildly depending on what our lives have looked like thus far. Unresolved trauma, damaging relational patterns, and neglect of our physical health often rear their head during this time, forcing us to reckon with what has come before. On the more positive side, if we've been lucky, we are resting more easily in our relationships than ever before, we have built up a professional reputation that we can leverage, and we are more comfortable in our bodies.

When we look to the future, if we are wise, we'll see that midlife is *the* moment to build a strong foundation for our sixties, seventies, and beyond. There is no better time to start eating right, exercising, and strengthening your social network. Spiritually and emotionally, we can begin the important work of reflecting on what we have and what we wish for ourselves in the second half of our lives. Do we have a strong purpose? Do we feel ready for what's ahead? How are we feeling about our mortality these days? Making these connections between past, present, and future helps us optimize middle age by taking control of what we can—how we face what happened in our past, and how we will prepare for the future.

Another aspect of midlife that makes it such a pivotal moment is the profound link to both older and younger generations. By embracing the role of a bridge between this divide, we have the opportunity to not only mentor and support those younger than us, but care for and connect with those in their elderhood. We can glean wisdom and meaning from relationships on both sides of the age divide, but just as importantly, we are contributing and caring, which are both well-evidenced approaches to boosting your life satisfaction quotient. Generativity—the quality of care and concern for others—is at a high point in midlife. By focusing on the positive aspects of this unique position and mitigating the more draining aspects of being a caregiver or mentor, we can find a lot of meaning in our usefulness to others. Mid-lifers have valuable skills to teach and wisdom to impart. By doing so we can be filled with the sense that we are making our mark on the world and positively impacting others. This is truly a win-win, because the peaks of generativity we experience in midlife benefit others greatly. Mastering this balance between concern for others and care for ourselves is a test of boundaries to be sure, but it can also become a superpower that helps carry us through the obstacle course that is midlife.

The beauty of being in the middle is that we can move in so many new directions if we choose, whether our tweaks are small or our changes radical. When people make big moves during this time, some think of it as a midlife crisis (more on this in the first chapter). Yet, if we see midlife as the pivot point it truly is, then it is natural to expect ups and downs and movement in different directions.

In midlife, we find ourselves truly in the middle—not just of our lives, but in the middle of other people, and in the middle of whatever tasks we are trying to complete. This often creates conflict, tension, stress, and a need to prioritize competing demands from those older and younger at home and those who are more senior or junior in the workplace. The need to balance roles and juggle demands can be a primary source of problems and stress, creating an urgent need for multitasking with little time for leisure. All of this transpires in the context of physical changes in health and fitness, hormonal upheaval, and cognitive changes in memory, mental flexibility, and reaction time. It's no surprise that being in the middle of life can be a challenging time, but it can also be deeply rewarding. Until now, much of what we've known about midlife has been born of stereotypes, fear, and a vacuum of information and data. Luckily, now we have science to fill in the blanks.

The Science of Midlife

As the director of the Lifespan Lab at Brandeis University in Massachusetts, I conduct research to better understand the psychosocial and behavioral aspects of midlife and how they can either help protect our health or increase the likelihood or risk of decline and disease. I am one of a small group of psychologists who study the midlife period from a lifespan developmental perspective. What this means is that we consider how and why people change physically, cognitively, psychologically, and socially before, during, and after midlife. The lifespan view doesn't focus on one age, per se. To understand midlife, we examine the processes of change from early to late adulthood. While the focus of my research is midlife, we consider what came before to impact it, and what comes later because of it.

Many of our studies revolve around testing out strategies that can help mid-lifers adapt to the inevitable changes in functioning that they will face so that they can live happier and healthier lives. For the last thirty years the focus of my work has been on tracing the nature of midlife to define its characteristics *as it is being lived*—not as it is being portrayed by memes and deep-seated societal fears. The aim of my research is to better understand what is really going on in the lives of mid-lifers and find evidence-based answers to the most pressing questions about this time period: Does everyone go through a midlife crisis? What are the losses of midlife that hit us the hardest? What are the parts of aging that make us feel more confident and hopeful than ever? How can we regain a sense of control in a time that often feels stressful and chaotic? How will this stage of life affect our physical health and functioning and what can we do about it? What can we do in midlife to ensure that we stay healthy and happy into old age?

In a time of great uncertainty and change, our sense of control is dwindling, with stress and anxiety rising not only among those in midlife but among younger generations as well. Major events and experiences such as the pandemic, school shootings, violence, climate change, crumbling infrastructure, inflation, political divisiveness, and misinformation leave us all on shaky ground. These circumstances can undermine our sense of security and agency, and many feel helpless with the belief that even if you do everything right, things are unlikely to go as planned. For people in midlife right now, focusing on maintaining health and well-being becomes even more important given how out of control the outside world can feel. Recent research findings regarding deaths of despair due to overdoses and suicide and the loneliness epidemic show us that many, many people are indeed struggling in midlife.

Plus, getting older is often just strange. And hard. And confusing.

In this book, we will look at the surprising research around midlife with an eye toward understanding how those who are managing to find happiness and health are doing so despite the many challenges. We'll grapple with the reality that it is inevitable that we will experience both gains and losses and learn how to tip the balance in favor of gains. I've come to believe that the middle years are so central and so misunderstood and undervalued that I want to share insights and strategies that are based on my life's work, and the work of many others. The science of midlife is young but robust, and tracing its lineage can help us understand why the misconceptions and hidden opportunities of this time period are just now coming to light.

The Lifespan Perspective

When I started studying psychology in the 1970s, scholarship on midlife did not exist. Developmental psychology was solely focused on infancy, childhood, and adolescence, while the fields of gerontology and geriatrics focused on the problems of old age. What was ingrained in students of psychology by the writings of classic scholars such as Sigmund Freud and Jean Piaget was that by about age twelve, we reach the final stages of emotional and cognitive development. Even though their contemporaries Carl Jung and Erik Erikson had paved the way for the possibilities of development throughout life, for many more decades personality trait psychologists believed we are born with our personalities, which remained stable throughout life. We now know that a static adulthood is a fiction and that it is possible to change in meaningful ways throughout life.

I was fortunate to be at the right place at the right time when views of human development were shifting. My senior year of college I met Freda Rebelsky, whose name was apt—she was a sort of scientific rebel, a trailblazer who had the pluck to teach a course called Post Adolescent Development at a time when almost no one believed there was such a thing. In her class there were many new terms and concepts I found intriguing, and sometimes baffling. I decided I wanted to learn more about this approach, and I applied to graduate school to work with the psychologist Paul Baltes, whose first book, *Life-span Developmental Psychology*, was the text we used in Rebelsky's course. I consider myself lucky that he was assigned as my advisor, and I met him on my first day of graduate school.

Under his guidance, it wasn't long before I was hooked on the life-span perspective. At the most basic level it espoused the simple, and at the time novel, notion that it was possible to grow and develop throughout adulthood, which I found fascinating and compelling. While this is something we now take for granted, trust me when I say that back then it was radical.

In the beginning, most of the lifespan research on adulthood and aging was cross-sectional. Which means it compared people from two different age groups rather than following the same people over time as they age, which is called longitudinal research. For example, a cross-sectional study on cognitive abilities might compare test scores of older adults, ages sixty and above, with college students ages eighteen to twenty-one, usually from introductory psychology classes. Typically, the older adults performed worse on these assessments compared to the students, and the findings painted a rather bleak picture of abilities in later life. Scholars such as Baltes, John Nesselroade, and K. Warner Schaie put these results in perspective, showing that the younger and older age groups came from different birth cohorts (generations) and comparisons did not necessarily shed light on what happens as people age. Most of the older adults in the studies either had not gone to college or had been out of school for over forty years. No wonder they didn't fare well in comparison to students who were very familiar with taking these types of tests.

Lifespan researchers knew it was critical to understand how people aged, rather than just to examine those who were already older, as the gerontologists were doing at the time. To do this, they decided to focus on the processes of aging by following the same people over time. We considered the early origins as well as the more recent influences on development. This would require longitudinal studies, which were expensive and hard to get funded. Luck broke our way in the 1990s and would forever change the course of my career as a result.

In 1990, sociologist Bert Brim proclaimed that midlife was "the last unchartered territory of the life course." At that time most of what we knew about midlife was from clinicians, which painted a picture of midlife primarily as a time of crisis and difficulty. I was invited to join a group of twelve experts on human development who would meet several times a year to plan extensive research about the middle years. Our Research Network on Successful Midlife Development, named MIDMAC, was funded by the John D. and Catherine T. MacArthur Foundation and later by the NIH. MIDMAC helped put the scientific study of midlife on the map. One of our crown jewels is the Midlife in the United States (MIDUS) study. We wanted to know what comes before, during, and after middle age, so we have studied a group of over ten thousand people ages twenty-five to seventy-five from across the country. This huge age spread has enabled us to capture data on how people change in the transitions from early adulthood to midlife, then midlife to old age. We've followed them for over thirty years, resulting in one of the largest and most significant longitudinal studies on midlife. The findings and insights in this book are drawn from MIDUS as well as other research studies that I as well as others have done. It's no accident that MIDMAC's logo is an hourglass that is half-empty or half-full depending on your perspective. Much of what we have found about midlife shows that both perspectives are valid, which of course deeply contradicts the mostly glass-half-empty perspective we are fed from an early age.

In view of the thirtieth anniversary of the MIDUS study, while we still have much to learn, it's safe to say that we now know a lot about what really happens in midlife and what feeds into whether or not someone is more or less happy and healthy at this time in their lives. One of the concepts that anchors the insights in this book is the overarching principle of lifespan psychology—that there are both gains and losses throughout life. However, the balance of increases and decreases also shifts *across* life, as is illustrated in the lifespan image. In fact, the two trajectories depicted are the individual data points that constitute the arc of decline versus growth with their intersection in midlife. In childhood and early adulthood, the primary motivation in all endeavors is toward growth. We add to our repertoire as we learn the ways of the world. As we enter the middle years, a primary goal is to preserve what we have and make sure we use our expanding experience and knowledge for the good of ourselves and others. In later life, a key focus is to deal with or avoid decrements as much as possible. As physical and mental abilities start to wane, concerted effort is needed to counteract decreases in functioning and to compensate for any unavoidable losses. Throughout life, the overarching goal is to maximize the gains and minimize the losses.

While the framework of gains and losses in midlife is the fruit of MIDUS and the north star of this book, there are other concepts from the lifespan approach that are important to our understanding of midlife. The research we have done over the last thirty years has shown:

✦ **Each of us is unique.** Some people are happier and healthier than others. It seems obvious, but the reason is that people change over the course of their lifespan based on highly individual factors like genetics, personality, trauma, and behavior. In other words, there is no one midlife template. Any cultural characterization that tries to act as a stand-in for everyone's experience of midlife is never going to be accurate.

✦ **The seesaw effect.** There's also variability in the midlife experience *within* an individual person. How people feel in midlife fluctuates. Some days they might feel younger and other days they might feel their age. As aches and pains, conflict and contentment come and go, we see that each person can have ups and downs and differences over time. That's why it's critical to not just compare one person to another, but the same person from day to day, month to month, or year to year. Only then will you get a clearer picture of their true experience of midlife.

✦ **You are more flexible than you think.** When we understand plasticity—how changeable, flexible, modifiable, and resilient—we realize that what you see is not necessarily what you get. There is always room for improvement. While the natural course of aging is one of decline, there are plenty of things you can do to minimize the decline or delay it. Even if stamina declines, there is evidence that muscle strength and mobility can be increased well into the nineties with high-resistance weight training. Cognitive training programs lead to learning new things and increasing synapses. Aerobic activity can lead to increasing blood flow to the brain, benefiting memory. In other words, it's never too late.

+ **You can't escape cause and effect.** Research on midlife shows clearly that what you do, and what has happened to you, has consequences. In our studies we focus on the long-term and short-term changes that play out over the course of a life. You might not think that early childhood experiences can reach into midlife and impact your health, but they can. However, it's important to remember that given neuroplasticity, our destinies are not predetermined—there's plenty we can do to mitigate the damaging effects of early childhood trauma and toxic stress.

+ **Consider the context.** If you think that what affects your experience of midlife is solely about genetics or behavior, you'd be mistaken. There are age-graded influences—things that typically occur around the same age for most people (menopause, retirement). There are historical influences—things that happen to everyone regardless of age, but they may have different effects *depending* on your age (pandemic, Great Recession). And, of course, there are nonnormative influences—things that affect you but are not common to everyone, such as divorce, car accidents, winning the lottery, or a health crisis. And finally, there are contextual influences—environment, culture. Life is all about context, so before you blame yourself too much for the parts of midlife that you are struggling with, consider the role that context plays!

+ **There's a model for that.** In midlife, decisions start to take on more weight, and there is a way to make better decisions. It's called the SOC model, which stands for Selection, Optimization, and

Compensation. Selection means choosing wisely and being selective, understanding that you can't do everything. Optimization is where you smooth the way for your decision to be a success by practicing, gaining experience, and anticipating different outcomes. Compensation is all about having backup plans, finding alternatives, new opportunities, substitutions, and modifications so you can follow through on your decisions and not get derailed. When it comes to locking in an exercise routine or meeting a goal of learning a new language, the SOC may get you further than old habits.

+ **What happens in midlife doesn't stay in midlife.** Lifespan researchers have validated what we already know but may not always put into practice—you have better outcomes on all measures of health when you nip a problem in the bud. We know that when we focus on actions in early adulthood, we may be able to prevent problems in midlife, and when we look at actions in midlife, we may be able to prevent problems later in life. Whether it's high cholesterol or low muscle mass, taking care of the problem in midlife means that it won't grow into a nightmare later on. Early detection, screenings, and blood tests can provide a baseline for your health in midlife and identify where you need to take action.

These concepts are both the gifts of the lifespan psychology approach and the themes that this book will come back to again and again in the context of real lives. In the chapters to come, we'll see how myths, personality, health, time, relationships, curveballs, and decisions in midlife affect real people by highlighting stories of mid-lifers in the thick of it all. We'll see how the research findings of MIDUS and many other studies can help us better balance the gains and losses, the challenges and joys of midlife.

Writing Your Own Midlife Story

The research on midlife—MIDUS and beyond—shows us a more nuanced and hopeful picture of midlife than fits comfortably in a pithy newspaper headline. What we have found is that the picture of midlife resolves into something altogether more beautiful and fascinating than the one-dimensional depictions we've been imbibing all our lives. Midlife can be a time of reckoning, but it can also be a vehicle for transformation. It can drive us crazy with its demands on our time but also lift us up when we finally sit back to look at just how *full* our lives have become—full of love, challenge, joy, and deep meaning. Much of this ache and exaltation happens on its own; this time of life is a fast-moving train you're on whether or not you realize you bought a ticket. Once we know what the opportunities are in midlife instead of just the challenges, we can get off autopilot and be more intentional in working toward making the most of your "one wild and precious life," as the poet Mary Oliver famously put it, and setting ourselves up for a happier, healthier life for years to come.

So, whether you are just entering middle age or have been navigating it for some time, by using this golden moment in the middle to look both backward and forward, you have the opportunity to make the changes that lead to greater control over your health and well-being so your present *and* your future can be bright.

Primetime offers you a new, evidence-based lens with which to see midlife, and a fresh set of tools to navigate the terrain so that you find yourself enjoying more ups than downs. The chapters ahead will provide you with plenty of room for reflection, helping you to make sense of the past and imagine future possibilities. Beyond that, where there are strategies for enhancing gains and compensating for losses, I provide some tools and the guidance to help you use them.

This book presents an up-to-date account of the latest scientific research on the middle years of life and covers what we know about the physical, psychological, cognitive, and social changes that accompany our middle years, illuminating the potential to harness a sense of control, mastery, and well-being in the face of the challenges and constraints, gains and losses. Far from a lost horizon, midlife is a unique and profound vantage point. We have a chance to assess what truly matters. And, having lived a good while, our experience in life can give us the confidence to pivot, be it a little or a lot.

This is a far cry from the view of aging and midlife that many people are bringing to the book. So many people on the cusp of midlife are confused, sad, and fearful about what the rest of their lives are going to look like. They want to know if it's going to be hard and if there's a chance to make it better. The answer to both is yes—this is a period of life, like all the others, that has its tough moments. But we can also make it better. Especially when we peel away the layers of stigma that hide the possibilities for joy and discovery that are available to us all.

Which is why before we jump into how to make midlife our best life, we have to take a closer look at the myths and misconceptions, so we know exactly where to start.

DEBUNKING MYTHS and REWRITING the STORY of MIDLIFE

Chapter 1
The Myth of the Midlife Crisis

Hoping for the best, prepared for the worst,
and unsurprised by anything in between.

—MAYA ANGELOU

When the pandemic hit in early 2020, three college friends decided to start up a group chat on Marco Polo, a video-messaging app. They were all turning forty within the next six months, which was how it all started—birthday messages. Eventually, they realized how nice it was being in touch again, so they kept sending video messages back and forth. It was a good way to stay connected (despite living in different time zones) and help each other through what they hoped would be a short-lived, though frightening historical blip. Four years later, the pandemic habit had stuck, and they were still swapping videos of themselves recorded while they waited at the bus stop, made coffee in the morning, or walked to pick up a kid from school. Reflecting back on the group chat, they marveled at how much had changed in the last four years for each of them when it came to jobs, relationships, emotional ups and downs, and health challenges.

Life in the intervening years had looked very different for each of them. Ravi lost his job at a tech company where he'd worked since he was fresh out of college. At age forty-three in a youth-obsessed industry, he failed to find steady employment for six months before he decided to open his own consultancy and pray that clients would follow. A year later it was going okay, but finances were tight since he and his wife had their third child. Every time one of the kids needed to go to the doctor (which was all the time, it seemed), he winced thinking about the bill they would get. Between the stress of hustling for new clients and the lack of sleep, his lifelong struggle with depression fired up again. He was drinking too much beer and staying up late binge-watching British police procedurals, yet he assured his friends he was muscling through. His wife, of course, had a front-row seat and insisted he go see a therapist; he agreed it wouldn't be a bad idea. After the first ten emails he got back from prospective therapists letting him know that there was no availability or they didn't take his self-employed insurance, he gave up. For the time being, he felt like talking with his friends Emily and Skye over Marco Polo was keeping him grounded, and he was begrudgingly considering cutting back on his commitment to expensive microbrews.

On the other side of the country, Emily watched this all play out on Marco Polo and felt bad that Ravi was having such a rough time. Some days it felt hard to give the report on her life because things were going shockingly well. The relaxing of work-from-home rules during the pandemic allowed her to leave a job she hated but was tied to because of its flexibility. Now there were plenty of other design firms that needed account executives and would let them work from home. She not only got an offer from a much better company across the country, they also gave her a substantial raise. Then, unexpectedly, she got pregnant. Already a stepmom to two middle school boys, apparently she and her husband were adding another one to the mix. At forty-three, she had given up on the idea of having her own kids, even though she wanted them. She had met her husband only two years earlier and he'd been clear from the beginning that he didn't want more children. Emily thought she'd made her peace with it, but the reality of a life growing inside her changed everything. After weeks of painful back-and-forth, her husband changed his mind too—they decided to go for it. When the pandemic started, she had thought her life was going in one direction, but this last, sweet little curveball made her realize just how fast things can change—even in your forties when you think everything is settled.

Then there was Skye. Just a few years earlier she would have had a hard time hearing about Emily's unexpected news. When they first started Marco Polo-ing, it was difficult to admit to her friends just how overwhelmed she felt. She and her husband Drew had been through fertility hell trying to get pregnant and it had exposed all the painful cracks in their relationship. Fighting about whether to do IVF was just the beginning of a seismic year of couples therapy, separation, and eventually, divorce. Even though Skye acknowledged that she and Drew had grown apart, letting go of a fifteen-year relationship stirred up insecurities and fears she didn't even know she had. And it also brought up questions about the kind of relationship she really wanted to be in. The idea of divorce was something she had never considered before; it was against her core values. She had worried about how her family would react as she knew that her parents and siblings believed you should do whatever you can to work things out in a marriage. While still healing the wounds of her breakup, Skye forced herself to start dating again. At one point Ravi joked that he was surprised she didn't need a spreadsheet to keep track of all her dates. While she remembered dating as a special kind of hell in her twenties, Skye was shocked to find out that dating in her forties was actually fun. A lot of fun. She had less inhibitions, she knew who she was (for the most part), and now she definitely knew what she didn't want. Seeing it reflected in the eyes of new friends and lovers, slowly she realized that she was becoming more and more herself, a person she liked in a way she never had before. As she fell in and out of love, went to dinner with new friends, and traveled the world with her sister, Skye was always updating Ravi and Emily, who were genuinely thrilled for her.

In just four short years at the beginning of their forties, these three friends saw each other through ups and downs both large and small. They continued sharing about their lives in real time, and also started trading ideas about where they should get together to celebrate their fiftieth.

———————

This may seem obvious, but there is no one experience of midlife. As the three stories above illustrate, it hits everyone differently. Some have ups, some have downs, and many are on autopilot, barely noticing they have entered this transitional zone. That being said, our ideas about midlife—what it looks like, what it feels like—are often flattened and distorted by pop culture, misleading statistics, and clickbait headlines. These ideas about middle age tend to skew negative, no matter the cause. Yet the most prevalent negative interpretations of midlife are not supported by the research. The truth is so much more hopeful and frankly, interesting. As with most rites of passage like puberty, marriage, and parenthood, the realities of midlife are far more nuanced than the cultural perceptions, or even our own fears, would have us believe.

Until relatively recently, our understanding of this time of life has existed within a scientific vacuum, so it's no wonder that our notions of what it means to be middle-aged have been less than comprehensive. Luckily, a lot has changed, and the latest research on midlife deeply complicates the cultural narratives that developed in lieu of science. While there could be a whole book written on debunking the myths of midlife, *this* book will devote just two chapters to the most pernicious and problematic. Because before we can begin to embrace the full reality of midlife, we have to understand more about why we're either dreading it or ignoring it.

Myth: The Midlife Crisis Is Inevitable

If you ask someone what comes to mind when they hear the word *midlife*, 99.9% of the time the answer will be very specific: crisis.

That's why many people might look at the surface details of what Ravi and Skye went through and identify it immediately as a midlife crisis. The trope of the midlife crisis is so deeply embedded in our cultural lexicon that it's easy to think we know what it is and how it operates. This is unfortunate, even disempowering. Instead of prompting us to look deeper, it often leads people to dismiss these experiences as either "just a phase" or evidence of a character flaw. Cultural shorthand and stereotypes like the "midlife crisis" are a failure of curiosity, and they can lead to alienation, misunderstanding, and loneliness for those in the thick of midlife. They are at once totalizing (as if *everyone* goes through a crisis) and deficient. It captures the challenge but not the transformation.

This time of life is associated almost universally with struggle and turmoil, which is why the notion of the midlife crisis makes for juicy novels, television shows, and movie plots. Divorce, radical career changes, substance use disorders, and obsessions with maintaining a youthful look all get pinned on the midlife crisis. Considering how solidly the midlife crisis is embedded in our collective consciousness, we'd be forgiven for thinking that it is a theme as old as time. Surely our ancestors were stricken with the same midlife maladies—after all, they were human and a good midlife crisis is a rite of passage, right? It's a natural human phase, no?

Not exactly.

The origin of the midlife crisis can be traced to a 1965 article by Canadian psychoanalyst Elliott Jaques—only sixty years ago. He observed that the creativity of artists plummeted in their mid-to-late thirties and he attributed this to existential anxiety and the fear of impending death. He also introduced the idea of life going "downhill" after forty. Interestingly, it wasn't Jaques who came up with this, but a patient he quotes: "Up till now life has seemed an endless upward slope, with nothing but the distant horizon in view. Now suddenly I seem to have reached the crest of the hill, and there stretching ahead is the downward slope with the end of the road in sight—far enough away, it's true—but there is death observably present at the end."

Since then, the midlife crisis has remained lodged in our cultural consciousness. But only recently was there a blip on the scientific radar that *seemed* to support it.

Enter, the U-shape of Happiness.

In 2008, economists David Blanchflower and Andrew Oswald began plotting happiness on a graph using data from thousands of surveys of people all over the world. The surveys asked people to rate their happiness or life satisfaction on a 10-point scale from 0— the worst possible life—to 10, the best possible life. Scores typically ranged from 7 to 9 across many different ages but the result showed a distinct U shape, in which those in their late forties and early fifties reported the lowest life satisfaction and as a result were hanging out at the bottom of the curve. The nadir is said to occur at age 47.2— right smack in the middle of midlife. So, according to this research, our happiest years are our twenties and sixties, with a lot of struggle in between. In 2012, Oswald even published a research article claiming the U-shape findings are present across species, with apes also showing evidence of more negative moods during middle age.

This work, done primarily by economists, seemed to revive the cultural appetite for the midlife crisis. The news that happiness plummets in midlife became fodder for many a media headline, making its way to the pages of *The New York Times*, *The Economist*, *The Guardian*, *The Washington Post*, and many others. *The Atlantic* even published a story in 2014 with an image of a man slumped woefully over the door of a bright red convertible.

At this point, all signs seemed to point to the midlife crisis as being a done deal. A psychoanalyst identified it, economists proved it. What more can be done other than to bite our nails when we turn forty and hope for a mild case? But as with most cultural phenomena and popularized science, there's much more to the story than that. It turns out that the bend of the U shape isn't quite as dramatic (or even solid) as the headlines would have us believe.

Reality: There Is No Universal Crisis

Thanks in part to the popularization of the concept by journalist Gail Sheehy, who wrote the best-selling book *Passages: Predictable Crises of Adult Life* in 1976, and the U-shape research, one of the most prevalent myths of midlife is that the midlife crisis is universal, meaning that it's something normal that we *all* go through. But in the 1990s, as part of the MIDMAC research network, MIDUS investigators quietly turned this myth on its head. Initially the midlife crisis wasn't on the docket for evaluation, but with all the hubbub animating the concept, we felt compelled to investigate it in a large representative sample. Up until then, most of what was known about it came from clinicians who were treating people who came to them with problems big and small.

In our MIDUS surveys we found that only a small percentage of people reported having a midlife crisis, in the 10 to 20% range. Other studies have backed up our central findings, but also added the nuance that a significant portion of respondents reported having a midlife crisis either before (25% of men and 18% of women) or after middle age (9% of men and 17% of women). Now, 10 to 20% of people having a midlife crisis is certainly *some* of us, but it's definitely not *all* of us. Far from universal, this amounts to about one out of every five people experiencing what they describe as a crisis in midlife. And some research suggests that those percentages could be even lower because of the wide disparity in definitions of what a midlife crisis actually is. Only about 10% of people surveyed had what might be called a midlife crisis in the sense that their concerns were tied to this specific age, that is, worries about getting older and running out of time, or feeling dissatisfaction with where they ended up. Others who reported having a midlife crisis actually only reported on having experienced difficult times, such as losing a job or getting a divorce, which of course could happen at any point in their lives. Either way, this is a far cry from the life-shattering, ego-dissembling portrayal of the inescapable midlife crisis that we have all become so accustomed to. It's neither inevitable nor universal.

When news of the U shape came out, those of us who study psychological development in midlife were left to make sense of the disparities in the findings. When we looked closer at the U-shape data we discovered that the graph itself, while visually compelling, was problematic. Feeling the need to correct the record, I, along with my colleagues Nancy Galambos, Harvey Krahn, and Matthew Johnson, wrote a review of the U-shape research in 2021 suggesting that their conclusions were overblown and misleading. We pointed out that there are a couple of problems with taking the U-shape findings as gospel. First, the giant dip in the graph isn't as significant as it appears from the image—in fact, the average rating for midlife happiness on a scale from 1 to 10 was only about .5 lower than for those younger and older. This could be more reflective of the normal stressors of this time of life than a huge, splashy crisis.

Another issue is that the U-shape research relies most heavily on cross-sectional data, which compares people from two or more different groups at a moment in time, rather than the same people over a long period of time. Cross-sectional studies look at different birth cohorts, which can be valuable—but you have to be careful because being in different generations can really change things. For instance, the most recent survey of the World Happiness Report published in 2024 revealed that in the US, Gen Z, who are in their mid-to-late teens and twenties, and millennials, who are mostly in their thirties, are unhappier than older generations. This worsening of mental health among more recent generations in the US has also been found for depression, anxiety, and loneliness. Many speculate (reasonably) that the combination of lost rights, the missing COVID-19 years, reliance on social media, economic pressure, and increased political polarization is to blame. It stands to reason that the level of life satisfaction that these generations will feel when they make it to midlife may be quite different from the generation that is in midlife right now. If you followed them longitudinally, you would see with more accuracy if there really is a dip in their midlife happiness. But if you don't, then you're just comparing them to a group of people whose life circumstances in both youth and midlife were radically different. In this way, generational differences can skew the results and lead to misunderstanding the picture of middle age.

After the evidence showing the prevalence of mood disorders and anxiety among young adults began to stack up, even Blanchflower couldn't ignore the data. He now says he was wrong about the U shape. What he has now observed is precisely what we had identified in our 2021 paper. It is young adults who seem to be at a low point, showing increasing evidence of mental health issues. This shows us the importance of considering both age and generation when discussing trends across a lifetime. The most recent results do not change the levels of life satisfaction that the middle-aged adults reported when they were studied by Blanchflower and colleagues from 2010 to 2017. What is different now is the *interpretation* relative to the younger age groups who report worse mental health than those currently in midlife. There is no longer a giant U shape to point to, despite the fact that for those in midlife things have largely gone unchanged.

It's worth noting that these young adults who are showing increases in depression and anxiety are the children of middle-aged parents. This understanding is important to lifespan researchers not just because my colleagues and I were onto something based on our studies, but because the mental health of their children is a central concern for those in midlife. As Jonathan Haidt has described in his important book *The Anxious Generation*, Generation Z, born 1997 to 2012 and ages thirteen to twenty-eight in 2025, are suffering from mental health problems, especially anxiety and depression, at an unprecedented level. He argues that much of the difficulty is tied to the proliferation of social media and technology, which can affect the well-being of both children and their parents. As a result, those who are parents and teachers in midlife are faced with increasing pressure to deal with their own mental health as well as that of their children.

While it's certainly true that midlife is a time when things may be in a state of flux and turmoil, it's usually not as totalizing an experience as many would have us believe. Research shows that when you look closer at those reporting a crisis, people might mention things being rough in one area of life (e.g., work) while things in another domain (e.g., family) might be going more smoothly than ever before. They report both ups and downs throughout midlife, and even during a single day. Looking back on my sojourn through midlife, this tracks with my own experience. What I felt during midlife was a fair amount of stress from juggling kids and career, and also a lot of success and excitement about where I was going and what I was building. Times when I was being evaluated for tenure or promotion, or helming a big research project with kids at home, tended to be more anxiety-filled. On the other hand, I remember huge swells of relief and happiness when I finally got tenure or took a sabbatical or received a grant. And I thoroughly enjoyed seeing my children reach milestones and accomplish goals despite the trials and tribulations. Midlife for me was characterized by both highs and lows. And all the research I've done since then has shown me that my experience is far from rare. I'd argue that the single U-shape curve doesn't capture the essence of midlife. In fact, a more apt depiction of midlife would look more like this:

Others have found that people tend to stay fairly stable in terms of their average happiness across their lifetimes. This phenomenon is called "hedonic adaptation" and was popularized in Dan Gilbert's

Stumbling on Happiness, where he points out that we have a happiness baseline we tend to return to no matter what happens. If we win the lottery, find new love, or get our dream job, our happiness will increase initially, but eventually (and often sooner than we think) it will return to baseline. The flip is also true—when bad things happen it can lay us low for a while, but as some studies have shown, even those with serious injuries after catastrophic accidents eventually return to their happiness baseline. What this means for the U-shape study is that we are missing critical information when we ask people at one point in time how happy or unhappy they are. A person who reports feeling a certain level of unhappiness at age forty-seven may well have reported that same level of unhappiness if you had asked them the same question at twenty-seven or thirty-seven—in fact, it's pretty likely. For the most part what the MIDUS investigators found is that when you follow the same people, there are some who have a low point in midlife, although most of them expect things to get better. People who were the happiest and most satisfied to start were also the happiest and most satisfied decades later.

This is why it's important not to put too much stock in one type of study; what is captured in longitudinal data (looking at the same people over time) is far different from looking at the snapshot of cohorts of different ages at one single point in time. Both are important and give us valuable insights, but neither gives you the full picture. One does not negate the other. There is no doubt that some semblance of a happiness U shape exists, but is that indicative of a full-blown midlife crisis epidemic? Not a chance. It's far more nuanced than that, which is why the problem is not actually the numbers—it's the narrative.

Breakthrough vs. Breakdown

When Skye's marriage ended in divorce, she was quick to pin her breakup on a midlife crisis—as were a number of the friends she confided in. But as her experience of this time in her life deepened, the idea that this was just some cut-and-dry "crisis" felt increasingly untethered from her experience. For her, the challenges she was facing in healing from her divorce and exploring a new self were undoubtedly difficult and painful. But they were also inextricably linked with what would come next—a positive transformation.

Part of what is such a problem with the so-called midlife crisis is the very definition. A crisis implies a sense of danger, threat, or dysfunction, which is not what most people experience, even if they do fall into that 10 or 20% of people who report having a midlife crisis. In fact, it's something much closer to a *challenge* than a crisis, which is much less scary. Experiencing a prolonged challenge followed by a period of growth is a predictable and healthy process that happens at many points throughout our lives. In fact, it can make our lives better.

In the 1950s, child psychoanalyst Erik Erikson developed his famous theory on human development. He believed that humans go through eight distinct stages of psychosocial development, noting that how we move through these stages is influenced by a host of factors from the biological to the social. In 1963, Erikson postulated that it may be necessary and even adaptive to experience turmoil in order for growth and development to occur in the first place. To explain this phenomenon, Erikson used the word *crisis* (which probably contributes to all the confusion!), but his definition characterized crisis as a period of uncertainty or a choice point that included internal conflict. Like a wave rising and falling, Erikson's "crisis" involved tension and resolution, which then helped move a person toward the next stage of maturation.

Psychologists Daniel Levinson and Roger Gould were highly influenced by Erikson's work on these transitions from challenge to growth. Levinson wrote, "The primary tasks of every transitional period are to reappraise the existing structure, to explore possibilities for change in the self and the world, and to move toward commitment to the crucial choices that form the basis for a new life structure in the ensuing period." Far from being unique to midlife, these shifts from crisis to catharsis have been shown to happen throughout our life course. A series of six studies by psychologists Adam Alter and Hal Hershfield looked at people who were "on the 9s"—meaning they were age twenty-nine, thirty-nine, forty-nine, fifty-nine, sixty-nine, and seventy-nine—to see how being on the cusp of a new decade impacted self-reflection, existential angst, and behavior. As expected, the study found that the decade years (thirty, forty, fifty, etc.) were widely considered to be major symbolic milestone years, and as such, in the year *before* those birthdays people were more likely than those at other ages to say that they were searching for meaning or looking for purpose in life. They also were more likely to set new goals such as running a marathon for the first time. In this study, for example, researchers discovered that "9-enders" were represented to a greater degree among first-time runners than those at other ages in the marathon database.

This shows us yet again that midlife is not the only time people are prone to existential self-reflection and inner turmoil. As Erikson pointed out decades ago, as humans we are in a constant state of becoming.

The so-called midlife crisis is one of many important transition periods available to us as we move through our lives. Whether it is puberty, a quarter-life crisis, or a rocky shift into retirement, there are a variety of external forces at every age conspiring to throw us into temporary tumult before cannonballing us into a new version of ourselves. When we are at the beginning stages of adolescence, we are contending with bodies that are rapidly changing shape, surging hormones, and new social challenges that we have no idea how to face. During the so-called quarter-life crisis of the twenties, people are making the leap *out* of adolescence and into full-fledged adulthood, which comes with its own challenges: learning how to fend for yourself financially, navigating the professional world, and trying on different identities. Often when people retire after many years in the workforce, they can become temporarily destabilized and experience feelings of loss. In order to find our footing at each stage, in each new reality, and to keep growing and learning and becoming, change is necessary. And it can be uncomfortable. Why would midlife be any different?

By looking more closely at both the numbers and the narratives of midlife, it's clear that there is more to the story of the midlife crisis than we've been led to believe. Far from being a universal experience, for some people this time of life is the peak, while for others there might be a more mixed bag of struggle and success. For people like Skye, who do go through a more difficult life change during these years, talking about the crisis without the growth misses a deeply important part of the process. So now the question becomes, why should we care? Why does it matter that how we look at midlife is overtaken by the myth of the "midlife crisis"? What do we lose?

How Myths Hurt

In a survey of over a thousand millennials conducted in spring 2024—which included people age twenty-eight to forty-three—one out of ten respondents said that they had already experienced a midlife crisis, while a full half (one out of two) expected to have one by age forty-four. The survey also asked millennials to rank the experiences they thought they were likely to have when their midlife crises hit. The top three were career change, attending therapy, and changing their appearance. In what feels like an ode to the 1980s, a full 36% believed they were likely to buy a sports car during their future crisis. Right now, millennials are the largest generation—over 72 million people in the US, exceeding even the baby boomers in terms of sheer numbers. Poised on the cusp of middle age, they are saddled with different challenges than their parents, but regrettably, they are hanging on to the same cultural clichés and fears about the next chapter of their life.

As a midlife researcher, this is worrying to me because I know just how pernicious these legacy beliefs can be. Debunking the myth of the midlife crisis isn't just about correcting the record—it's about harm reduction. Cultural notions have a real-time effect on our perception of our health and well-being in our middle years and, if the "information" is more myth than reality, that can have negative effects on our physical, psychological, and cognitive health. Research done by Becca Levy, professor of epidemiology and psychology at Yale, and summarized in her book *Breaking the Age Code*, has shown the power of both negative and positive beliefs about aging to impact our health span and lifespan in a number of ways. Levy found that those who had more positive images of aging (e.g., being healthy and active) lived longer than those with the more stereotypical views about older adults as weak, forgetful, and slow. She also found that those with a more positive mindset about aging were healthier, with lower blood pressure and a lower risk of developing Alzheimer's disease.

Breaking the Age Code looks at the differences in beliefs cross-culturally, from one country or part of the world to the next. In the US, an extremely ageist culture by almost every standard, we are taught to *expect* that aging means certain things—frailty, cognitive decline, and helplessness. While in countries like Japan, aging is celebrated. Older Japanese are both revered and *expected* to live full lives where they travel, exercise publicly, and pick up new hobbies, elevating them to the status of "aging rock stars." The puzzling difference in longevity and long-term health outcomes (people in Japan live an average of six years longer than those in the US) is what inspired Levy to look more closely at how our ideas about aging intersect with our physical health. What she discovered in her lab was that what we think of as age-related illnesses like cardiovascular disease and dementia are in part a result of the beliefs we hold about aging itself.

This is the root of the harm caused by the myth of the midlife crisis. We absorb ideas about aging and about certain life periods unconsciously. Whether it is listening to our parents talk negatively about aging or passively ingesting these notions while we watch a popular movie, it's not our fault that so many of us have defaulted to this negative narrative of midlife, but it is our problem. If, like the millennials in the survey, we think we are bound for a midlife crisis, we put ourselves in danger of cultivating a self-fulfilling prophecy. From Levy's work we know that this isn't speculation—our perceptions matter greatly, impacting, as she writes, "health through psychological, biological, and behavioral pathways."

In a longitudinal study my MIDUS colleagues and I conducted over the course of nine years, we found that one of the most feared aspects of aging—memory decline—is affected by our emotional states. Those who had a more positive outlook experienced less memory decline than those who were less positive. Intuitively, this makes sense. Viewing things negatively or expecting failure causes stress and anxiety, which we all know is public enemy number one when it comes to our health and our memory. But it also makes a difference in our behavior. If you expect that you're going to start getting injured and achy in middle age, you might back off skiing or running because you're "too old" for those kinds of high-impact sports. Maybe you get invited to a party that is supposed to carry on until the wee hours of the morning, but you decline because you think that time of life has passed you by and you should instead opt for more sleep. But when you curtail your physical and social activities because you are trying to conserve energy, avoid injury, or play a role that society has carved out for you, you are accelerating the aging process—not slowing it. If you believe you've entered a time of life where it's "normal" to feel worse, do less, and become more forgetful, you may be hastening the arrival of exactly what you fear.

Subscribing to the myth that the midlife crisis is inevitable and dysfunctional is similarly problematic and intersects with ageist beliefs. Not only does this myth promote stereotypes and cultivate fear about a time of our lives that can be incredibly joyful and productive, it can also serve to downplay real and serious suffering. One of the most nefarious twists of the cultural cliché of the midlife crisis is that it stokes fear while simultaneously making a joke out of real suffering. What this does is take the focus away from the people in this stage of life who are really struggling, and for very good reasons. As in any life stage, depression, anxiety, and other mental illnesses can upend people's lives. This was Ravi's experience. Even as his depression deepened, he half-jokingly shrugged off others' concerns, reassuring them that he was just going through "the midlife crisis thing." Eventually, his attempts to push down the suffering stopped working, and he did find a therapist who helped him get back on track. But what if he hadn't had this cultural meme to hide behind, what if he had seen this depressive episode as what it really was—a legitimate experience that wasn't a joke.

Unfortunately, for many, the specter of the midlife crisis can eclipse the truth. If a woman in her fifties whose children have just left the nest goes to see her physician about feeling excessively fatigued, depressed, and sleepless, the cliché of the midlife crisis makes it more likely that her concerns will be dismissed. This can lead to misdiagnosis for more serious conditions such as depression, autoimmune disorders, or hormonal deficiencies, which if recognized can be treated properly. Many people experience great pain and suffering in midlife, and it deserves to be taken seriously and treated appropriately. While far from commonplace, what researchers call "deaths of despair" have increased greatly in the last twenty years. These include suicides, fatal drug overdoses, and complications from alcohol abuse. Every day, people going through a *true* crisis like this are not met with the support they need but instead may hear from friends and family something along the lines of, "Oh, it must just be a midlife crisis, it'll pass." Collectively, our focus should be on expanding resources for the people who really need them, not disregarding people who are in crisis or scaring an entire generation on the cusp of turning forty.

Together, we can do better—but it all starts with us as individuals. Now that we've dragged the midlife-crisis monster out from under the bed and seen that it's not so bad after all, we can begin the work of dismantling these negative, unhelpful beliefs and start to tell ourselves a story about midlife that is much more hopeful, positive, and reflective of the science.

Flipping the Script

While it's hard to predict exactly who will have this experience, it's likely that between 10 and 20% of people in midlife will go through some intense period of challenge and growth. For those folks, it's important to remember that *this isn't a bad thing*. First of all, we know that the "crisis" is only part of the story, and not even the most interesting part. Whatever challenges you face are likely to be followed by changes to your life that will help you become freer, stronger, and more tuned in to what you really want for yourself in the second half of your life. Sometimes there are patterns, behaviors, and beliefs about ourselves that are holding us back from living our best lives. If we want to live authentic, joyful, easeful lives, it serves us best to deal with our issues head-on, no matter what time of life they crop up.

One of the best ways to set ourselves up for success when the sea of life starts to get choppy is to pay close attention to the way we are thinking about our story. What turned things around for Skye was editing the narrative of her divorce, changing it from "My life blew up" to "I have a real chance here to be happier." Whether we know it or not, we are always telling ourselves stories in order to make meaning out of what happens to us and how it makes us feel. When we're going through a rough patch, it helps immensely to take control of the narrative—moving from a negative frame of mind to a more hopeful one that emphasizes agency and opportunity. Midlife is a great time to revisit old stories and even consider some rewrites and new beginnings.

On the opposite end of the spectrum from folks who enter midlife ready for battle, many enter midlife on autopilot. Maybe they are happy, or maybe they are just in a period of overwhelm so considerable that they feel they don't have time to even ask the important questions. Many don't even think to reflect on their newfound status in the middle. Some assume they are stuck with the decisions made early in adulthood. Others want out but don't imagine the alternatives or can't see ways to improve circumstances. Either way, it's important to remember that it is possible to make tweaks or small changes in midlife; they don't have to be radical ones. One of my colleagues on the MacArthur Foundation Research Network on Successful Midlife Development used to say, some people are so fed up at work that they quit their jobs in frustration, when all they really needed was a two-week vacation. When we sleepwalk through midlife, at best it's a missed opportunity for growth, and at worst it simply delays the challenges that will inevitably surface. What we know from the research is that middle age—whether or not you go through a "crisis"—is *the* time to reflect and make change. What you do now has ripple effects that extend both forward into the future, and outward to the people who you love and are tasked with caring for you.

For those who don't know where to begin when it comes to reflecting on their life story and even changing it, there is good research to suggest that a "life review" can help. The life review was first introduced as a tool for well-being by gerontologist Robert Butler in the 1960s and was tied to understanding why older adults liked to reminisce. He thought that successfully navigating this transition into the last part of their lives required a review of life with the goal of accepting and appreciating life as it has been lived rather than regretting what one has or has not done. This life review is often used as a therapeutic device for helping older adults come to terms with the end of life. But a life review can also be of value in midlife. What better moment to take stock, reflect, and ask questions such as those provided at the end of this chapter. Unlike at older ages, in midlife the goal of the life review is to look back but also forward to where you are going. In this way, I like to think of midlife as halftime in sports: Some of the important plays have been made, but not all. You have the opportunity to breathe, examine what has come before, and start analyzing what you need to do next to reach your goals or modify them. There is plenty of time left after midlife, so this kind of reflection can help people see how they might move in different directions.

Aside from the myth of the midlife crisis, one of the biggest impediments to embracing the kind of midlife change that can make people happier and healthier is the myth that *we aren't supposed to or able to change* during this time of life. Whether or not one has lived their early adulthood life script as intended, by the time we reach middle age it can feel as if it is a static period and that we are stuck with who we are. In the next chapter we'll look at how personality and identity develop through midlife and how longitudinal research has completely upended what I call the Myth of Midlife Stability.

Tools: How to Do a Midlife Review

When we reach midlife, many people tend to naturally reflect on the first half of their lives. This can lead to dissatisfaction or even despair if what we find are unmet goals and milestones. It's always better to do this kind of look-back with more intention and positive framing. While a little discomfort with the poor choices of our past isn't a bad thing, getting mired in regret isn't something that helps anybody (we'll talk more about this in chapter 5). When done well, a midlife review can help you make sense of the past and bring clarity to your life's goals moving forward, even providing motivation for taking things in a new direction.

In the interest of doing a midlife review in a healthy way, there are some guidelines that may help make this a springboard for positive change and growth.

When to Do It: One strategy is to do life reviews every five or ten years at the decade milestones, forty, fifty, sixty, and possibly at the halfway marks, forty-five, fifty-five, and sixty-five. These are the periods that Daniel Levinson suggested are transition points. Another strategy is to do the review when there are significant life events that might require some readjustments: if you have a new child, or your child is leaving home for college or starting a job, or there is a divorce, or a death of a spouse, or a job loss or transition. Any of these moments can be a good time to reevaluate and think about possible changes. If you think you are having a midlife crisis, ask yourself whether it's really a crisis or if it's just that you're not happy with how some things are going. Maybe it is just a time to make some changes.

What to Ask:

+ Ten (or five) years ago, what did I think I would be doing at this age/time?

+ Which of these things am I doing and which am I not doing?

+ What is going well and not well? Am I happy now with what I am doing?

+ Are there things I am not happy about doing or not doing? What changes do I want to make?

+ What is essential and what is less important? What are my priorities?

+ Where do I want to be in ten (five) years? What things do I want to be doing in ten (five) years?

+ What changes do I need to make to get there?

+ What do I need to do to reach these goals?

+ Are my expectations realistic or unrealistic?

Reality check: It is important to keep in mind that it is unlikely you will have accomplished everything you expected by age forty, fifty, or even sixty. And it is unrealistic to think you will be happy with all areas of your life.

Chapter 2
The Myth of Stability: Can People Really Change in Midlife?

At 50, I began to know who I was. It was like waking up to myself.

—MAYA ANGELOU

Before she had kids, Anna ran everything from turkey trots to ultra-marathons and spent every Tuesday evening sprinting around Manhattan with her runners' club and going regularly to the theater with friends. Now, in her mid-forties, she is a mom consumed by the stress of caring for her three young children and is lucky to lace her sneakers up more than once or twice a week. Some days she wakes up and wonders what happened to the person who pushed and pushed until her legs almost gave out and then turned up the next day for more. It seemed, without her even realizing it, that identity was gone and had been replaced with someone who drives carpools, does dishes, and scrambles to get in a workout or get together with friends. She would often ask herself, Is this who I really am? Or is it just a tempo-rary glitch?

It wasn't until Joe met Sylvia that he realized just how bad he was at dealing with other people. Compared to Sylvia's easy way with friends and family, Joe felt like an antisocial curmudgeon. All his life he'd been in and out of conflict with friends and romantic partners. Friends seemed to come and go more frequently than the seasons, and his search for a girlfriend who didn't drive him nuts was a constant source of disappointment. Generally, he found people frustrating, confusing, and needy. And he'd been told more than once that he was insensitive, defensive, and manipulative. Sylvia, on the other hand, seemed to have endless compassion for people and trusted them in a way he didn't know was possible. One day he woke up and realized that the company of his plants and dogs, while wonderful, wasn't entirely fulfilling. He liked Sylvia and wanted her to stick around, but worried that his disagreeable tendencies were going to drive yet another person away. He wanted to be more like her, but wasn't sure it was even possible. After all, how much can you really change at fifty?

The questions Anna and Joe are asking—who am I? Do I really like who I am? Can I change the parts of me that aren't serving me well?—aren't unusual; we all find ourselves in the midst of these queries at some point in our lives. But they can be upsetting and disconcerting to many people who have been hoodwinked by yet another myth about midlife: the notion that by midlife, you should have this all figured out and you are stuck with who you are. I call this the Myth of Stability, or the idea that by the time we reach midlife, we are set—in who we are and what we do. This is, to be frank, a load of garbage. Unfortunately, many people buy into it, judging themselves and others when they arrive at midlife and discover there are some changes they want to make, or some new identities they want to try on. This can be a huge source of distress for those who wish to reclaim or change parts of themselves, or for people who find themselves chafing at the bounds of their personalities, wishing to be more of this or less of that. Or maybe they just don't feel like *where* they are in life fits who they really are, which in turn causes anxiety because they think it's too late to make such big moves.

But the real truth is that it's completely natural and normal to still be in the process of solidifying and integrating who you are and how you want to live your life. As we saw with Skye's story in the last chapter, sometimes our authentic selves can elude us for longer than we think is "normal." But once we look at our self-concept (personality and identity) as naturally mutable, we can reflect on who we are *now* and what it might mean for our experience of midlife. If you're in midlife and things aren't going well, looking to make some shifts in personality can help set you up not only for feeling better now but also for thriving in the future. In this chapter we will look more deeply at how who we are impacts our experiences of midlife. But first, let's begin with a simpler question—what defines us?

What It Means to Be You

When self-concept researchers ask people to answer the question "who are you?," most start off with the predictable responses. I am a mother, a teacher, a husband, a doctor, or a surfer. Then, usually, people will continue by listing their strengths and weaknesses—I'm a good listener, I'm a great friend, I'm a terrible cook, I'm always on time. Self-concept is how we view ourselves. It is a mash-up of all that we know about ourselves, from the roles we play to the unwelcome tendencies we try to hide. It is our understanding of who we are in the world, how others see us, and how much we value ourselves. Personality and identity are two important aspects of our self-concept that directly impact how we experience the world, how successful we are in it, and how we act, from the smallest transgression to the most consequential decision. Our self-concept matters greatly in all stages of the life cycle, but midlife is an especially important time. Research shows that late in midlife is when our personalities and identities crystallize and solidify in a more permanent way than ever before. It's unique to the individual, of course, but overall people in their forties are still exploring, tweaking, and integrating their self-concept based on the life they've lived before and the transitional period they now find themselves in. When folks move into their fifties things indeed begin to settle, setting the course for the rest of their lives.

Personality can be defined as the patterns of thoughts, feelings, and behaviors that shape how we interact with the world. It includes the characteristic ways in which we describe ourselves to others, and the ways in which others see us. Personality is something that may look different depending on the context we're in, shifting and stretching depending on our motivations and fears. (Who among us hasn't found ourselves acting more agreeable and extroverted when meeting our in-laws or a new client for the first time?) But more concretely, empirical studies of personality have led psychologists to agree on a fixed number of traits that comprise personality. These are often called the Big Five: openness to experience (creative, curious), conscientiousness (your ability to stay on task and get things done), extroversion (how outgoing and social you are), agreeableness (how well you get along with, trust, and feel compassion for others), and neuroticism (emotional instability).

Our adult personalities are determined by both genetics and experiences in childhood and beyond, and as a result there is both continuity and evolution. As any parent will attest, there are aspects of our personalities that have been evident from as early as our infancy. This is backed up by twin studies that suggest genes contribute anywhere between 30 and 60% to our personalities. Of course, that still leaves a lot of room for our environment to be a great shaper of who we become. From childhood trauma to the varied experiences of being human, our environment and our genes intersect and integrate, shaping our personality traits in unique ways. Even identical twins can seem wildly different, with one displaying extreme introversion, for instance, while the other is consistently the life of the party, depending on how their life experiences play out.

The traits we develop as a result of this collision of nurture and nature impact not only how we are perceived but also play a big role in how we behave. Psychologists have found that people are more likely to show their personality's true colors when they are in what we call "weak situations," where there is ambiguity as to how one should behave. In weak situations individuals will behave differently, so their personalities shine through. (This is also true in times of stress.) For example, when a traffic light turns yellow, some people will speed up to go through the light. Others will slow down and stop before the light turns red. These different approaches to the world reflect personality, helping us see whether someone is a risk-taker or perhaps more cautious. The same person may also fluctuate in whether they stop or slow down depending on the circumstances. If they have their grandchild in the car even a risk-taker might slow down at the yellow light out of concern. On the flip side, someone who is more cautious might speed up at a yellow light if they are late for their best friend's wedding.

Identity is another aspect of our self-concept that shapes our experience of the world, but through slightly different pathways. This dimension of who we are is less about thinking/feeling/acting and more about what we believe to be true about ourselves, the commitments we have, and how we define ourselves in a social context. There are multiple domains for identities: occupational, gender, political, cultural, religious, sexuality, lifestyle, and relationships. Sometimes we have a clear sense of identity in one domain, and a fuzzier understanding of identity in another. For instance, someone might identify strongly as a mother, but less strongly as a Catholic. Because of the environmental context and the social dimension of identity, our choices and actions can strengthen or weaken the identification. If you're a young entrepreneur and you choose to join a start-up incubator where you work alongside other entrepreneurs, that identity will deepen through those social bonds. In contrast, if you are a lesbian living in a small town with no queer community in sight, you might focus less on your sexual identity and feel more defined by your other identities.

Personality *Can* Change in Midlife

For most people, trying on new identities and personality traits is an ongoing process that kicks off early in our lives whether or not we arc aware of it. Research shows that identity exploration is necessary for overall well-being, definitely in adolescence, and likely throughout our adult lives. However, for many years people believed that the only time to play around with identity and personality *was* in adolescence. It was thought that personality and identity were formed during those early years and then remained fixed throughout adulthood. Well into the latter part of the twentieth century, psychologists believed that by age thirty personality was "set like plaster," as documented in a famous paper titled "Still Stable After All These Years." This is no longer accepted by most scholars of human development. In fact, we know there is a huge amount of variation in how we navigate through the adult years, whether that's exploring new identities or flexing our personality traits.

Who we are can, and often does, change significantly over the years, allowing for a great deal of personal growth in midlife and beyond. How much someone's personality changes through their lifespan varies, with some people maintaining their lifelong traits, and others showing adaptive changes such as becoming less neurotic or more conscientious, in contrast to less desirable changes such as becoming more rigid and close-minded. Psychologist Brent Roberts used longitudinal data to test whether the Big Five personality dimensions remained stable or not. He found clear evidence that personality can change in adulthood and indeed well into midlife, and also that on average people become more conscientious, more agreeable, less open to experience, less extroverted, and less neurotic as they age. He also found that personality begins to stabilize after age fifty. Likewise, Bernice Neugarten, one of the earliest researchers in the psychology of aging, reported that the decade of the fifties is an important turning point in personality, with increased introspection and reflection.

Research on identity draws similar conclusions; one may have a clear identity in some domains and less clarity in other domains, but that can all change throughout the years. A study of identity in the adult years through midlife found that identity was still in flux for many adults. When it came to the different domains—religious beliefs, political identity, occupation, intimate relationships, and lifestyle—this study showed that for the most part, around age fifty most people are pretty settled in their identities, though not necessarily in all domains. For those whose identity was still in flux at fifty, it was primarily in the domains of lifestyle, relationships, and occupation. This suggests what we already know anecdotally from the experiences of people like Anna and Joe, that while we may be feeling like our authentic selves in some areas of life, there is still plenty of room for movement in others.

Looking at the Myth of Stability from a commonsense perspective, it seems obviously wrong to imagine that once we cross some magical threshold to adulthood that we're stuck with the personalities and identities we've developed so far. In reality, who we are is constantly changing and morphing throughout our lives—this jives with most people's experiences of aging. We know that our sense of self is largely constructed by the varied circumstances we encounter, the dynamics of our physical and mental health, and our relationships with others. With so many variables in play, of course self-concept is still in flux during midlife! For most of us it is a time when our lives are really changing—social roles shift, hormonal changes descend, and long-held relationships can come into question. And how we react to the changes of midlife and what we choose to do about them is profoundly impacted by personality. While we might think of self-concept in light, pop-psychology terms like the sixteen types from the Myers-Briggs personality test, it's actually much more consequential than most people know.

Why Does Personality Matter?

How much do you think it would be worth to you, in dollars, to be a little less worried, anxious, and emotional? A little less *neurotic* (in the words of personality researchers)? Well, a study highlighted in *The Atlantic* put a number on it: $314,000. If you were able to change this personality trait by lowering your neuroticism by only one standard deviation (a measurement of how far you are from the average), your happiness would increase as much as if someone plopped $314,000 into your bank account. If you increased your openness, conscientiousness, and extroversion by one standard deviation, the correlating cash value in terms of well-being would be $62,000, $92,000, and $225,000, respectively. As the article points out, the latest research tells us that "personality changes can even be a *better* predictor of life satisfaction than many of the external variables that are normally considered in economic models of happiness." Those variables could include how much you make, your level of education, and even your access to quality housing. All of these are aspects of life that we know push our sense of well-being and life satisfaction up and down significantly—but not as much as personality can.

When we take a moment to look at "who we are" as more than just low-stakes idiosyncrasies, we see that personality actually impacts everything from our earning power to our health and longevity. Reflecting on identity and personality at midlife is hugely important because we know that the higher you rate in agreeableness, conscientiousness, openness, and extroversion, the more likely you are to have strong relationships and excel at your job. If you score high in neuroticism, however, you're more likely to experience financial hardship. You're also more likely to develop a mood disorder like anxiety or depression, not to mention other health challenges like autoimmune disorders and cardiac issues. People with higher rates of neuroticism are also more likely to encounter challenges in midlife that hew more closely to the stereotypical "midlife crisis." This is likely because the hallmark of neuroticism is a compromised ability to regulate emotions, which simply means managing your emotional reactions and feelings in adaptive ways.

The nature of midlife will vary dramatically depending on our self-concept because each characteristic is a tool that is either more or less helpful. For instance, those who are flexible have an easier time dealing with unexpected events, while those who are neurotic may have more difficulty coping. Those who are open to experience may seek out new, better opportunities with more ease than those who are lower on the openness scale. Agreeableness and the social cushion that it provides can enable us to better get along with others and handle interpersonal conflicts. (Of course, being *too* high in agreeableness can also be problematic—think extreme people pleasers who neglect their own needs.)

The reason personality and identity have such a large impact on our quality of life boils down to behavior. Remember that yellow light? We are faced with "weak" situations all the time in our day-to-day lives—from deciding whether to let your teenager go on a weekend trip with only her friends to figuring out whether to blow the whistle on your terrible boss. How we meet these decisions, every single one of them, is driven by *who we think we are and how we think others will react or see us.* The accumulation of all these decisions is what shapes the arc of our lives.

Personality and its influence on our behavior and choices really becomes clear when we look at the realm of health and longevity. For instance, conscientiousness—being organized, goal-oriented, and responsible—is critical to maintaining the exercise regimens and healthy diets that add years to our lives. And those who are more conscientious show less age-related decline in cognition. This is likely, in part, because they are engaging in cognitively stimulating and challenging activities that keep their minds active. In addition, higher openness and conscientiousness are associated with better cognitive performance and a higher self-rating of memory (called subjective memory), whereas higher neuroticism is associated with slower processing speed and worse subjective memory. In another study, MIDUS participants who showed a decrease in extroversion, agreeableness, openness, conscientiousness, and emotional stability (the flip side of neuroticism) showed greater decline in their cognitive abilities over twenty years.

While personality matters to our health and happiness throughout our lives, midlife is a good time to reflect and even change the parts of your self-concept that aren't serving you. Think about it like playing with your personality "settings," which can truly shift how you feel. If you're unhappy or discontented in some parts of your life, looking more closely at your identities and personality traits can help you figure out what parts of you could use some calibration, and which parts are working just fine. Midlife is not too late to explore new ways of being, work on being a little more conscientious, and set yourself up for an easier ride in the second half of your life. The good news? It's not as hard as you might think.

Midlife Personality Glow-Up

What if you could change the things you don't like about yourself by using an app—no therapy, medication, or major life upheaval required?

This was the question at the heart of a study spearheaded by Mirjam Stieger, a former postdoctoral scholar in my Lifespan Lab at Brandeis. She and her coauthors wanted to know if it was possible to help people either dial down or turn up one of the Big Five personality traits that shape our patterns of thinking, feeling, and acting, and are so important to our health and happiness. Earlier research had already made it clear that personality traits could effectively be changed by psychotherapy in a relatively short period of time. For instance, in one meta-analysis, Brent Roberts reviewed the findings on psychotherapy as well as nonclinical interventions to change personality. Those unhappy with their personalities were able to achieve changes in a remarkably short period with traditional psychotherapy. Across all types of interventions, the two most common changes were for lowering neuroticism and increasing extroversion, and the average period of change was twenty-four weeks.

What Mirjam and her collaborators wanted to know was just how quickly those changes could be made by someone on their own, and how long it would take to see results. Also, considering the problems of access embedded in the mental health industry (high fees and low insurance coverage, for one), the team thought there might be an easier, more democratic way to mimic those interventions. So, in a randomized controlled trial of over fifteen hundred people, Stieger and the other researchers developed an app that would act as an intervention—kind of like a personal coach—helping people change the parts of their personalities they didn't like.

In the last section we talked about the big-picture reasons you might want to change your personality—better health and longevity, happiness and life satisfaction. But there are smaller, yet more immediate and practical reasons that someone might want to calibrate parts of their personality. Maybe someone's lack of conscientiousness at work is getting in the way of a promotion, or their lack of agreeableness means they often find themselves in conflict with the people around them. Perhaps they've met a partner whom they care for deeply, but who loves to go on adventures and travel in a way they aren't yet open to. Who we are is a unique constellation of personality traits that you can think of like settings on a phone for key volume, ringer volume, and brightness. We all have default settings, but we also have the ability to change them. With that understanding, the first step of the trial was to ask people which dials they'd like to turn up or down. Then researchers and developers tailored their app interface to interventions that would help participants achieve their goal. The trait people most wanted to change was neuroticism (no surprises there), which they wanted to decrease, while the runners-up were conscientiousness and extroversion, which they wanted to increase.

Over the course of three months, participants in the research group interacted daily with their app. They were asked to complete tasks and record their observations and actions in a diary, while also keeping an eye on a dashboard that tracked their progress. The control group, on the other hand, was asked their goals and then effectively put on ice—a one-month "waitlist." At the end of the three-month period, researchers compared the progress of both groups toward their goals and found that the participants who used the app showed significantly more change than the control group when it came to achieving their goals. While these results were self-reported, the study also included another validating factor—the observations of friends and family, who could corroborate the reports. To see if these results would stick, researchers also checked back in with participants at two points—three months and a year—after they stopped using the app and found that the changes persisted.

The results of this study, and others like it, point to a sea change in psychology over the last twenty-five years. It's now widely accepted that people *can* change, and as Mirjam's study shows, with far more ease than they might have otherwise thought possible. It's important to note that the participants in the app study were mostly in their twenties. However, there's no reason to think this kind of personality shifting doesn't happen for those in midlife as well—in fact, over two hundred of the participants in her study were in their thirties, forties, and beyond.

Both within and beyond academia there is an emerging interest in what is called volitional personality change (intentional personality change toward one's desired goals). Psychologist Shannon Sauer-Zavala suggests that you can change personality by trying different ways of feeling, thinking, or behaving to reach a goal. She gives an example of someone who wants to become more dependable. For example, if you are someone who typically shows up late for meetings, you can work on becoming more reliable, an aspect of conscientiousness, by changing your behavior so that you arrive early or on time. This change might involve setting an alarm or using appointment reminders, or checking on traffic to see how long it will take to arrive at your destination—and don't forget to figure in the time it will take to find a parking place. Cognitive behavioral techniques can be used to change personality as they focus on adjusting how you think and behave. In several studies I have used cognitive restructuring to help middle-aged and older adults change neurotic misconceptions and self-defeating beliefs about losing their physical and cognitive abilities and being too old to learn or try something new. These techniques involve identifying faulty narratives about the inevitability of losses and the potential for gains. The next steps involve modifying your outlook to enable more adaptive beliefs to support desirable outcomes such as feeling more confident about one's memory or ability to try a new exercise routine. This can include providing strategies to improve one's skills through practice and encouraging more accurate self-appraisals and positive emotions. Setting specific goals is an important first step for changing one's personality.

Stacey accepted that she was introverted and knew that it was adaptive in her field of accounting. Her quiet demeanor helped her to be highly productive. She didn't spend a lot of time talking with coworkers at the water cooler. She was close with her parents and her siblings and spent most of her free time with them. She had a few friends from college who lived nearby but she had not seen them in ages. At age forty she decided it was time to venture out and get a life. Her goal was to become more extroverted. She knew that meant being around other people. She got up the courage to call her college friends, who had all kept in touch. They were happy to hear from her and invited her to dinners, parties, and other social events. Before long Stacey was planning activities and inviting them to join her. She noticed she was even more outgoing at the office, getting to know her colleagues better and going out with them after work. She had indeed become more extroverted and much happier too.

In a follow-up to Mirjam's personality app study, I joined forces with her to look at how personality change drives behavior changes, *specifically in midlife.* We wanted to focus on this age demographic, and we also needed to make sure those changes in personality could lead to downstream positive effects as well. In other words, we needed to test how personality shifts were related to changes in behavior. So, we conducted a seven-week trial of an intervention designed to increase participants' physical activity by improving their self-control, which is a facet of the conscientiousness trait. We recruited participants who said they wanted to exercise more. What we found was that those who received the intervention and increased their self-control the most showed greater increases in physical activity compared to those who did not receive the self-control treatment.

This is good news because one of the great opportunities of midlife is that we are in a stronger position than ever before to close the gap between who we are and who we want to be. Using personality change as an avenue for improving the way you think, feel, and behave is a new and underutilized tool. What this new science shows us is that in midlife, positive change is possible in all the areas where personality matters— which is in your professional life, your personal relationships, and your health. Health, in particular, is a big one because it's more important than ever to start locking in good health habits now to increase your odds of being healthy well into your later years. Our study shows that not only is personality change possible, it can actually boost our ability to make the kinds of positive behavioral changes that really improve our quality of life, such as exercising more or eating a healthier diet.

Does *Who* We Are Fit with *Where* We Are?

By midlife, many of us have tried on a number of different identities, played out the patterns of our personalities over and over again, and with years of failure and success to inform us, we can see more clearly than ever what feels right, what feels wrong, and what could use some adjustment. But embracing this kind of change in midlife isn't just about changing our self-concept from within. Sure, that's a large part of the work, but as we sink more comfortably into our authentic selves, we still might chafe at the intersection between us and our experiences in the world. What we need to look at, then, is what psychologists call the "person-environment fit"—which simply means whether the identities and personalities we have match up with the people and places we've chosen to surround ourselves with. Whether it's a spouse, friend group, community, or living situation, people are happiest when their environment meshes well with their self-concept.

Once we have a firm grasp of who we really are, which, as we talked about before, may not solidify and settle until well into our fifties, sometimes we find that the life we built or the person we chose to marry doesn't really "fit" anymore. Skye from the last chapter is a great example of this experience. As her identity changed and morphed in her late thirties and early forties, it became clear that she was no longer the same person she was when she married her husband. At one point, they were a good match, but after struggling through infertility and coming out of that process with different ideas about what they wanted for their lives, they no longer worked. What we call a personality-environment mismatch in the social sciences, you might just call "growing apart." Divorce and separation can be incredibly painful experiences. Many people castigate themselves for not being able to make it work, they feel guilty and judged when all along no one was to blame but the natural evolution of two people's personalities or identities. On the other hand, not all growing apart needs to end in schism; there are of course many ways to work through the differences and stay together. Understanding that this growth and readjustment period is natural (and not a clear sign one way or the other about the fate of the relationship) might help people lean into new ways of interacting without casting blame or giving in to hopelessness.

The same mechanism is at play when people start to feel bored, stagnant, and downright miserable about their chosen career paths. Many of us choose occupations in our twenties or thirties that match the person we were *then* but don't necessarily bring joy to the person we are *now*. Naturally, as we age priorities change, preferences shift, and what feels good and right can take a swift turn. These are just two of the big categories of common personality-environment mismatches. Of course, there are more—the city you live in, the groups you're involved in, the types of vacations—but jobs and relationships are the biggies. They are the parts of our lives that tend to confront people in midlife with the biggest sources of turmoil, in no small part because of the misconception that we should have everything "settled" by the time we are in our forties or fifties. A source of great suffering in midlife is the expectation that we should have it all figured out by now and that there's something wrong with us if the person we chose or the job we fought so hard for are no longer making us happy. These mismatches are challenging and painful in the best of circumstances, and they are made so much worse by blaming ourselves for what is actually an incredibly natural and healthy part of aging.

It Gets Better

There's good reason to embrace the challenge that our forties often provide in terms of exploring and calibrating who we are and how we feel in our lives: Sooner rather than later, things are likely to solidify.

While it's true that our personalities and identities can shift well into our fifties and beyond, the science tells us that for *most* people, our self-concept starts to fully integrate with our lives and become stable in our fifties. This shouldn't feel like a scary deadline you have to meet—*I have to find my authentic self NOW?!*—but rather a reminder that it's normal for things to be shifting in midlife and that they won't be in flux forever. If there are patterns of behavior or thinking that you've struggled with for a long time, or you've been questioning whether a relationship is working after all these years, it's a good time to face it and act. On the other hand, if you're someone who is already pretty happy with who you are, there's no need to change a thing—you've probably already gone through this integration process. The good news about this time of life is that no matter whether you're someone who is still questioning or someone who is fully content, you'll find that time typically smooths out your rough edges. Studies show that over time, as you ride the midlife wave into your fifties, sixties, and beyond, as you age, you're likely to become more comfortable and content with who you are.

Far from being a period of stability, midlife is a time of increasing change and opportunities to seize control of our health and happiness at this pivotal crossroads. Self-concept is just one lever we can use to push ourselves in the direction we want to go. In the next chapter we'll take a deeper look at how exactly we can make the shift from believing our lives are on middle-age autopilot to seeing just how much control we really have.

Chapter 3

Mastering Midlife: Balancing the Gains and Losses

There is a fountain of youth: it is your mind, your talents, the creativity you bring to your life and the lives of people you love. When you learn to tap this source, you will truly have defeated age.

—SOPHIA LOREN

If you ask writer Catherine Newman about the biggest, sneakiest sadness of her life in the last two years she'll tell you: It was the shoes.

When her kids were at the end of their high school years, she began to worry about all the ways she would miss them when they went off to college. Despite working full time, she'd deeply identified as their mother, a role that gave a sturdy shape to her life for almost two decades. Plus, she just really enjoyed their company. She knew she'd miss them in all the day-to-day ways: the sweet gangs of kids who were always coming and going, rifling through her refrigerator and playing music in the living room; the unexpected peals of laughter from the next room while she was responding to work emails; the hilariously cutthroat family board game nights. "I was dreading the last of that, and I was right to dread it. It was terrible."

The biggest surprise was how she choked up every time she walked into the house and spied the heartbreaking lack of shoes beside the front door. There were her husband's beat-up sneakers, but otherwise, it was just a sad, empty space compared to the forty-shoe pileup that had been a permanent fixture there for so long. Shoes of course meant feet, and feet of course meant people. People meant family. And family meant love and togetherness. It felt like a mental reminder that she was about to enter the dead zone of empty-nester land.

Catherine makes no secret of how difficult that first year and a half was. Between dealing with the hormonal roller coaster of menopause, missing her two kids, and trying to navigate what felt like an entirely new relationship with her husband, she felt incredibly lost. Both she and her husband, Michael, were reconstituting their identities, trying to nail down who they were when they weren't so consumed by the daily tasks of parenting, all the while trying to figure out what that meant for their relationship. This took some time, but slowly they found opportunities for expansion and reconnection; they began cold-water swimming together, playing tennis, and seeing more live music. To their surprise and delight, they were having fun together, and there was a lot more headspace to enjoy it. No longer did they have to make sure they were home to greet the kids or rush back to make sure they weren't missing precious time with everyone. She joked to friends that she was "retired" even as she was publishing one book and writing another.

But for Catherine, what really exemplifies her life at fifty-five are her semi-regular trips to the doctor. Recently, she started to display symptoms that required her to leave her home in Amherst, Massachusetts, and make trips to Boston for diagnostic testing and appointments with specialists. Because she doesn't like to drive on the highway, her husband takes her to all her appointments. They use the time to talk, listen to podcasts, and try out new music. Because they don't have any kids to get home to, they can take their time, stop for lunch on the way back, take the scenic route, decide to stay in Boston for the night, or do whatever they want. Catherine talks about how strangely poignant these drives are. Here she is in midlife, her health suddenly a question mark (illustrating in full living color the inevitabilities of aging), and yet she's also experiencing what she calls "the incredible dearness and solidity of this relationship that I've been in for thirty-five years." For her, it's emblematic of how this time of life is a head-spinning tour de force of yin and yang. The nasty hot flashes and mood swings of menopause, but also the sweet new cold-plunge friend and the time to go out for coffee. There is the almost unrecognizable older lady in the mirror with her deepening wrinkles and softening belly, but also the bliss of moving through the world invisibly, free of the male gaze and all its attendant hassles. It's all of the hard stuff and all of the good stuff of aging, slamming together in so many beautiful, poignantly human moments. A time when the newer, deeper losses of midlife are curiously sweetened by the unexpected gains.

Catherine's story isn't only about the midlife phenomenon of the empty nest, it's much bigger than that. It's about how we can thrive in midlife: by balancing the ups and downs and embracing the hidden opportunities of midlife.

Lifespan research tells us this midpoint is all about trade-offs. Unexpected deaths, new health problems, and professional down-shifting are all losses that can sneak up on us, but they are equally met with the gains we see in confidence, sense of self, and the ability to synthesize the entirety of our life experience into gleaming jewels of insight. In psychology-speak, we call these trade-offs "gains and losses" and the balance or imbalance of these positives and negatives are at the heart of what makes midlife so unique and full of potential. As we move through this new life stage, how we approach, think about, and act in the face of this balance/imbalance is what defines how content, joyful, and empowered we feel moving forward.

It's undeniable that, with age, our bodies and minds begin to slow down and display other signs of aging. Yet there are things you can do to slow the aging process and there are distinct high points to mid-life as well. It can be a peak time in terms of work accomplishments and productivity, creativity, highest earnings (although often coupled with the biggest expenses), leadership in the family, and valuable con-tributions to the community, all topped off with newly accrued self-esteem, self-confidence, and wisdom gained from experience.

When we think about the gains and losses we have to navigate in midlife, it's important to remember that we're all individuals and our experiences will vary greatly. That being said, there are a few cate-gories in which most of us will experience similar shifts. The catch is this—many of us *think* we know the kinds of changes we can expect. However, in recent years research has shown that there is a lot more to the story. Things are likely to be less dire and more nuanced than you may think.

A Tale of Two Intelligences

One day, the forty-three-year-old mother of a bright and deeply competitive seven-year-old got trounced playing a unicorn memory game. Trying to model good sportsmanship, Lauren, the mom, gave her daughter a high five, asked for a rematch, and then spent the next three games losing. Much to her daughter's delight and her own chagrin, Lauren just couldn't seem to get a handle on the twenty pairs of different unicorns. Where was the other unicorn with the mushroom necklace again? Despite the motivation to win and recover her dignity, Lauren kept getting distracted. While her daughter was taking a turn, her mind was all over the place: She was keeping an eye on the oven timer so as not to burn the brownies; she heard the washing machine downstairs sing its "I'm done" tune so she made a mental note to put the laundry in the dryer right after her next turn; she looked at her daughter's clawlike toenails and got up to grab the clippers; she had to recall whether or not she called the doctor to reschedule an appointment when her husband popped his head in with an inquiry; and in between all these thoughts was the creeping worry that maybe she was in fact losing her once-stellar memory. But really, she just couldn't focus given the myriad things she was juggling at the moment, which is true of many people at this stage of life.

The next night, the whole family played Scrabble after dinner. The dishes were done, everyone had eaten, and their family of three had settled in for the parents' favorite game. Precocious and already reading chapter books, their seven-year-old did well, but by the end of the game she was still a solid hundred points behind each of her parents. There was pouting and grumbling, but as Lauren pointed out, Scrabble is about how many words you know, and they had had decades to build their vocabularies. In a game like that, the poor kid never really had a chance. After she put her daughter to bed that night Lauren felt some relief—the memory game humiliation had concerned her, but maintaining her Scrabble dominance made her feel better. Maybe she wasn't succumbing to the indignities of old age just yet.

Lauren was right to be relieved—after all, at forty-three, she doesn't really have anything to worry about. We refer to those who are concerned about their memory when their memory is perfectly fine as the "worried well." In the MIDUS study we found that 25% thought their memory was below average for their age when it was actually above average. In another longitudinal study, using the Health and Retirement Study data from the University of Michigan Survey Research Center, we found that 20% thought their memory had declined over a two-year period when it did not. At the beginning of midlife, while intelligence, cognition, and memory are starting to shift, they have not, as many people assume, started falling off a cliff. It's safe to say Lauren's memory is far better than she thinks. Because of the way we are culturally conditioned, many people *expect* cognitive deficits to begin rearing their heads around midlife, so naturally, we start looking out for them. Many people might crack a joke about aging when they hear the story of someone getting beaten by their seven-year-old at a memory game, but most people wouldn't even comment on the fact that she beat her child at Scrabble. That's because by the time we're in midlife, some people assume it's all losses and no gains, but when we look a little closer, we see that the gains are, in fact, very present. If only we step back and look at the whole picture.

What Lauren experienced is a perfect illustration of the complexity of the losses and gains we experience in the realm of the mind. As we age, our brains are literally changing, so it's natural that our abilities should change as well. The brain is an adaptation machine, and as the years roll on the nature of our intelligence and how cognition works changes to help us compensate for the natural losses we experience. How well our memory works, how successful we are at multitasking, how long we can maintain our focus, how quickly we can come up with novel ideas, and how good we are at synthesizing information are all affected by the march of time. But it's not a simple story of one-way deterioration.

One example of this is what I call a Tale of Two Intelligences, or how midlife can be seen as a transition from strength in one kind of intelligence to growth in another. Researchers have found that there are two components to intelligence: fluid intelligence and crystallized intelligence.

Fluid intelligence is all about quick thinking and innovation. It is the kind of intelligence that works regardless of how much knowledge or experience you have. When Lauren's daughter was zeroing in on all the matches with lightning speed, she was relying on her working memory, an aspect of fluid intelligence, which gives you the ability to quickly incorporate new information and hold it in your mind until it becomes useful. Fluid intelligence also involves abstract reasoning and solving complex, novel problems. It's the stuff of late-night breakthroughs, disruptive technology, and new inventions.

Crystallized intelligence, on the other hand, is the epitome of wisdom. It's most at home playing a game like Scrabble, which relies on experience, semantic memory, knowledge, and the ability to synthesize them all and apply it to the current problem. It takes its time, knitting together a dense weave of complex insights based on historical knowledge, which allows us to rise to the challenge.

These two dimensions of intelligence have different trajectories of change over the course of our lives. Fluid intelligence gradually declines with age, with some aspects starting as early as the thirties. In contrast, crystallized intelligence continues to develop and increase throughout the adult years well into the sixties and early seventies. Even though fluid intelligence may start to decline earlier, the changes are subtle and gradual. Most people in midlife will not even notice that these aspects of cognition have changed at all (unless they play memory games with their kids).

Compensation to the Rescue

When people read about the declines found in fluid intelligence in midlife, they start to panic, especially if they are professionals working in a field that relies on novelty and speed. But our brain is adept at compensation, managing declines in one area by boosting capacity in another.

While the findings we see showing a decline in fluid intelligence might feel alarming, all is not lost. Laboratories are not life. Because researchers are trying to show the extreme ends of the ability spectrum, the tests run to determine fluid intelligence are particularly challenging and assess things that are not usually encountered in everyday life. Poor performance or declines on these tests is not likely to translate into performance on the job or in one's daily life. That is because in daily life we seldom need to perform at our maximum capacity. We've also got to remember that fluid intelligence is just one of many components that contribute to how well we do on life tasks. For instance, Lauren's distraction and multitasking during the memory game may have contributed to her losses even more than any declines in fluid intelligence. But even when people do experience losses in some fluid abilities, they are able to lean more heavily on crystallized intelligence, their accumulated wisdom, or find situations that are more compatible with their skills.

Still more promising, there is research that suggests fluid intelligence doesn't diminish in a meaningful way as early as we once thought. K. Warner Schaie, who was director of the Seattle Longitudinal Study of intelligence and one of the preeminent scholars of intellectual functioning in adulthood, conducted longitudinal studies of fluid and crystallized intelligence with a large group of adults from their twenties through their nineties, testing them every seven years. Although the earlier cross-sectional studies suggested that performance on cognitive tests started to show meaningful declines in midlife, this was not the case when Schaie followed the same people over time with his longitudinal studies. In fact, his work found that the changes in fluid intelligence weren't significant until after age sixty.

There are also wide individual differences to consider. Some people show declines earlier and on some dimensions of fluid intelligence, while others maintain their functioning until much later, even into their seventies or eighties. Researcher Timothy Salthouse from the University of Virginia has found that much of the changes we see in fluid intelligence are attributable to declines in the speed of processing information. Interestingly, most intelligence tests have time limits that make it more challenging to finish all the problems, which leads to lower overall scores. Yet, when more time is given, performance typically improves dramatically. The ability is there, it's just a little slower to kick in.

Slower doesn't necessarily mean less sharp in the final results. For example, let's say you are given a deadline and need to write an article quickly. You don't have time to do much research or even check your work carefully. You can still produce something that is acceptable, but because you did not have time to reflect on what you wrote, it may have some errors and not be up to your highest standards. On the other hand, if you don't have a deadline and can take your time to check your sources thoroughly and incorporate different perspectives, it will likely be quite different (maybe more accurate) and something you're proud of as your best effort. Both are publishable, but one done without time constraints is a better reflection of your full abilities. This is yet another way in which the lab work on abilities is not the same as in life. While on an intelligence test you might have little time to show what you know, there are plenty of situations in everyday life in which your abilities can take their sweet time to come up with an even more elegant solution to whatever problems lie before you.

As we can see, experience can compensate nicely for the slowdowns of age. Even without the benefit of extra time, sometimes crystallized intelligence can outperform fluid intelligence in the realm of speed.

For instance, when I was a graduate student, I remember my advisor was able to read a manuscript and respond much quicker than I was. It took me a lot longer to read and figure out what I wanted to say and how to respond. This makes sense, considering he had decades of knowledge and experience in the discipline that I lacked. Naturally, as I gained more experience I began building my own crystallized knowledge in psychology and over time I was able to read, review, and critique papers and grants much faster than before, and even though with age my processing speed was dwindling my expertise in the field stepped up to compensate.

I've seen this context-dependent phenomenon play out in my own lab when during the MIDUS study we examined changes in cognition (the processes through which we apply our knowledge to solve problems or remember information). Over a ten-year period, we found that there was decline in some dimensions of cognition—but mainly speed—beginning in the forties. Memory and numerical reasoning showed significant declines starting later, from the fifties into the sixties. In contrast, the tests that required fast reaction time and measured how quickly people responded with their answers showed some declines in the forties. Again, the changes that we find with tests in the lab don't necessarily correspond to how we might perform in our daily lives. After all, our tests are designed to be novel and challenging because the goal is to test the limits of our abilities. In our day-to-day lives we have plenty of practice doing things that require us to leverage our cognitive abilities, like figuring out how to adjust the ingredients in a recipe for five people instead of the two servings that the recipe shows or pulling together an important presentation for work. Success in everyday experiences can serve us well in new and challenging situations, and it's important to remember that most tasks don't require lightning speed.

Different Kinds of Memory

The changes we see in the lab regarding memory, and how well that memory actually serves us in real life, are important to consider because what we *believe* about our memory is a key to maintaining it. We know that memory is a slippery thing even on a good day, even in your twenties. So many factors impact memory—from sleep to hormones to simply having too much to do—that it's pretty hard to parse out what can be chalked up to age-related memory loss versus outside factors. When folks enter midlife, they are more and more likely to attribute their slips in recall to aging, or what some may call a senior moment, whereas if the same thing happened in their twenties they likely would have just brushed it off. What accounts for all this confusion and paranoia around memory is that there are so many different kinds of memory, and each declines at a different time and a different rate. For instance, at all ages, people consistently complain about their memory for names. You may have the face clear in your mind but draw a big old blank when you try to recall the name of the neighbor down the street who just moved in. A likely reason for this is that the name never entered into your long-term memory in the first place. You were probably paying attention to something else and didn't bother to process the name so it would stick. It might have nothing to do at all with age.

On the other hand, *working memory* and *episodic memory*—the kind that Lauren and her daughter needed to rely on to remember where the unicorns were—are the kinds of memory that decline earlier than other aspects. Working memory involves trying to remember information at the same time you are doing something else with the things you have to remember. It's driving somewhere unfamiliar and remembering all the turns and landmarks in the directions you were given at the gas station. Thank goodness for GPS! It's flipping over a new card at the same time you are trying to hold in your memory where the rainbow unicorn was last turned. This kind of recall can begin to decline as early as our thirties, yet some people maintain strong working memory well into middle age and beyond. Episodic memory, which involves remembering specific events or images, such as the name of the movie you saw last month, may begin to show declines from the fifties into the sixties. Luckily, some aspects of memory seem to be preserved until later in life:

Procedural memory, which involves remembering how to do something like working a computer, riding a bicycle, or playing bridge remains pretty much intact.

Prospective memory keeps track of the things you need to do in the future such as pay your bills on time, take your medications, or bring brownies to the high school fundraiser. Calendars can come to the rescue as a backup.

Metamemory is the ability to know *how* to remember things effectively—in other words, knowing the strengths and limits of our memory as well as identifying memory aids to help us remember. Use of sticky notes, calendars, electronic reminders, and mnemonic devices such as ROYGBIV are all strategies that reflect metamemory. Meta-memory hack: Writing things down and taking notes is a great way to get the information you need to remember into your brain. In one of my studies we found that if you are given a list of words and then write them down you're more likely to remember them later. I find this works when I forget to bring my grocery list to the market; I am more likely to remember what I need to buy if I wrote everything down before I left. So even though my memory failed to help me remember to bring the list, I benefit from having made the list in the first place. I keep a pad and pen on my night table so when I think of something while in bed, I write it down. It not only helps my sleep; I am more likely to act on it the next day.

As we can see, when we look at the different kinds of memory, a very different perspective on how aging affects this core ability emerges. While there are certainly declines in some of the flashier aspects of memory, we're doing ourselves a disservice when we overlook the gains in others. As Lauren would tell you, never underestimate the joy of surfacing a word you learned decades ago to score Scrabble Bingo (using all your letters in one turn!).

Most people misunderstand how intelligence, cognition, and memory impact us as we age. Succumbing to fear and cultural narratives about decline, we cherry-pick the losses and miss the gains, ultimately ignoring the most important question of all—are we still able to do what we want and need to do? Can we solve problems, rise to the occasion, and function well in our day-to-day lives? Just because our brains are working *differently* starting in middle age doesn't mean they are worse.

An article by Melissa Lee Phillips in the APA *Monitor on Psychology* points this out by highlighting research done on airplane pilots, a group with notably heavy responsibilities when it comes to staying on top of challenges and thinking fast. They reported on a study from the journal *Neurology* that compared the performances of pilots between the ages of forty and sixty-nine, and looked at how well they did on two markers: learning to use the flight simulator and avoiding collisions. Despite showing the normal level of decline in their processing speed and working memory, it didn't affect the older pilots' ability to get the job done. They actually bested their younger colleagues when it came to avoiding collisions in the flight simulator.

This illustrates how both experience and specialized expertise can help compensate for some of the declines that are experienced with age and make a difference in performance when it really counts. As a scientist in the APA article pointed out, many people in midlife are quick to see the losses but slower to see the gains that ultimately lead to their outcomes being the same or even better. For instance, the young pilots in the study were undeniably quicker to figure out how to use the new simulator. But in this situation, it didn't confer a functional advantage—they still had more collisions than the older pilots. While being quick might be important in some contexts, there is a speed-accuracy trade-off—time pressure doesn't always help us; sometimes working faster leads to greater errors. Ironically, this loss of speed sometimes results in more thoughtful and effective outcomes.

As the old saying goes, haste makes waste. It is not always the first answer that is best; we want the correct answer. Sometimes being right requires taking your time.

Contrary to typical narratives surrounding midlife, research like the pilot study and many others reveals that growth and decline can balance out in such a way that there is potential for us to be at peak functioning in midlife—far from the downhill tumble we've come to expect.

Creativity and Innovation

A lot has been written about the effect that aging has on one's creativity in their forties and fifties as some aspects of fluid intelligence start to decline. This is a particularly panic-inducing specter for those entering midlife, and yet like so many other concerns about aging, it's not as dire as it seems. Most of the work in this area has focused on the top percentiles of achievement such as major inventions, famous artistic, musical, and literary works, or discoveries leading to a Nobel Prize or other prestigious awards. The studies of how creativity changes with age have looked at the number of creative works and also the quality of the works at different ages. Researchers looking at these accomplishments show that the likelihood of a major discovery in many fields peaks by one's forties and starts to decline beyond. But there's still a blind spot here.

Most people do not expect to win the Nobel Prize. You can be creative in everyday life with how you cook or decorate your home or how you dress or solve a problem at work.

For those of us who aspire to be creative and productive but don't aim to win a major award, it is good to be in midlife. Fortunately, for most of us who are trying to do good work in our chosen fields in midlife and beyond, crystallized knowledge can compensate to some extent for the slow loss of fluid abilities. There is much evidence that the brain uses compensatory mechanisms to adapt to these aging-related shifts. For example, when tasks are difficult, the older brain recruits more regions of the brain to complete them. Whereas younger adults might use one side of the brain, older adults may engage both sides in the prefrontal cortex, called bilateral activation, to ultimately solve the problem. This is an example of neuroplasticity, which involves the brain adjusting to changes with age. There is also evidence that as we age we become less self-conscious and worried about what others might think, which strengthens our ability to take more creative risks. Because of this kind of compensation and our growing crystallized intelligence, we have accumulated skills that are almost like second nature and we have gained the emotional freedom and confidence to explore creatively—both are critical to ongoing success in our chosen professions.

Recent research has revealed that the hectic, responsibility-laden aspects of midlife that many people struggle with may actually be good for the brain in the long term. We all have the potential to draw on what researchers call "cognitive reserve"—how agile your brain is, or how quickly it recruits various regions, adapting to help us reach our goals even when obstacles pop up. My colleague, neuropsychologist and researcher Anne Berry, hypothesizes that "the burdens and challenges of middle age are a kind of food for the brain—giving us the scaffolding we need to remain resilient later, when we really need it." One study she often cites shows that activities done in midlife such as playing a musical instrument, learning a new language, developing an artistic pastime, or traveling to another continent (even when controlling for education, age, and activity level in later life) are positively associated with fluid intelligence in older age, and this active engagement bolsters our cognitive reserves. The magnetic resonance imaging (MRI) data from this study found structural evidence by using brain scans to compare gray matter. They discovered that midlife activities contributed to cognitive reserves, which help older adults compensate for some structural changes in the brain such as declines in gray matter volume.

Bottom line: The more you use your brain for activities in midlife, even to do seemingly mundane things like juggle your children's sports schedules, doctors appointments, and various snack preferences, the nimbler and more resilient it becomes.

The Proof Is in the Patents

In my Lifespan Lab, we wanted to examine creativity and innovation in a more general population than was typically studied. My economist colleagues, Adam Jaffe and Mary Kaltenberg, and I were interested in whether there were age differences in the quantity and quality of innovative work as represented in inventions that had received patents. We were surprised to find that the U.S. Patent and Trademark Office does not ask information about age or birth date in their applications. Luckily, we found another way to get age information—by searching directories on the web and extracting the information. We were able to find the ages of over 1.4 million US inventors and linked them with more than 3,648,663 patents granted from 1976 to 2018. We hypothesized that midlife might be the most productive and fruitful time of life given the favorable balance of growth and decline. On the one hand, the processes that are declining—for instance, memory and abstract reasoning—are still running pretty well. In other words, they haven't yet reached their low point. At the same time, the things that are improving—knowledge, experience, self-confidence—are steadily rising toward their peak. Suspecting that this point of intersection between growth and decline just might lead to a golden hour for creativity, we applied this reasoning to the study of inventors who received patents. After our analysis of the data, we found out we were on the right track: US patent filers were the most productive with inventions during early midlife. Moreover, some inventors continued to be productive well into their sixties and beyond, and 22% of first-time patent filers were over fifty. We found that just as many career inventors were awarded their first patents in their early fifties as were awarded in their early twenties.

We also found a fascinating pattern in age differences when we explored not just the quantity but the quality of inventions, that is, how important they were. We determined this by looking at the number and types of citations associated with the patents, which are often linked to commercial success. Based on the analysis of the citations, we found that the nature of inventions varied by the age of the inventors. Inventions that have more citations to past inventions and rely on expanding these past inventions in new ways were more likely to be done by older inventors. Their inventions drew more on improving or expanding on things already invented—indicative of relying on experience and the domain of crystallized intelligence. In contrast, those inventions that involved more novel and forward-thinking ideas, as measured by the number of citations made by future patent inventors, were more likely to be done by younger inventors. We also found that when patents were filed by teams of inventors, the more diverse the inventors were in age, the greater the quality of their inventions, that is, they had more citations by future inventors. This is a hugely important insight for anyone tasked with bringing together intergenerational teams in the workplace. By combating stereotypes and embracing generational differences, we can more successfully leverage the strengths that each age group brings to the table.

Each generation brings different skills and experiences to the workplace. It is up to the leadership to help the team work harmoniously to blend their contributions so that the whole is greater than the sum of its parts, like a conductor who integrates the various instruments in the orchestra. In my Lifespan Lab I work with an intergenerational team, as do most science labs. It would not be possible to achieve the quality and quantity of research output without this kind of teamwork. The lab includes postdoctoral scholars, PhD and master's students, undergraduates, research assistants, as well as a group of other faculty collaborators, often at other institutions. We all work together to plan and carry out the research, including developing hypotheses, data analysis, presentation of research findings at conferences, and writing manuscripts for publication. Each generation has different strengths and goals. The younger generations know the latest technology and the cutting-edge statistical programs. They want to learn the ins and outs of how to conduct research, so they are motivated to do the hands-on work of recruiting and testing participants or data processing that the more senior investigators don't have time to carry out. The older generations have the conceptual expertise to know how to design studies and how to get grants for funding the research. We have a system in which everyone works together to help each other with what they bring to the table. Without this cooperation and different skill sets we would not be as productive and impactful in our work.

How to Leverage *All* Your Intelligences in Midlife

Once we know how the brain can adapt, the question becomes: How can we help it along? How can we be more intentional about compensating for our losses and live out Primetime on our own terms?

Here are three ways you can do that:

1. Be patient with yourself and remember that speed isn't always the most important thing—experience is the great equalizer;

2. Exploit both kinds of intelligence by teaming up with people of different ages; and

3. Be flexible and lean into the strengths you have *now* instead of fixating on what you used to be able to do in the past.

The knowledge that age-related decline isn't set in stone helps us retain our sense of control and our belief in our ability to master whatever comes our way. This is more than a nice-to-have benefit—it's the key to balancing the gains and losses in a way that keeps us both happy and healthy.

Fostering a Strong Sense of Control

If there's one thing that most psychologists can agree on, it's that much of our mental, emotional, and physical well-being relies on our sense of control over life outcomes. This is simply our belief in our ability to meet our goals and take charge of situations to bring about desired outcomes. A healthy sense of control is a foundation of mental health, and it's also a key to successfully balancing not only the gains and losses of midlife but also to addressing the unique constraints that we are confronted with during this time of life.

When we are young and busy doing the work of building our lives, naivete to the ways of the world can be a superpower. Confronted with a challenge, we tend to simply barrel ahead, taking risks with a "where there is a will, there is a way" attitude. By the time we enter our middle years, however, experience has taught us that sometimes—even though we feel fairly confident that we have what it takes to accomplish our goals—difficulties and obligations can get in the way. Maintaining a strong sense of control as we age is critical to successfully balancing gains and losses so that we can truly embrace midlife as Primetime. It also happens to be good for our health as we age. For instance, studies show that a sense of control is related to a wide range of good outcomes. This includes a reduced risk of mortality and numerous physical health outcomes, including a lower risk of stroke, lung disease, physical limitations, cognitive impairment, and chronic pain. A higher sense of control is also related to behaviors that boost our health, such as more physical activity, as well as higher psychological well-being, lower psychological distress and depression, and decreased loneliness.

So how do we know if we have a strong sense of control?

Personal Mastery and Perceived Constraints

My colleagues and I have identified two important factors that contribute to our sense of control: personal mastery and perceived constraints. At midlife, there is a growing awareness that we have the knowledge, skills, and competence to tackle life's challenges (our sense of our own personal mastery). At the same time, we also know from experience that there will be limitations on our ability to achieve what we want (the degree to which we perceive that there are constraints in our lives). Some examples of constraints that may surface in midlife are job loss, a sick child, parents who need care, a difficult boss, menopausal symptoms, joint pain, weight gain, divorce, or financial difficulties. Such constraints seem to come at us fast and furious in midlife, which can make life feel far heavier than it was in young adulthood. And yet, by midlife our gains in self-confidence, experience, and wisdom set us up to tackle unwelcome circumstances more successfully than we would have been able to in our twenties. Those in midlife typically have encountered and successfully navigated challenges and stressors before and have inner resources (and hopefully external ones as well) to come out on top with a sense of mastery and accomplishment, despite the constraints.

In my research, we often are interested in assessing someone's overall sense of control. To do this we measure a person's perceptions or expectations about their level of personal mastery or agency relative to their perceived constraints. We assess sense of control, or what I like to call a "can do" attitude, by asking people to rate how much they agree or disagree with simple questions like, "When I really want to do something, I usually find a way to succeed at it," which helps us assess their level of mastery; or "There are many things that interfere with what I want to do," which helps us assess their perceived constraints.

What mastery boils down to is really acknowledging one's abilities to get things done, while constraints are all about assessments of how big the obstacles are and can I get around them? The ideal combination is to be high in personal mastery and low in perceived constraints. This combination signals that you have a healthy sense of control, something that can buffer you from the slings and arrows of life.

Paradoxically, to gain a sense of control it is crucial to acknowledge there are many things one can't control. As we move through our middle years, increasing constraints tied to the aging process, unexpected challenges, interpersonal relationships, and the seemingly endless responsibilities that pile up in midlife force us to acknowledge our limitations. But the research on sense of control, beginning with Julian Rotter, who developed the related concept of locus of control in 1966, consistently finds that those who believe that internal factors such as abilities and effort are what determine outcomes do better across the board when it comes to health, happiness, and well-being than those who believe more so in the role of external uncontrollable factors such as luck or chance.

The challenge is that people want to have choices and be in control, but in midlife all the ups and downs can be difficult to navigate. While being in control is not something that is often associated with our middle years, the opposite is in fact true. A recent MIDUS study that I coauthored (the first to look at patterns of change in control beliefs across a twenty-year period) revealed that people's sense of control over their lives in midlife is stronger and more stable than in early or later adulthood. So why might it be that many people journeying through middle age are able to maintain a strong sense of control while others feel more of a sense of panic and helplessness? What is the secret sauce?

Primary vs. Secondary Control

Navigating life and building on your sense of control at this crossroads of gains and losses in middle age is challenging but if done well can pay big dividends in midlife and beyond. The key to contentment in midlife is to find ways to minimize, compensate for, or counteract the losses and declines by using assets, strengths, and skills. This is a lot like what the brain naturally does as it ages: It compensates for a loss in fluid intelligence with gains in crystallized intelligence.

Taking control can look like finding other ways of thinking about your experiences or finding ways to adjust your responses to the constraints that inevitably pop up. No one is immune to the complexities of midlife, yet those who feel a sense of mastery and control are better able to meet the challenges head-on and find effective strategies for reducing or dealing with stress. Our attitudes and behaviors reinforce our sense of control—or lack of control—over our lives. In our research we have found that planning for the future can help to foster a sense of control. Even when it seems something is not clearly within your power to change, it is possible to adopt control strategies. Making plans can help add structure and meaning to your life. For things that you can't do right away due to time constraints or lack of resources, it's helpful to bookmark it for another time when you might be better able to get it done. Plans can be both short term and long term, which is an effective management strategy, especially in midlife when people often have multiple responsibilities. Yet not everything can be expected to go according to plan. When this happens, the best we can do is remain flexible and open to adjusting our plans along the way.

According to Jutta Heckhausen, a professor of psychology at University of California, Irvine, two ways we can foster control are by taking charge of the situation or circumstances through what is known as "primary control," or by changing our perspective, views, or goals, which is known as "secondary control." Primary control requires persistence and a can-do attitude, meaning you don't give up until you get what you want. For instance, if you want to meet a romantic partner you could put your profile up on an online dating site even if you feel intimidated. You keep attending singles events and knocking out the first dates as long as it takes. Secondary control involves changing your perspective or view of the situation. Let's say you haven't met your dream partner after many dates and are not enjoying the search, so then you may decide to make dating a lower priority and switch your focus to building your close friendships. Research findings show that usually people strive for primary control and resort to secondary control if their primary control efforts are unsuccessful. Knowing when to relinquish primary control is a skill that is especially useful to develop in midlife. Getting good at secondary control—changing your attitude and adapting—is also critical for our emotional health and well-being. It comes in handy because sometimes you don't have control over the situation or outcome, *but you can control how you respond to it.*

The Adaptive Response

Some of my early research involved administering cognitive tests to middle-aged and older adults to see how their sense of control influenced outcomes on challenging tasks. What we found was that those who had more adaptive responses (i.e., accepting the challenge) were more likely to persist and perform well. In contrast, some had defeatist attitudes consistent with the idea they were too old for this kind of problem-solving. Some people laughed and said the tests were silly. Others saw their performance as a measure of their intelligence or abilities. They believed they did poorly because they are not smart or were "losing their mind." Still others would say they didn't try very hard and that accounted for poor performance.

These different responses, or what researchers call "attributions for success or failure," indicate how you explain an outcome. These attributions can make a difference in how people perform and the emotions they feel. A simple example of this is how you respond when applying for a job. If you get a job interview but don't get the job, you're likely to do better the next time if you use what's called an "adaptive attribution"—in other words, chalking up the poor or unsuccessful performance to something you can control or change. Maybe you tell yourself that you didn't do enough homework to learn about the company, or that you were off because of a bad night's sleep. Those are factors you can do something about. Whereas someone who blames their performance on something they can't change (such as their age or sex) or other things outside their control (like the interviewer was biased) probably won't do much better the next time, because they are more likely to throw their hands up instead of preparing more in advance. In the short run, you may feel better if you can blame the outcome on someone else. But this kind of self-defeating attitude, explaining failures with factors you cannot change, will likely lead to anxiety and despair, which can have negative consequences for future performance, and may lead to avoiding stimulating or challenging situations.

The way you explain successes also makes a difference. In order to be modest or humble, we often don't take credit for things that go well. Yet this is a key tactic for bolstering a sense of control. If you acknowledge the effort you made and how hard you tried, this can go a long way in the future to reinforce that your efforts paid off.

When it comes to things like memory, explaining the losses we experience with something that is modifiable is the adaptive response: You lost your keys so you tell yourself that next time you will pay more attention, or put your belongings in the same designated place every time. This is more adaptive than concluding you forgot something because you are old and getting dementia. Those who believe there is something they can do to improve their memory are more likely to maintain their memory functioning well into later life. Yet, many in midlife start to worry and go for cognitive workups in a memory clinic. Fortunately, for most, these memory slips or failures are due to carelessness, stress overload, or unrealistic expectations about the capacity of human memory.

Choose Your Own Perspective

How we look at each loss or constraint may vary, but the sum total of our ability to engage secondary control or adaptive explanations for failures and adapt to what comes at us determines our broader perspective. Each of us has our own conception of how our development will play out in midlife. Research and theory on aging by Alexandra Freund, at the University of Zurich, and colleagues describe three common viewpoints: loss-framed, maintenance-framed, and gain-framed.

The loss viewpoint is exactly what it sounds like, the belief that aging-related declines in physical, psychological, and cognitive health are inevitable and irreversible, and there is not much you can do about them. In contrast, the gain viewpoint sees it is possible to improve or increase abilities, health, and well-being. A maintenance view focuses on ways to keep things intact, maintain the status quo, and do what you can to avoid losses.

You can have a different viewpoint for different areas of your life with the emphasis shifting across adulthood. In young adulthood most people focus on the gains they expect to achieve and they don't think much about losses. As we enter the middle years, we begin to focus more on the losses. However, it is important not to lose sight of the possible gains, as we can continue to grow throughout life.

What becomes critical, at least, is to maintain what you have. If you can keep things stable in midlife, especially your physical and mental abilities, you will be ahead of the game. The secret to well-being is to maintain the things you recognize are important to you. It's okay, perhaps, to accept the losses for things you don't care about. You have some control over your choices for what to emphasize and invest effort in.

In midlife it becomes important to find strategies to maintain the aspects of aging (like physical health, which we'll dive into later) that are starting to undergo slow but steady declines. They may not have a big impact on one's everyday life in midlife, but left unchecked they will accumulate and can wreak havoc on your quality of life in later years. Each of these viewpoints on change in midlife can act as self-fulfilling prophecies, which is why it's important to not only identify which viewpoint you have on midlife (and in what domains), but also to understand that you can change it.

The bottom line: You can take control of the way you see life in the middle. And what you expect to happen plays an important role in the way things actually turn out. Those who believe they are in control of their lives are happier, healthier, and less likely to suffer cognitive declines. For those in midlife, there is plenty we can't control about what our gains and losses look like. Everyone is different. Some people start experiencing chronic pain in their joints at forty-five, while others are in the best shape of their life. Some people will find themselves caring for older parents and young children at the same time, while others will be child-free and focused on building a thriving business. No matter who we are, or what midlife looks like, gains and losses will come, constraints will tug at us, and we will have a choice. How do we want to look at our journey into midlife? Do we believe we can improve it to mitigate the losses and celebrate the gains? Or do we surrender to the fatalistic narrative of aging that we've been force-fed for so long? At the midway point of our lives, we are at a unique crossroads. We get to choose which viewpoint to carry with us as we age. And we know from decades of science that our outlook, mindset, and beliefs about aging profoundly determine the course of our lives.

Rewriting the Story of Midlife

In the first two chapters, we knocked down the mythology of midlife, seeing more deeply the ways in which popular notions of middle age are at best lacking, and at worst, harmful, and replacing those out-dated notions with the realities of midlife and the great potential it holds. In this final chapter of Part 1, we've seen that the path to thriving in midlife is about taking a clear-eyed look at the gains and losses we'll inevitably experience and taking control of both our responses and our mindsets.

Now we're ready to jump into the second part of the book to look more closely at the gains and losses of midlife in different domains—in health, relationships, and decision-making. We will dive deep into the intricacies of these midlife shifts as well as learn strategies to lever-age the gains we find along the way. You'll find that these chapters are intentionally "gain-framed" while still looking honestly at the dif-ficulties that folks in midlife have to contend with. Having a positive outlook on midlife doesn't mean we have to deny the reality of our overscheduled lives or its disappointments. It just means that we give equal airtime to the good stuff—the increased self-confidence, the ability to emotionally regulate, and the deepening relationships. To get started, we're going to look at one of the most feared domains of midlife: our aging bodies.

PART TWO

RIDING the WAVES of GAINS and LOSSES

Chapter 4
Healthy in Midlife

Middle-aged life is merry, and I love to lead it,
But there comes a day when your eyes are all right but your arm
isn't long enough to hold the telephone book where you can read it.
—OGDEN NASH

One day in the summer of 2024, Sarah's four-year-old daughter, Maren, was having a rough morning. Sarah was trying to get her out the door to preschool, begging her to sit down so she could put on her shoes, but Maren was not having it. Instead, she decided to wriggle free from her mom's grasp and throw herself face down on the rainbow rug by the front door. Kicking her feet, with a mop of ginger curls flopping back and forth as she shook her head, Maren was in full protest mode.

"Baby, *please* sit up so I can put your shoes on," Sarah said, painting over her frustration with the world's thinnest veneer of calm.

Maren rolled over, looked her dead in the eye, and said, "I can't, Mama. I'm *exhausted*."

Sarah felt amusement momentarily disrupt her annoyance. After all, Maren had just woken up from a luxurious twelve hours of sleep. But quickly, the familiarity of the phrase caught her in the chest. This wasn't something her daughter came up with out of nowhere—she was four after all, the ultimate sponge—in fact, it sounded a lot like *Sarah*. Tears welled up in her eyes as the realization dawned. She had been so, so exhausted for the last three months and, clearly, she hadn't been doing a very good job of hiding it from her kid.

Over the next several days, Maren would utter that phrase whenever she didn't want to do something that involved any amount of physical effort. And every time she heard it, Sarah braced herself for a deepening of the guilt, frustration, and the depression that had been following her around for far too long. If she was honest, her mood swings and sadness had been going on for the better part of two years. She kept saying over and over to her husband, "I just don't feel like myself." When he pressed her to elaborate, she had a difficult time pinpointing it. She didn't have the energy she used to have, and her joy seemed dampened. Maren seemed to be the only thing that reliably made her smile these days, everything else was just kind of *meh*. She had experimented with antidepressants but the ones she tried either did nothing or destroyed the sliver of libido she had left. Instead of chasing a diagnosis and burning herself out with doctor's appointments and testing that went nowhere, she decided to just focus on making it through the day, hoping things would eventually turn around.

Unfortunately, at the beginning of the summer—her absolute favorite time of year in Vermont—she came down with a case of crushing exhaustion. She was sleeping fine, usually a solid eight hours, but whenever she opened her eyes in the morning, she just wanted to close them again. By the time she sat down at her at-home office desk around ten in the morning, she found herself looking longingly at her bed. Workdays became an exercise in stealing time. Whenever she could she'd squeeze in a twenty-minute snooze between meetings or use a nap as a reward for churning out yet another excruciating marketing report. She felt like a sleep addict—she just couldn't get enough. Evenings were by far the worst, though. Sarah would zombie her way through family dinner with her husband and Maren, put Maren to bed, and not even go back downstairs again. After doing the dishes her husband would come up and find her asleep—another day when they hadn't found more than ten minutes to talk, never mind hug or kiss. It had been going on for months now and even though he was supportive, Sarah felt terrible about being so absent. He had been valiantly shouldering almost all the housework and childcare while she either slept or scoured the internet trying to figure out what the hell was wrong with her. Was it just depression? Being tired all the time was a symptom, after all. But something about that didn't feel right to Sarah. Unfortunately typing "fatigue" into Google and hitting search was basically asking for an avalanche of diagnoses from cancer to parasites. She went to her primary care physician, who checked her thyroid (normal) and told her that she probably just needed to exercise more (infuriating), but otherwise the doctor didn't seem all that worried. "It's likely just stress—you've got a young kid after all," she said.

Fortuitously, the answer to her prayers came on her birthday. Her husband had insisted that they do *something* to mark her forty-fifth birthday, even though at first she protested. If she had to sneak away from her own party to go lie down, she thought it might break her spirit for good. Sarah had been at a real low for days, deeply depressed and finally understanding why people contemplated suicide. She wasn't thinking about it for herself, but she could viscerally understand why someone might. This was scary enough to jolt her into at least trying to reach for some joy—so she said yes to a short, casual backyard birthday party.

That day, after eating too much cake, she found herself trying to focus on what her friend's new girlfriend was saying. The second time she asked the woman, Georgia, to repeat herself Sarah got embarrassed and explained that she was feeling fatigued and foggy. After apologizing she gave Georgia the details of what had been going on with her lately. This friendly stranger nodded sympathetically, reached out to touch her arm, and said, "You know, it sounds a lot like perimenopause." All Sarah heard at first was the word *menopause*, so she replied that no, it couldn't be that—she still got her period. Although, she admitted, it *was* being wacky lately. Georgia then launched into an explanation about how perimenopause is the five-to-ten-year period before you stop menstruating when your estrogen gets wild and causes all these unfortunate symptoms—including mood swings and fatigue. And it can start as early as your late thirties. Sarah was intrigued, but it wasn't long before Maren came running to her with tears streaming down her face and she had to excuse herself from the conversation.

Later, she began researching this developmental phase of womanhood that she had never heard of, and quickly made an appointment with her ob/gyn. At the appointment a couple of weeks later she learned that Georgia was right, it *was* possible she was experiencing perimenopause, but the doctor wasn't sure. She wanted to run some tests first—iron levels and vitamin D. What they found was that Sarah's vitamin D level was low, but there was no way to tell which it was, vitamin deficiency or perimenopause—or both? Either way, Sarah felt a sense of relief that there might be a fix to this nightmare. So, she decided right then and there to throw everything modern medicine had at the problem. She asked her doctor to put her on hormone replacement therapy (estrogen and progesterone) and treat her for the vitamin D deficiency.

Within two weeks of beginning the estrogen and progesterone, as well as the humongous doses of vitamin D, Sarah started feeling like herself again. It was a little like resurfacing after diving deep; everything suddenly felt brighter and clearer than it had in a long time. One night at dinner, her husband cracked a joke, and she convulsed into an unbridled belly laugh that pretty much stunned her family. Her husband reached over, squeezed her hand, and said, "It's nice to hear you laugh." Sarah smiled and felt, not for the first time, profound gratitude for the stranger at the party who had so casually given her her life back.

Of course, Sarah still felt tired now and then, and her current good mood was often interrupted by thoughts about the years of her life spent *not* feeling good. She had Maren at forty-one, and knew time with her was a precious commodity. The months this past summer—an entire season of her life—were lost in a fog of sleep and sadness. It made her angry and depressed at the same time. She was especially angry about the fact that her doctor never proactively mentioned the possibility to her that her depression and fatigue could be perimenopause related. After doing more reading and identifying other symptoms she didn't know were symptoms (thinning hair, joint pain, inexplicable weight gain), she was convinced low estrogen was the real culprit. She also realized she wasn't alone: Many women her age would go through this, even if their symptoms differed. And yet her doctor didn't seem informed and very few women she knew were talking about it. How could such a major physical change that all women go through be so invisible and surrounded by silence? She decided to be like Georgia and if any woman her age complained about mysterious symptoms, she would share with them everything she had learned about perimenopause.

———————————

It's a common saying that if you don't have your health, you don't have anything. While that may sound dramatic, anyone who has been sick or injured in any serious way knows it rings true. When considering the balance of gains and losses in our lives, age-related health losses are top of mind. The physical changes that come with aging are among the most obvious and overt that we will experience. The aging process and our awareness of it can feel gradual, or it can seem like those crow's-feet sprung up overnight. For people like Sarah, some of these changes can be incredibly disruptive and obvious, while for others, they can remain hidden until the day we get a surprising lab result that needs to be addressed.

Many people believe that these aging-related changes are all negative, inevitable, and uncontrollable. But both the research and the lived experience of so many middle-aged people tell us the opposite—yes, our bodies start to change in midlife, but our lives don't have to be worse because of it. We can find relief from symptoms, *and* we can start addressing any early signs of chronic illness that age has revealed. As science advances, we have more and more tools in our toolbox to deal with everything from perimenopause to prediabetes. Excitingly, some of the biggest disruptors of physical and mental health—like hormonal changes—are finally getting the attention they deserve, leading to better awareness and utilization of treatments that make a huge difference in health and well-being. As ob/gyn and author Mary Claire Haver says, "Aging is normal, but suffering is not."

We can take action to mitigate unnecessary suffering. Probably the most important message of this chapter is that environmental and life-style factors have been found to be *more important than genetics* for your health and how long you live. The National Research Council wrote that "[r]ecent estimates suggest that human behavior accounts for between 40 and 50% of the risk associated with deaths before the age of 75 in the United States." That gives us a lot of opportunity to take control and do things to alter our life course. But before we look at some of the ways we can control our health and longevity, it's important to know what changes are typical in midlife—both the obvious *and* the invisible.

Hallmarks of Aging

As we age, physical changes occur from head to toe. We experience more dryness in many parts of our body such as our skin, mouth, and eyes. Things may become narrower, including our spinal column, esophagus, and arteries that get clogged. If we have an injury or acute illness, whether it's a broken bone or the flu, it takes us much longer to heal or get better than it did in the past.

When it comes to the types of physical changes we should be aware of in midlife, they generally fall into two major categories—the seen and the sneaky. The obvious changes, like creaky knees or wrinkles, tend to get the most attention, but the sneaky changes that impact our long-term health are just as important to attend to. Let's look at both:

The Seen. The seen (and felt) hallmarks of aging are driven by changes in virtually all body parts and systems.

Physical appearance: We may notice thinning and wrinkling skin, age spots, gray hairs, hair loss or balding, and changes to our voices.

Musculoskeletal: You might experience newfound stiffness in your joints and more muscle soreness and injuries.

Reproductive system: We experience the symptoms of hormonal changes from mild to wild during midlife, with some men experiencing a drop in libido due to testosterone dips starting in their fifties, as well as erectile dysfunction, and women in perimenopause or menopause who might experience a slew of symptoms from painful sex to frozen shoulder. For women, perimenopause is the period of fluctuations in the balance of hormones, estrogen and progesterone, that usually starts about five to ten years before actual menopause (which occurs on average at fifty-two but can happen as early as forty-five) and can lead to sleep disturbances, mood swings, vasomotor symptoms, or hot flashes.

Sleep patterns: While these change in midlife, it's often gradual and may not be as noticeable until later in life. It takes longer to fall asleep; you may wake up more during night and take longer to fall back asleep; and REM (rapid eye movement) sleep is disrupted, which is the phase of sleep in which dreams occur and the body repairs itself. Older adults spend less time in slow wave deep, which is important for memory consolidation, which transforms new memories into more long-term ones.

Reaction time slows down due to changes in central nervous system processing speed and may affect our ability to respond quickly when driving or trying to remember something, like on *Jeopardy!*

Shortness of breath is more common during vigorous exercise due to changes in lung capacity.

Our senses: Our sensory systems can begin to lose their sensitivity, resulting in vision changes such as presbyopia (difficulty focusing on close objects), hearing loss, as well as diminishing balance, taste, and smell.

If this list sounds terrifying, don't worry—almost no one experiences *all* these symptoms! In fact, some people experience very few, and for others the changes are so gradual as to be almost invisible in midlife. Aging is nothing if not an individual process, even if some of the age-related changes are more common, like needing reading glasses. For the most part, all the "seen" changes you might experience are mild in nature, at least during middle age. More dramatic issues with loss of memory, mobility, and vision/hearing don't hit until we are past midlife. This gives us the unique opportunity to start managing any encroaching, unpleasant side effects of aging before they start to erode our quality of life.

The Sneaky. There are a number of systems that affect your functional health that undergo gradual, sometimes invisible changes. These changes are usually not as apparent early in midlife but may start to cause difficulties later if no action is taken. These include bone loss, decline in muscle mass, cardiovascular changes such as clogging of the arteries, metabolic changes, and weakening of the immune system, which all are happening, although we may not be aware of them.

This is why seeing your doctor regularly in midlife for routine tests and scans is critical. Cancer, heart disease, or dementia can start to develop some ten to twenty years before the symptoms are manifested. Changes in the brain, in amyloid or tau deposits, white matter, and neurotransmitters, can start at least ten years before overt indicators of memory loss. You might not be able to stop decreases in brain volume, but you can certainly lower high blood pressure and cholesterol and drastically reduce your likelihood of heart attack or stroke, and yes dementia, which is associated with cardiovascular disease. Once we know what we're up against with sneaky changes like these, we can begin to set up the medical and lifestyle changes we need to live healthier, happier lives.

One of the biggest drivers of both seen and sneaky changes (the aches, pains, *and* scary lab results) for women is something that until very recently has flown under the radar. A lack of research, education, and misinformation have led generations of women to either suffer in silence because of stigma or live in the dark about what is causing their symptoms in the first place. While entire books are devoted to the subject, no book about middle age would be complete without a discussion of perimenopause and menopause. Let's dive in.

It's Not Your Mother's Menopause

When it comes to midlife misconceptions, menopause is an excellent case in point. Many women understand at least a handful of the symptoms that go along with the menopausal transition and declining reproductive hormones (like hot flashes or mood swings), but most don't know that symptoms can begin well before menopause itself—as early as the late thirties and early forties. The average age of menopause is fifty-two, which simply marks the one day in your life when you have been without a period for twelve months. In pop culture, menopause has been portrayed as a bit of a farce, with older women sweating copiously, peeling off clothes inappropriately, and snapping at their spouses. But the truth is much more nuanced. Some women—like Sarah—begin to experience symptoms of menopause years before it happens and their symptoms might not include hot flashes at all. During this phase hormone levels become more volatile, leading to irregular menstrual periods and other symptoms of low estrogen. While 75% of women experience hot flashes and night sweats in perimenopause, others float straight into menopause without experiencing any noticeable symptoms at all. Some people might have only one symptom, while others may have multiple. The symptoms themselves can range from merely annoying to incredibly disruptive to life-altering. For those who do experience symptoms of perimenopause and menopause, the path to finding both understanding and relief is strewn with obstacles.

Perimenopause may be having a cultural moment right now, but there are still legions of women out there who are going to their doctors with a laundry list of perimenopausal and menopausal symptoms and getting nothing but a pat on the back or a scrip for antidepressants. While surely these doctors are trying to help, the fact of the matter is that medical schools and residency programs are not sufficiently educating doctors-to-be about perimenopause and menopause care. A 2024 editorial published in the journal *Menopause* revealed a frustrating lacuna in medical education. Researchers found that only 31% of ob/gyn residencies offered a curriculum *with any menopause training*, and only 6.8% of the residents felt adequately prepared to manage women experiencing menopause. While many doctors will likely recognize the most well-known symptoms, there are over thirty lesser-known and sometimes subtle symptoms such as kidney stones, migraines, muscle aches, pain during intercourse, jaw pain, crawling skin sensations, vertigo, brain fog, insulin resistance, dental problems, sleep apnea, anxiety, and chronic fatigue syndrome. Doctors' inability to recognize the root cause of these symptoms is often not their fault, but women pay the price for the medical system's failures with their health, happiness, and productivity.

Unfortunately, even when women are diagnosed properly, the legacy of misleading science and a media maelstrom from the early 2000s means that they are not always able to get the treatment they need. Before 2002, many women were taking hormone replacement therapy (HRT) to combat their symptoms of menopause. But in 2002 a study looking at the effectiveness of HRT (called the Women's Health Initiative) was halted due to fears that the data showed estrogen caused cancer. This was a huge story that led the evening news and resulted in a lot of press coverage. It was so influential that between the years of 2001 and 2008 prescriptions for hormone therapy dropped by 70%. Doctors began warning women away from hormone therapy, and a new era of women suffering in silence kicked off. In fact, I was one of them. Because my mother died of breast cancer at an early age, I was warned not to take HRT.

There are many reasons why the "estrogen-causes-cancer" takeaway from this study was overblown and misleading—too many to go into here—but suffice to say, it is now widely accepted that the data were misinterpreted. Taken at the right time, in the right dose, with the right formulations, hormone replacement therapy can safely offer women relief from some of their most disruptive and painful symptoms. But just as importantly (contrary to the 2002 message), new research has shown that HRT, when taken before menopause or within ten years of reaching menopause, can reduce both cardiovascular disease and all-cause mortality. While research is still in the works to determine how HRT impacts other major health conditions like Alzheimer's disease, type 2 diabetes, and osteoporosis, early studies suggest that it may be both neuroprotective and helpful in reducing the incidence of diabetes and bone loss.

Going on hormone replacement therapy is a decision every woman experiencing symptoms deserves to make in an informed way with her healthcare provider. The symptoms of age-related hormone changes don't need to be gritted through, and luckily there is more help available now to women than there has been in a long time. Currently, there is a resounding call not only for a renewed conversation about menopause, but research to broaden and deepen our understanding of it. There's no reason that the 75 million women who are in perimenopause, menopause, or post-menopause shouldn't get help. Especially since one Mayo Clinic study found that 15% of the women they surveyed who were experiencing menopause-related symptoms had either missed work or cut back on hours because of their symptoms. They estimated that the annual cost of missed days at work for women with menopausal symptoms was $1.8 billion in the United States. It is statistics like these that are finally getting corporate America to pay attention. After all, women are 51% of the population and 57% of them are in the workforce, although the numbers have been declining.

One of the biggest problems associated with perimenopausal and menopausal drops in estrogen is inflammation. In fact, a 2020 article in the *Journal of Neuroinflammation* referred to perimenopause in the title as a "systemic inflammatory phase." The article goes on to describe how inflammation during this period may contribute to major health events like Alzheimer's disease and stroke. But inflammation isn't just something that occurs during perimenopause. In fact, for both men and women, it is a midlife phenomenon that may be at the root of many of our age-related health problems.

Inflammaging

One of the most important immune processes in our bodies is inflammation. It comes in two flavors—acute and chronic. Acute inflammation happens when there is an injury or an illness that the immune system needs to take care of immediately. Like a crew of firefighters, it blasts the area with immune mediators that try to put out the "fire"—this leads to the redness, soreness, and swelling you see when you've got a nasty cut or a sprained ankle. When things go well, this kind of inflammation is intense but short-lived. But sometimes, the immune system does its job a little too well. This is when the problems begin.

If acute inflammation is a fire hose, then chronic inflammation is like the slow drip, drip, drip of a spigot that someone neglected to turn all the way off. Over time—months and years—this constant drip can do a tremendous amount of damage. The immune system triggers this low-level, chronic inflammatory response for a handful of reasons: exposure to toxins and chemicals; autoimmune disorders like rheumatoid arthritis; fungus and parasites; and of course, chronic stress. Whatever the cause, chronic inflammation is such a driver of negative health-related changes as we age that an immunologist at the University of Bologna named Claudio Franceschi decided to coin a new term to describe it: inflammaging.

The idea behind inflammaging is that chronic inflammation is a major driver of age-related health problems, increasing the risk of chronic disease. It plays a role in a range of conditions including asthma, neurodegenerative diseases such as Alzheimer's and Parkinson's, as well as metabolic disorders such as type 2 diabetes, fatty liver disease, sleep apnea, multiple forms of cancer, musculoskeletal disorders such as osteoarthritis, osteoporosis, and sarcopenia (loss of muscle mass and strength), and cardiovascular diseases such as cardiomyopathy, atherosclerosis, and stroke. Name a disease state, and it's likely that inflammation is either to blame, or is fanning the flames.

While we can't do much about some things that might be driving chronic inflammation, like autoimmune disorders and parasites, it's worth looking more closely at one of the biggest drivers of all: chronic stress.

As we've talked about before, we all experience stress, but midlife is a time when stress can peak. Cellular aging is thought to be implicated in changes in immune system response (like chronic inflammation) and it is also accelerated by stress. Telomeres are the DNA at the tips of our chromosomes that protect them from damage during the cell division process. Each time there is cell division, your telomeres shorten, and eventually, when they get too short, the cells can't replicate. That's when tissue begins to age. As a result, measuring the length of telomeres can give an indication of cellular age. This is important because telomere length impacts both health and lifespan. Telomere length has been shown to correlate with mortality. In one study, for example, those who had shorter telomeres had a higher mortality rate from a variety of diseases including cardiovascular, digestive, musculoskeletal, and respiratory conditions.

Stress shortens telomeres through a process called oxidative damage—which basically means that important molecules in your cells are out of balance. There are more unstable molecules (free radicals) that can cause damage to cell structures than molecules that neutralize them (antioxidants). When this happens, bad things follow. For instance, caregiving is associated with higher oxidative stress, shorter telomere length, and lower telomerase activity (which helps to maintain telomeres)—known determinants of cell death and longevity. A study of parents who were caregivers of children with cancer showed that those who had more stress had shorter telomeres than parents whose children did not have cancer. Negative interactions with family are also associated with shorter telomere length while positive social interactions and support are associated with longer telomere length. Other studies have found that those who were the most optimistic had longer telomeres and this was particularly the case for those who had experienced stress.

While genetics plays a role in both inflammation and telomere length, recent research has made it clear that reducing oxidative stress is something we can do to mitigate the invisible damage lurking in our cells. For mid-lifers who find themselves in the sandwich generation, have high levels of stress from caregiving, or deal with autoimmune disorders, managing stress levels is doubly important.

Getting a handle on our stress is only one of the ways we can beat back inflammaging. Just as there are anti-inflammatory foods (blueberries, salmon, broccoli, and turmeric, to name a few) and nonsteroidal anti-inflammatory drugs (aspirin, ibuprofen, naproxen) to treat acute inflammation, there is another class of anti-inflammatories that can help manage chronic inflammation: what I call the psychosocial anti-inflammatories.

Psychosocial Anti-inflammatories

Although for years there have been unsuccessful quests to find the fountain of youth, some of the secrets of a longer lifespan have in fact been discovered. There are things we can do to increase the likelihood of maximizing our health throughout our life. The goal is to live as long as possible in good health—this is called health span. Ideally, we can delay the onset of chronic diseases and slow the biological changes that come with aging.

One of the best ways to kill these two birds with one stone is to address inflammation. We talked about how chronic inflammation can lead to disease and early mortality. To beat back inflammation, we must look at the psychosocial factors that can fuel it. Stress, we've covered, but there's also what can stoke the stress fires—discrimination, anger, trauma, neuroticism, depression, anxiety, bereavement, negative attitudes, pessimism, conflict, and social strain. And just like you might treat inflammation resulting from a torn ligament or a sprained ankle with an anti-inflammatory like ibuprofen, you can treat psychosocial inflammation as well.

In a study I worked on as part of MIDUS, we discovered that there are psychosocial anti-inflammatories that we can use to help mitigate the inflammation caused by the psychosocial stress in our lives. These include having positive beliefs such as purpose and meaning in life; having a sense of control; stress reduction with effective coping; optimism, positive affect (pleasant emotions and feelings), and social connections.

There is much evidence that these psychosocial factors are associated with better health and greater longevity. Those who have a higher sense of control, a stronger sense of purpose in life, and greater social support also have lower levels of inflammatory markers such as interleukin 6 (IL-6) and C-reactive protein (CRP). A narrative review of twenty-eight studies found that positive affect serves as a buffer against the effects of stress on inflammation. And although stress is associated with inflammation, the effects were reduced for those with a more positive attitude. Several studies have found that greater social strain is associated with higher inflammation levels. In contrast, social support and social integration were significantly related to lower levels of inflammation in a meta-analysis.

How exactly do psychosocial anti-inflammatories mitigate all this stress and inflammation? Obviously, there are many mechanisms at play, and most are still woefully under-researched. But we do know that increasing our levels of oxytocin (the so-called love hormone) is one possible pathway. When we both give and get support from people in our social network, oxytocin may act as a buffer against inflammation. Another mechanism is that those who have more social support engage in more health-promoting and less health-damaging behaviors than those without support. Also, feelings of mastery and control can reduce cortisol, the stress hormone, and increase endorphins, which reduce anxiety and promote well-being. Those who have a high sense of control and strong sense of purpose in life are more likely to be motivated to act in fulfillment of their goals, including health-promoting actions.

Move Your Body

By now, the science is clear that physical exercise is a panacea for just about anything that ails us. In middle age, it's even more important to keep stress, inflammation, and chronic illness at bay. Exercise is the one thing that has consistent and strong evidence for benefits in all the aspects of physical, cognitive, and mental health that change with age. Important for improving our day-to-day aches and pains, movement is one of the best ways to slow or prevent problems with the muscles, joints, and bones. A moderate exercise program can help you maintain strength, balance, flexibility, and strong bones. And regular physical exercise can reduce the risk of age-related conditions such as muscle loss, falls, disability, frailty, osteoarthritis, cancer, heart disease, Alzheimer's, and even early mortality. Last but not least, physical activity has also been shown to preserve telomere length, potentially lengthening our lives as well.

Of course, despite the widespread knowledge of the many benefits of exercise, only about 25% of adults engage in the CDC-recommended levels of exercise (i.e., 150 minutes of moderate to vigorous aerobic activity per week and two days per week of strength training), and this percentage decreases with age.

We know that those who have a higher sense of control are more likely to engage in physical exercise, which in turn leads to lower daily stress. But what about everybody else? The Boston Roybal Center for Active Lifestyle Interventions, which I direct, seeks to answer that question. Our goal is to find ways to help sedentary adults become more active. To that end, we have tested a variety of innovative behavior change methods, tools people can use in their own lives to stay healthy and fit through midlife and beyond. One of our interventions used Implementation Intentions (developed by psychologist Peter Gollwitzer) to motivate a more active lifestyle in middle-aged adults who were having trouble finding the time to exercise. The idea behind implementation intentions is that you have a goal with specific plans for how to accomplish it. The goal is to specify what you are going to do, when you are going to do it, how you are going to do it, and ideally with whom. Some people actually put exercise in their daily calendars, so they set aside a specific time that does not conflict with their other responsibilities. It is also important to have contingency or backup plans when something comes up that throws you off your routine—let's say it's going for a walk every morning, but you have trouble sticking to it. Life keeps happening and excuses keep rolling. The dog is sick, and you need to take him to the vet. You woke up feeling a little under the weather. You forgot that you had an early-morning meeting. And on and on. The success of Implementation Intentions boils down to specific planning around how to meet your goals and also building in if-then plans or contingencies for when life happens. For instance, if you must take your dog to the vet instead of going on your scheduled walk, then you would have a backup plan for fitting it in later in the day.

In a study with former doctoral students Stephanie Robinson and Alycia Bisson, we developed and tested an implementation intention intervention to increase step counts with middle-aged adults who wanted to exercise more. Our study found that by using personalized schedules and plans to nail down the specifics of how they were going to meet their goals, subjects walked more. One of the goals was to help people develop self-efficacy or a sense of mastery for regular walks despite the obstacles. We focused on addressing time constraints, which is one of the biggest obstacles to exercise, so we recruited participants who said they wanted to exercise more but just couldn't find the time. Our focus was on helping them plan how they would meet their exercise goals in spite of the time crunch. We gave participants a goal to increase their steps a realistic amount each week, so they could reach their goal in a manageable way.

To support the behavior change, we provided participants with customized maps with detailed walking routes based on their suggestions. If someone wanted to walk seven thousand steps, we gave them information about how they could achieve that on a particular route. And we provided other ways to increase steps in a daily routine, such as park in a distant space at the grocery store, take the stairs rather than use an escalator or elevator, or go for a walk during a meeting with your coworker instead of sitting in your office. We compared the implementation intentions group to a control group that did not receive the goal-directed materials. Compared to the control condition, the intervention condition increased significantly more in steps and time spent in moderate to vigorous activity. Those who achieved their walking goals also showed an increase in their time-related exercise self-efficacy. That is, they became more confident that they could find time to achieve their walking goals and they experienced more positive affect.

Given that midlife is a busy time, implementation intentions can be critical for those of us who find it hard to find the time or motivation to take care of ourselves. Often in midlife we are focused more on the health of our children or parents, but there are strategies for doing both at the same time, such as going for family walks or cooking and enjoying healthy meals together. The most important part? Knowing and believing that you *can* change for the better.

The More You Know

Having healthy attitudes, including the belief that you can influence your health outcomes, is key. It can determine how likely we are to engage in the healthy lifestyle behaviors that will, in turn, lead to real health benefits in midlife and beyond. This is one of the reasons that people who have a sense of agency and control in their lives are better at making physical activity a part of their everyday lives. Beliefs are powerful. Many in midlife feel that age-related changes are inevitable and uncontrollable. If you're not careful, this becomes a self-fulfilling prophecy. The truth is that there are many things you can do to take control of the aging process. Physical activity is just one. Here are some critical steps we can all take to improve our age-related woes, and make sure we are keeping chronic illness in check:

+ Regular checkups with your doctor and age-appropriate scans, immunizations, and blood tests. Many screenings, tests, and inoculations are tied to turning forty, forty-five, or fifty, with physicians recommending colonoscopies and prostate exams, bone density and breast cancer scans, shingles vaccines, and a bevy of blood tests for things like cholesterol and blood glucose levels. Don't be tempted to put off these important checkups and tests just because everything "seems fine"—the earlier problems are identified, the better. Even if your tests are normal, you've established an important baseline that your doctor can refer to later and use to make informed decisions about your ongoing care.

+ Eliminating the use of tobacco products and minimizing the use of alcohol.

+ Getting the recommended 150 minutes of physical activity every week and lifting weights or using resistance bands at least twice a week.

+ Eating a healthy, whole foods diet with plenty of fruits, veggies, whole grains, and protein.

+ Managing stress, strengthening your social network, and maintaining a sense of purpose.

+ Getting seven to eight hours of sleep a night.

+ Engaging in cognitively stimulating activities like attending lectures, reading books, doing puzzles, or playing card games, and learning something new that can create new pathways in your brain.

This may sound like a lot of work to do in between the million other obligations and responsibilities we must attend to every day, but the more, and sooner, you know about what your health baseline is (blood pressure, cholesterol, bone density, etc.), the more runway you will have to reverse any damaging processes that are in motion.

 **The Usual Prescription for Healthy Aging**

- ✓ *Exercise regularly*
- ✓ *Cognitive (brain) stimulation*
- ✓ *Get restful sleep*
- ✓ *Low-fat diet, antioxidants, fruits, veggies*
- ✓ *Low BMI/waist circumference*
- ✓ *No smoking*
- ✓ *Low alcohol consumption*
- ✓ *Use sunscreen; avoid midday sun*

 **A Psychosocial Prescription for Healthy Aging**

- ✓ *Find purpose and meaning in life*
- ✓ *Have a sense of control*
- ✓ *Maintain supportive social connections*
- ✓ *Be optimistic*
- ✓ *Stay positive*
- ✓ *Reduce stress*

Increasing your physical activity and engaging more with your social network may feel hard to fit in, but the juice will be worth the squeeze. You'll find yourself with more energy to tackle the other parts of your schedule, with a better mood. We may not be able to stop the march of time, but we can certainly make it more enjoyable.

Hopefully, understanding what may be in store for your physical self in midlife makes it less scary and confusing when age-related issues crop up. For women especially, untangling the symptoms of perimeno-pause from the day-to-day stresses of life can be tricky, which is why having a good doctor and educating yourself is critical. Often when we feel a sea change in our physical health it can lead to emotional distress, as if this is the beginning of the downhill slide we've been dreading. Whether it's your knees creaking on the way down the stairs or your cholesterol creeping upward, try not to panic and try to give yourself some grace. These changes are quite common—you are not alone. And there is almost always something you can do to make yourself more comfortable, even reversing some of your most bothersome symptoms.

Changes to our physical health in midlife are nothing if not a reminder that time is passing, maybe faster than we'd like. In the next chapter we'll look at time from a different perspective—how we experience it as a constraint, a loss, and if we're in the right mindset, an opportunity.

Tool for Implementation Intentions for Behavior Change

You can apply this strategy when developing a new habit, such as starting an exercise plan. Or it can be used to break an old pattern or habit, such as eating too many sweets. It is best to start small rather than trying to do too much at first. Specify something manageable that you want to accomplish. You can always increase the difficulty of the goal and add more of a challenge later on. Small successes add up and enhance motivation.

Answer these questions:

✦ What is your goal? What is it you want to do?

Example: I want to get 8,000 steps in a day.

✦ What are the obstacles or barriers and what will you do to overcome them?

Example: I work behind a desk for eight hours a day, my time is limited after work. I could take several short breaks throughout the day and get up and walk around, or I could go for a long walk on my lunch break.

✦ How will you carry out your goal?

Be clear about what the changes will look like. It is harder to accomplish vague goals.

Example: I won't schedule any more "working lunches" and will instead go for a walk.

✦ Where will you carry out your goal?

The setting is important for supporting goals. Make sure it is a location that can support what you want to do.

Example: I work from home, so I will just take a walk in my neighborhood.

✦ When will you do it?

Providing details about the specific times you have available to incorporate steps into your daily schedule is helpful for building the changes into your everyday life.

Example: I will do it at lunchtime, and if I can't for some reason, I'll wake up early and do it.

✦ With whom will you do it?

It can be helpful to plan these changes with another person so you can support each other and be accountable.

Example: I'll go by myself most days, but I'll try to get a friend to join me whenever possible. Or I will take a walk with my daughter before dinner.

✦ If you are unable to meet a particular goal on a given day, then what will you do?

Example: It's okay to miss a goal once in a while. I can still get back on track tomorrow.

Backup plans are helpful. And don't get discouraged if you don't accomplish your plan on a given day. You can just pick up where you left off or adjust your plans as needed.

Chapter 5
Time Is on Your Side

Never give up on a dream just because
of the time it will take to accomplish it.
The time will pass anyway.

—EARL NIGHTINGALE

When Eve walked into a party organized by some fellow doctors at her practice, she wasn't expecting much. At forty-six, she'd been in the dating game awhile, so she knew that while theoretically she could meet "the one," it was more likely she would meet, well, none. After a few laps around the appetizers, she looked around for the restroom. What she found instead was the impossible: him. When she saw the dark-haired man with a slim build and wide smile that made the skin around his eyes crinkle up at the corners, she thought to herself, *That's my guy.*

Her reaction not only surprised her, it also scared her a little. *Don't be ridiculous!* a voice in her head countered after the initial flush of excitement. She spent the rest of the evening irrationally trying to avoid him. But when he came up to her right as everyone was leaving, she knew she couldn't run away from the tingling tightness in her chest any longer. So, she stayed well after the last guests left and continued to talk to her guy: Mark.

They dated for a few months before it became abundantly clear that despite their chemistry and compatibility, Mark wasn't interested in a committed relationship. He was freshly divorced with two young kids, and Eve knew she wanted nothing to do with a half-in, half-out relationship. They decided to go their separate ways before things got too sad and strained. For Eve, it stung more than usual. While she was no stranger to the vicissitudes of dating, she was sure there really *had* been something different about this guy and their chemistry. But as a deeply practical person, Eve never threw bad money after good. She cut ties with Mark and moved on.

Finding a life partner, having kids, those were all goals she had had for herself for as long as she could remember. Things had gotten really rough in her thirties when all of her friends were getting married and having babies, and she was still looking for someone to share her life with. Despite the ups and downs of dating over the years, she never considered settling. She knew she was a catch, and she had an amazing life. A career she loved, friends she adored, hobbies that fulfilled her, and financial stability. Her biggest problem seemed to be time. By her late thirties, she knew she was running out the clock on her fertility. She considered becoming a single parent, but ultimately decided it wasn't for her. By her early forties, she had made peace with not ever having the chance to be pregnant and have a child of her own. The sadness would never leave her, but acceptance dulled the ache. Eve made a point to build strong relationships with the children in her life who weren't her own—her nieces, her friends' kids, and even her coworkers' kids. She loved those relationships and found the more she gave, the more they filled her up.

After Eve met the-almost-one, she rounded off her forties and entered her fifties feeling happy with the life she had built. She wasn't giving up on finding a partner, but she also wasn't going to let the pursuit of a relationship define her life—she'd always been clear on that. Eight years after she had first met Mark, Eve went to see a Motown quartet that was playing a show in Central Park, where she met him a second time. He spotted her first, coming up to her and her friend and introducing his children. By now the kids were teenagers, and Eve was so excited to see Mark again that it didn't even feel awkward. In fact, she still felt that spark.

Which is how they started dating again, and not too long afterward, marrying. At their wedding, the song for their first dance was "At Last" by Etta James—a classic that fit their story.

And so, at the age of fifty-five, Eve found herself in a committed partnership with two step kids. It was almost as if she was at the beginning of a whole new life, one she never fully expected but always wanted. Someone to take walks with after dinner, someone to give her a hug after a hard day at work, someone to share all of herself with.

As Eve is fond of saying, "just go for it," and when it comes to romance, she is proof "it's never too late."

This is what we know about time: Our perception of it shifts in mid-life. Looking back on our past, we sift through the choices we made, measuring them against how our lives have turned out. At the same time, we begin to look ahead, imagining what might come next when our children are grown and need us less, or if we retire or pivot in our careers and suddenly have more time on our hands.

Each of us experiences this middle period of the life course differently. It could be panic-inducing—we're so behind, and we're almost out of time! Or the ticking clock could be motivational, helping us get clarity and focus on what we need to do next to "win." For someone like Eve, the countdown clock was always in the background, but she didn't let it dominate her perspective. There is no getting around the fact that we are, in fact, mortal—our time here is limited. And yet how we each approach that constraint varies greatly. Some people choose to view time as a challenge rather than a limit, investing in age-defying wellness trends and trying to maximize physical health through biohacking and extreme exercise. Others see time as a cruel demon chasing them with a stick. These folks tend to be in a rush to get everything done NOW, at the cost of enjoying the present. There are mid-lifers who are blindsided by long-held regrets that steal their joy and keep them stuck in pits of self-loathing. While some people are so overwhelmed by the day-to-day obligations of their burgeoning responsibilities in midlife that they don't even have time for a break in which to contemplate how things are going—they just put their head down until something unexpected happens that forces them to reevaluate their lives. It could be an injury, divorce, job loss, or other major life changes. This is all to say that there are many ways we can respond to the time constraints that midlife makes apparent.

How we look at time in midlife is incredibly context dependent. For instance, people are living longer and healthier lives now, but there has also been a drastic shift or delay in when the average person hits major life milestones like getting advanced degrees, marrying, and having children, not to mention that many are deciding to skip those milestones altogether. A person who had kids in their late thirties or early forties and is caring for both young kids and older parents in their late forties and early fifties is going to have a much different perception of time than someone who had their children in their twenties. The forty-something about to be an empty-nester might have a more expansive view, finally able to think about life beyond endless laundry and car-pools, while the forty-something who is staring at almost another two decades of caregiving might feel that time is a little less forgiving.

Many in midlife are in fact at the top of their game, as we learned in the last chapter when we talked about the power of experience and crystallized intelligence. If we can allow ourselves the time we need to accomplish our goals versus worrying that we missed some mythical "right" moment, it is possible to accomplish many, many things in midlife and beyond. This approach to handling regret requires us to stretch and expand our time-with-a-big-T perspective so we can see that the hourglass is in fact half-full.

Researchers have studied the shift in future time perspective (how constricted our view of time in the future is versus how expansive) using questions such as those developed by Laura Carstensen, a

Stanford psychologist, and her colleagues. They ask people to describe themselves with statements such as "There is plenty of time left in my life to make new plans" or "I have the sense time is running out." Respondents are asked to rate these items from 1 = Very untrue of you to 7 = Very true of you. They find that future time perspective starts to become more constrained in later life. But in midlife, despite the realization that some doors may be closing, and some decisions need to be made posthaste, most people still have a sense that there is a lot of time left.

When people perceive that time is running out in some way (maybe they have an illness or are about to retire), they have a contracted experience of time. This is not always a bad thing—in fact, it can lead to what is called a "positivity effect"—because folks in that situation are far more focused on prioritizing feel-good, short-term goals, especially involving close relationships. They reach more intensely for what will make them happy *now*, which is probably why they are more likely than young adults to actively try to shift their current moods. On the other end of the time continuum, when we are younger, we feel like we have plenty of time to reach our goals, placing the emphasis on exploring and moving toward what we *think* will make us happy in the future. This is yet another way that midlife is an amazing opportunity for balance. Folks in their forties and fifties aren't done reaching for their goals or even developing new ones, but many also understand the poignancy and importance of enjoying life as it speeds by and appreciating the time that does remain. As Eve's story illustrates, even when you think the buzzer is about to sound, you might just find yourself in overtime with a second chance you never anticipated.

Inaction Regret vs. Action Regret

In a podcast interview with Hoda Kotb, Mitch Albom, the best-selling author of *Tuesdays with Morrie*, spoke poignantly and at length about regret. When he and his wife were in their forties they began to feel deep sorrow that they did not have children. Albom described himself as having "dragged his feet" on this important decision, and as the sands of time slipped through the hourglass, eventually it was too late. Or so he thought.

While the author might be best known for selling over 40 million books globally, he and his wife are also committed philanthropists who have both started and volunteered their time at charities since the late 1990s. It's no surprise that when an earthquake devastated Haiti in 2010, killing over 220,000 people, the Alboms left their home in Detroit, Michigan, to help. By this time Albom was in his fifties, and thoughts of parenthood were largely in the rearview mirror, even if the pain of regret was still riding shotgun. In Port-au-Prince, he found himself touring an orphanage that had been damaged during the earthquake. "I happened to ask the guy who had been running it, 'How come the kids aren't eating?' and he said, 'Well, I don't have any money to operate this place. And I'm 84 years old.'" At the time, Albom said to himself: "Well, I could probably do this. How hard could it be?" Not long after, he took over the orphanage and has been running the Have Faith Haiti Mission & Orphanage ever since. After years of hard work helping the children in his care, Albom now thinks much differently about not having kids. "It's probably the biggest regret of my life, but God works in funny ways, you know, because now I've got 53 children and so does my wife and we look at them as our kids."

When we feel regret, we look back in time at something that happened (or didn't happen) with a sense of sorrow or disappointment. There can be a certain disbelief that we lacked control over an event or situation—or that we did have control, but failed to exercise it. Maybe we feel that we made a mistake, made bad choices, or simply didn't do something that would have made us happy. Some people spend years and years of their lives recalling what happened—or didn't happen— and questioning the universe or just questioning themselves.

The ups and downs of midlife, including regrets, are best seen in findings from longitudinal studies such as the MIDUS, which we have covered throughout the book. One of my favorite longitudinal studies is from Michael Apted's *Up* film series, which followed the same people every seven years from age seven to sixty-three. When his film subjects were age sixty-three, Apted posed them an interesting question: Do you have any regrets and, if so, what are they? One man said, "I don't think life is there to be regretted." Another said, "Life is what happens while you are waiting for something else." One man's response stood out to me because I have heard it many times myself: He regretted not spending more time with children and family. It is often said that no one who reflects on their life says they wish they had spent more time at work. Try to keep this in mind before you turn down a chance to attend your child's or grandchild's play, concert, or sport event to attend a meeting at work instead.

While we can feel regret at any point in our lives, midlife is a time when we're well into our professional and personal lives, having made plenty of decisions along the way that are cannon fodder for regret. In one study conducted by Dan Pink, author of *The Power of Regret*, he found that 82% of Americans occasionally feel regret when they look back on their lives. He also discovered that as we age, people more frequently regret the things they didn't do, as opposed to regretting the actions they took. In other words, midlife is a time when our *inaction regrets* start to outnumber the *action regrets*. Whether it's regretting not having children, forgoing advanced education or the more lucrative job, or really, really wishing you had started contributing to a 401(k) in your twenties or a 529 education plan for your children in your thirties, there are plenty of decisions to blame for things not turning out the way you wished. It could be an unmet goal, a bad decision, the mucking up of a loving relationship, and everything in between. Dan Pink's survey of regret found that some of the most common regrets were staying in a bad marriage too long, not getting advanced degrees, and living what feels like "someone else's life." Regrets such as not getting married, not having children, or not pursuing a particular career path may surface in middle age. As you get older, the options for pursuing these dreams may become more restricted. There are fewer eligible partners, the biological clock is ticking louder, or there is ageism in the workplace that works against getting a job offer. In this way, midlife is the perfect time to deal with feelings of regret. You're motivated by the dearth of time, but not yet overwhelmed by it, and many doors are still open.

Not dealing with regret has consequences. Like any unpleasant or negative emotion, it is information that, depending on how it is used, can be either a blessing or a curse. On the positive side, the anticipation of regret (or fear of it) can help us make better decisions. It has even been shown to improve decision-making and emotion regulation in children because it helps them rein in their impulses and think more clearly about future consequences. For adults, feelings like regret and guilt can act as correctives for bad behavior, helping us smooth out interpersonal rifts and maintain relationships. On the negative side, letting feelings of regret fester is bad for your mental, emotional, and physical health. One study looked at people who had lost their jobs during COVID and found themselves stuck in unemployment; they regretted the loss of their jobs and were unable to find new ones in their field because of the pandemic. Researchers discovered how unhealthy it is to focus on a goal you can't achieve. Those who continued to ruminate about their job loss instead of pivoting to a new field or project saw increases in their levels of stress, anxiety, and depression.

So what can we do?

Change It or Let It Go

Lifespan psychologist Carsten Wrosch, from Concordia University, and his colleagues have studied how to best adapt to feelings of regret. From this work we know that there are two simple, healthy choices to deal with the negative feeling of wishing you had done something differently: change it or let it go.

In order to do this, you have to know what you're dealing with.

Is it truly something you can't change?

Some past decisions can be changed; for instance, the goals we once had can be met at a later date. You might *think* that running a marathon after a knee replacement is off the table, but in reality, if you're willing to work hard, go slow, and spend plenty of time at physical therapy, it's possible. Late-in-life career changes might also feel daunting, but if passing up a career in law or education is a haunting regret, it is possible (with a certain amount of privilege and/or determination) to make a change or begin again.

For people whose regrets are changeable, the best way to approach regret is to do everything in your power to change the conditions that led to the regret in the first place—in other words, exert primary control. This might mean a belated apology to the friend you treated poorly in college. It might mean exploring new ways to find a partner, and remaining tenacious about achieving your goal, like the way Eve never gave up on love. Or if writing a novel was your life's ambition, it could be as simple as making a commitment, changing your routines, or finding a writing coach. For every regret we have in midlife, we should look more closely and ask ourselves the tough questions: Is it *really* impossible, or are we just unwilling to do what needs to be done? That could mean leaning into discomfort and even fear. You can also find ways to modify the goal. Write a short story for a magazine instead of a novel. Or volunteer in a school or a legal office to satisfy unfulfilled desires for an education or legal career.

After asking the hard question of whether you can do something about your regret, many people find that there are indeed some constraints that are too overwhelming and costly to try to change. Professor Jutta Heckhausen of UC Irvine examined what she calls "developmental deadlines," which occur when the opportunities to accomplish a goal have diminished or disappeared. This is the case for someone like Mitch Albom and his wife, who in their late forties changed their minds about kids. But it could look like a person who wanted to travel the world but realizes all their savings must now go to kids' college expenses or retirement. Or it could be a professional tennis player who is sidelined by a career-ending injury, never having won a major tournament. For situations like these, Heckhausen and colleagues determined that once the deadline is approaching or has passed for people who are struggling with a life goal that they wish they could achieve, the most adaptive step is to disengage from the unobtainable goal and adjust accordingly instead of returning to the "failure" again and again.

Re-visioning Regret

When there are circumstances we can't control, what we *can* do is try to find alternative pathways—we can call this "re-visioning."

Instead of dwelling on what may no longer be possible, we can focus our energy and resources on modifying our goals or exploring other options. In other words, finding another version of what it means to meet that goal. A large body of research supports the idea that being able to disengage from unattainable goals and reengage in alternative goals can lead to improved levels of psychological well-being and physical health. In contrast, people who find it difficult to shift course in the face of regret can experience greater distress, release of stress hormones, inflammation, and other physical health problems. The Alboms, for instance, were able to change their perspective on regret by reaching their goal in a totally different way. Yes, they would never have biological children, but the joy and fulfillment gained from taking care of children in need was still available to them—they just had to embrace a different perspective. For many others who want children later than biology allows, there are options such as finding an egg donor, surrogacy, or adoption. Just because things don't play out exactly the way you want doesn't mean you can't still achieve the essence of your goal and fulfill dreams in a different or even more creative way.

Just Shelve It

Another way to exert control is by choosing to view the goal as not in the cards for you *right now* and instead save it for later. I call this the "shelve it" approach to managing regret. Maybe the crush of responsibilities you find yourself pinned under in midlife is not the best time to do that two-month silent meditation retreat you've always dreamed of. Maybe the time isn't there *now*, but that doesn't mean it won't be there later. A friend of mine, Steve, is a prime example of how you can "shelve it" successfully. When he was in his early thirties, Steve was three-quarters of the way through a PhD program in anthropology when his mentor switched universities, and his wife got a job in another state. Seeing the writing on the wall, he gave up on his PhD, followed his wife to Virginia, and started a successful business. Raising kids and growing a business kept him happy and busy, so Steve didn't look back until he was in his late fifties. Around that time, he was starting to get restless and really wanted to sell his business and finish his degree. Unfortunately, this was when the 2008 recession hit, and no one was buying.

To stave off regret and frustration he decided to shelve his goal and wait out the recession. Ultimately, he sold the company and finished his PhD at the young age of seventy-five. His proud wife, children, and grandchildren all cheered for him as he walked across the stage at graduation. Since then, he has been happily writing, researching, and teaching. Steve's experience isn't as unique as it sounds; plenty of people decide to put their dreams on ice. In fact, research has shown that goal shelving is a strategy that leads to less regret in the long term when compared to giving up on your goals altogether. As a result, it is particularly important in midlife to consider ways to reimagine how you can fulfill unrealized goals in new ways—while you still have the luxury of time.

As for the regrets that you aren't able to shelve and you can't do anything about, you can still disengage from the regret in a healthy way by changing your internal perspective on the matter. Practicing self-compassion, zooming out and seeing things from a distance, and reorienting ourselves to *new* goals can all mitigate the negative effects of regret. As Albom aptly put it: "It's not just other people we need to forgive. We also need to forgive ourselves. For all the things we didn't do. All the things we should have done. You can't get stuck on the regrets of what should have happened."

Blame History

When we look back during midlife, we see the ways that the passing of time and the impact of our decisions has shaped our lives. Because we're so close to regret, it's easy to see and feel. But beyond regret there is another aspect of what I call big-T time that is harder to see but impacts midlife just as much—*historical time*.

As we go through our middle years focusing on all the things (and people!) we must attend to, it can be easy to lose track of what is going on in the world that might be impacting our own lives. And these days with climate change, political divisiveness, economic volatility, and rising gun violence (just to name a few), there is a lot. Such historical factors have both practical and psychological impacts on our health and well-being as we move through midlife.

To understand how historical context can play a role in shaping your life, take the Great Depression as an example. It is well known that the Great Depression had a major short-term and long-term impact on employment, work life, finances, and health in 1929 and the early 1930s. Life course sociologist Glen Elder found that the timing of the Great Depression in one's life made a big difference. He called it the principle of historical time and place: that "the life course of individuals is embedded in and shaped by the historical times and places they experience over their lifetime." Those who experienced financial difficulties when they were younger (he studied those who were born 1928–29) were more vulnerable, with greater long-term negative consequences into adulthood, than those who experienced them when they were older (he also studied those born 1920–21). Elder surmised that this was in part because those who were younger were more dependent on their parents' finances than the older group during the difficult financial times. The older group could draw on resources from earlier, more prosperous times and could work or enter the military to help earn extra money for the family as they came of age and entered their teenage years.

Lifespan psychologists Frank Infurna, Denis Gerstorf, and I have been investigating historical shifts in loneliness, depression, and mental health in middle-aged adults from different generations in the US and Europe. The findings are striking in that a recent cohort, Gen X (born 1965 to 1980), and especially in the US, seems to be showing more problems than earlier cohorts of baby boomers (born 1946 to 1964) and the Silent Generation (born 1928 to 1945).

Likewise, millennials (Gen Y, born 1981 to 1996) have experienced many events at critical periods that may affect their midlife differently than those who experienced them at younger or older ages. All living generations experience the same events, although at different times in their life course. The timing of major events such as 9/11, the 2008 recession, and the pandemic varied for Gen X, Gen Y, and baby boomers.

The implications of this for the sense of control and midlife experiences are noteworthy. For example: The oldest of the millennials experienced the school shooting at Columbine in 1999 when they were in or about to graduate high school, 9/11 when starting college, and the recession of 2008 when they were entering the job market. COVID occurred just when millennials were in the thick of trying to balance work and family life, often with young children whose schooling and day care were disrupted. Such monumental events would have been experienced differently (and may not have had the same profound effects) by those who were older and more established in their work and family roles. Yet unpredictable and unexpected events like these can contribute to feeling a loss of control regardless of one's circumstances. A key message these uncontrollable events convey is that what you do or how much you prepare does not always make a difference in preventing bad things from happening or vast external obstacles to your goals suddenly appearing.

For millennials in particular, these events have had a hand in delaying important life milestones like advanced degrees, professional achievement, economic stability (and security), marriage, and starting a family. When we hit certain milestones in life much later than expected, it can feel like we are attempting to defy nature—or at least stop the clock. The time at which people now tend to get married is a case in point. The median age of marriage has been increasing over the past seven decades. In the US it is now age thirty for men and twenty-eight for women. But in 1950, for example, it was twenty for women and twenty-four for men. The median age of having a first child has also been rising—age thirty for women, up from age twenty-four over the past two decades. Over the same period, the fertility rate (the number of children born to women of reproductive age) has declined. Millennials, currently the largest generation, are less likely to have a spouse and children than previous generations. And that's not all . . .

Adults nowadays are:

✦ Getting more advanced education

✦ Marrying later

✦ Less likely to marry

✦ Having fewer children

✦ Having children later

✦ Launching adult children later

✦ More likely for women to be in the workforce

✦ More likely to have work/family conflict or balance

+ Engaged with a greater proliferation of social media

+ Using technology more regularly

+ Likely to have parents who are living longer, and

+ More likely to be sandwiched between caring for children and their parents.

What people want in their lives and when they might want it is changing. This delay is sometimes conscious and sometimes unconscious or unplanned, but either way our personal decisions are playing out against a larger backdrop of historical moments. Looking at the historical trends that are affecting not just you but everyone moving through midlife with you can be comforting and take some of the onus off you. After all, you can't control the historical time you live in.

Your timetable for reaching work and family goals may not always match what others and society at large expects, which can create tension and distress. In the late 1960s psychologist Bernice Neugarten wrote about being "on time" or "off time" in terms of what she called a social clock. She noted that on time means that you are accomplishing the milestones of adulthood in keeping with the conventional timing of cultural norms. In contrast, off time means you are either early or late, which Neugarten suggested can have negative consequences for well-being. Anyone who has done anything in their lives a little "off time" can relate to being prodded by parents or grandparents about when they are going to finish graduate school, get married, or have children. We feel the subtle societal pressures when all our friends are getting married at the same time but we're still single, or when it seems like everyone is going back to grad school but we're perfectly content in our current job.

The important thing to remember is that it's your timetable that matters, especially because, as we've seen, cultural norms shift dramatically from generation to generation. A parent asking for the millionth time when you're going to start having kids is likely operating from a timetable based on an outdated cultural norm and perhaps even their own fears about not achieving their desired goal to become a grandparent. The best we can do to navigate these disconnects in historical time is to separate our own goals and desires from what is inherited or passed down from other people. Being "on time" is better determined internally, not externally.

That being said, the timing of marriage, childbearing, and parental caregiving all have consequences. If you have your children at twenty-five versus forty, that's going to significantly alter your experience of midlife. Whether or not you graduated during a recession and struggled to find the first rung of the corporate ladder has implications for your long-term earning power and how financially stable you are in midlife. Whether or not you are living in a historical time when a woman can be pregnant in the office or take time off to care for a sick child or parents, and not be discriminated against or fired, greatly impacts the trajectory of your middle years.

When it comes down to it, what the slippery nature of historical time teaches us is that timing *does* matter and that we can't always control it. Understanding these two principles can go a long way toward helping us reframe how we look at midlife. If we are living in regret, if we are struggling with what feels like everything happening at once, or, on the flip side, if we are skipping through midlife without a care in the world, we would be wise to remember that we are not the sole architects of our life's trajectory. We live in the world, and we are influenced by it mightily. When things are tough, look around, see what you've lived through and how it might have impacted your choices—and then cut yourself some slack. You can't do anything now about when you had your children, so give yourself grace and acknowledge what you can't control. But—and this is a big but—you should never lose sight of the fact that you still have a measure of control over how you use the time that is left to you. Similar to regret, how we think about the buffeting forces of historical context and time is critical to maintaining that sense of control that we know is so important. We acknowledge what we can't change and then adopt a mindset that allows us to live with that reality, while still pursuing present happiness.

Dealing with Little-*t* Time

So far, we've covered the way our past choices shape our present, and how historical events and the mere timing of our birth can radically alter our experiences. In other words, the impact of time with a big T. But what about our experience of time with a little *t*? What about the discrete moments of our daily lives? The crush of obligations that seem to gobble up our days, weekends, and months? Part of maintaining a healthy sense of control is feeling like you have agency not only over the life events that unfold over a longer time horizon, but the more quotidian concerns of the calendar.

Unfortunately, many people in midlife find themselves beholden to the calendar, or what one of my friends affectionately calls both "the dictator" and "the savior," depending on the day. Increased obligations to family and deepening ties to friends mean that most midlifers are no longer just taking care of their own day-to-day needs. They are often taking care of many others, or at least their lives are intertwined with the lives of others they care about. As a result, one of the common complaints of middle-aged adults is that they have little or no "me time," chunks of time when you do only what you desire (preferably alone).

There are so many daily tasks and responsibilities that finding time for oneself can take second (or third or fourth) place. In many families both parents work, leaving less time for childcare, housework, and friends than ever before. And yet, changing norms in both parenting and economics mean that not only are more women working mothers today, but they are also paradoxically spending even *more time* caring for their children than stay-at-home moms did in the 1970s. Moms today are doing less housework, spending less alone time with their spouses, and ramping up the multitasking in order to accomplish this herculean feat. A recent Gallup poll found that women reported having a more difficult time than men balancing work and family. "Fifty-one percent of working women in the U.S. report feeling stressed a lot of the day yesterday (vs. 39% of men). Additionally, 42% of working women said their job has had a somewhat or extremely negative impact on their mental health over the last six months (vs. 37% of men). . . . [And] women with children (64%) are nearly three times as likely as men (22%) to strongly agree they are the parent or guardian expected to address unexpected childcare issues."

For family types and child-free mid-lifers alike, schedules are packed: Job demands, community service, social networks, and appointments all need to be tended to. If you have aging parents who need care, or are supporting other family members, this adds yet another layer of time constraint. And then there is everything else: the cooking, cleaning, calling the doctor, scheduling appointments, buying groceries, staying ahead of deadlines, getting your oil changed, finding a new babysitter, buying your kid new shoes, getting your dog groomed, knocking on doors for local elections, attending graduation parties, planning your next vacation, picking up a prescription, bringing dinner to a sick friend, calling your senator, investigating that weird smell in the fridge, getting your eyesight checked, renewing your license, registering your car, getting a quote from an arborist, babysitting your nephews, and on, and on, and on. Finding time with a little *t* to take care of your mental, physical, and emotional health can feel like a fraught game of calendar Tetris. Luckily, there is a strategy that can help.

Temptation Bundling

Despite the challenges, those who do well with the demands of time with a little *t* are predictably the ones who intentionally take a step back, look at the calendar, and get creative. Chris, forty-four, and Kyle, forty-seven, are raising two beautiful eight-year-old twin girls. They each have full-time jobs and busy social lives, and for years they were at odds with what to do and how to organize their time. They were drowning in diapers and doctor's appointments with little room to even *consider* their own fulfillment. As the years went on, the mad dash of time with a little *t* suddenly turned from days into years.

They realized they were on an unhappy sort of autopilot—just barely getting through the days until they woke up to do it all over again. Grumpy and disconnected from each other and themselves, one night they sat down and made a list of things that were important to them that they never got to do anymore. They made a commitment to be supportive of each other taking time to do what they enjoyed given their busy lives balancing work and parenting. Then, they figured out a way to cleverly stack their responsibilities with their desires. Sometimes Kyle takes the long route to walk home from work and listens to a podcast before helping Chris get dinner on the table for the twins. In turn, Chris likes to combine Saturday afternoon grocery runs with some extra time to poke around in a bookstore or visit a museum exhibit. Compared to the luxurious hours they used to spend seeing art and reading books, these small pockets of me time seemed laughable at first. They weren't sure it was going to work. How could a half an hour at the bookstore make that much of a difference? To their great and enduring surprise, these little moves made a huge difference. Not only did each of them feel more like themselves, but they also felt more connected in their mutual support for each other. It turns out these little moments went a long way to improving their sense of control over their lives, and as an ancillary benefit, it set them up to be better partners and parents as well.

The solution that Chris and Kyle stumbled onto has a name: temptation bundling, a strategy recommended by Katy Milkman, a behavioral economist at the University of Pennsylvania. Simply put, temptation bundling means doing two things at once—something that is required or necessary at the same time as something enjoyable.

Watch your favorite TV show while folding the laundry or exercising on your spin bike. Take a hike and get in your exercise while also spending time with family or friends. Use your lunch break to work on that novel-in-progress instead of mindlessly scrolling through the internet at your desk. These might seem like paltry scraps of "me time," but as Chris and Kyle discovered, they can make time with a little *t* feel more expansive and meaningful.

As hard as it may be, it's critical to take care of yourself and find time for leisure and relaxation in midlife. Almost everyone experiences stress throughout their adult years—there's no avoiding it. Stress may be more intense in middle adulthood given the extra responsibilities and constraints of time and other resources. Which means it's more important than ever to respond to stress in a healthy way. In any given stressful situation, there are a multitude of ways to interpret and handle it. As most of us know by now, too much stress can make us sick, so it is important to find ways to tackle stress to minimize the effects on one's health. Managing our time wisely (e.g., temptation bundling) and making time for relaxation and joy (me time) are just a couple of ways to successfully and healthfully manage stress. Exercise, meditation, and social connection are three more critical tools we have to mitigate the physical and emotional impact of the stressors we can't avoid.

Managing midlife stress is not only for the well-being of the middle-aged. It is important to recognize that the mental and physical health of those in midlife affects their children. For example, the risks for anxiety disorders, major depression, and substance dependence are three times as high in the offspring of depressed parents as in the offspring of nondepressed parents. And poor physical health in a parent is associated with more disruptive child behavior. It goes both ways. Certainly, having children who have anxiety and depression can take a toll on middle-aged parents, and we can't blame the parents for all the problems. In fact, today's mid-lifers are raising Gen Z, a group of young people with the highest rates of anxiety seen in decades. Nevertheless, middle-aged parents who work on their own mental health are doing a favor not only for themselves but also for their kids and the future they will experience together.

There is no denying the time famine in middle age—it's a fact for most people, a part of this dizzying transitional time in our lives. At the same time that we are snowed under with daily responsibilities, the middle years themselves go by fast. It can become a habit to not stop and process or think about what we are doing. Meanwhile, we can lose track of time and suddenly find ourselves at sixty or seventy wondering how did I get here? Where did the time go? Instead of just putting our heads down and *getting through it*, we can absolutely find ways to mitigate the most negative effects of this time crunch and take ourselves off autopilot. When we pay attention to how fulfilled we feel, we can adjust our priorities and get creative.

No Time Like the Present

In midlife, despite the realization that some doors may be closing and some decisions need to be made quickly, people who have a higher sense of control (regardless of age) are likely to remain optimistic in their future time perspective. This shows us that we can successfully manage time's most unfortunate side effects (regret, stress, overwhelm). By changing what we can and reframing what we can't, we can take the sting out of regret. By understanding the impact of the historical moment we're in, we can distance ourselves from the idea that we're "behind" on important life milestones. And by being intentional about building in time for joy and pleasure, despite our busy schedules, we can balance the overwhelm with the biggest perk of being in midlife—knowing who we are and what we like to do. The beauty of being in the middle is that there's no need to race to get everything done—we can shelve some goals for later, so we can linger in the beautiful present moments that we have.

The Age of Generativity: The Dynamic Social Network

Life is a seesaw, and I am standing dead center, still
and balanced: living kids on one side, living parents on
the other. Nicky here with me at the fulcrum. Don't move
a muscle, I think. But I will, of course. You have to.

—*SANDWICH*, CATHERINE NEWMAN

John felt like he was playing a half dozen leading roles in his life and failing at all of them. As an employee, husband, father, friend, and son he was doing the best he could, but it was nowhere close to enough.

Just when the pandemic lockdown was over and he thought things would get back to normal, his mother (who lived alone and didn't drive) was diagnosed with colon cancer. With the added responsibilities of taking care of her, bringing her to appointments, and witnessing her mental health deteriorate, things felt crushing. Instead of exercising or taking a walk, he was going flat out from morning until night. When his wife got home from work, he either took his mom to get her radiation treatments, picked up her prescriptions at the pharmacy, made her dinner, or did her grocery shopping and laundry. Sometimes he would bring his two kids over to cheer her up, but no surprises, her persistent depression got a lot worse after the cancer diagnosis, and John was worried about her.

He also didn't know what to do. Everything was on his shoulders. He was always his mom's rock and his older sister and brother each lived more than an hour away. He didn't really question what he was doing for his mom, he just did it. If anything, she was getting worse, needier and more depressed by the day. He found her distress and moods impacting his own. And on top of that, he was facing pressure from his boss to increase sales, which made him pretty miserable at work.

Most nights he made it home from his mom's for a late dinner with his family but felt himself looking at the clock over their heads, counting down the minutes until he could excuse himself to go smoke a cigarette—a bad habit he restarted recently. It felt like the *one* thing he could do for himself. When he first started this routine, his wife didn't like it, but she let it slide. After a couple of weeks, she started getting worried, then annoyed. Before they got married, he had promised to quit smoking for good. He had, or so he thought. The truth was, his wife was just as stressed out as he was; working as a nurse was demanding and draining, and as soon as she got home, she immediately took over watching the kids and making dinner while he went to tend to his mother. It wasn't easy for her, and instead of being there to support her at night, he was ducking out to chain-smoke, sometimes going for a drive and not coming back for an hour. The reality meant that bedtime kid meltdowns were all on her, and then when she came downstairs to relax, she didn't even have her husband to talk to. He'd come home drained, trudge up to bed, and fall dead asleep until about three in the morning when his panic attacks would wake them both up. This wasn't what she signed up for when she married him, and he knew it. John knew he needed to pull himself out of this tailspin he was in, but figuring out how would require leaning on other people in a way he never had before.

Everyone's Counting on You

There is an old *Doonesbury* cartoon that I have pinned up on my bulletin board because it so succinctly captures what midlife can be for some of us. In the cartoon, one of the recurring characters, Joanie, is pictured on the phone with her mother discussing travel arrangements for her mother's upcoming visit. Her husband, Rick, overhears the conversation and remarks that Joanie has reached the age where you use the same tone of voice when speaking to your parents as you do with your children. Joanie is exasperated and tells Rick that she doesn't even want to think about what this means. Rick responds, "It means don't die. Everyone's counting on you."

One of the most extreme examples of the way our social responsibilities shift in midlife is the phenomenon known as the sandwich generation. This is a cohort of people in midlife who are caring for children under the age of eighteen and their aging parents at the same time. At this age many people are drowning in caregiving responsibilities. According to Pew Research, 54% of Americans in their forties are caring both for children under age eighteen and an aging parent.

"By comparison," the study says, "36% of those in their 50s, 27% of those in their 30s, and fewer than one-in-ten of those younger than 30 (6%) or 60 and older (7%) are in this situation."

Whether or not you will be sandwiched depends to some extent on how old you were when you had children and how old and healthy your parents are. For some people, their parents may not need help until after the children are launched (let's call it the open-faced sandwich). But for those caught in the middle, like John, taking care of the two generations sandwiching you involves providing physical help, financial help, emotional support, and/or logistical support. This is all on top of everything you need to do for yourself or *should* do for yourself to help get through it all: work, exercise, maintaining a social life. And because more Americans live far away from their family than ever before, the simple fact of physical distance can further complicate these obligations. Trying to care for an ailing parent who lives across the country is expensive, time-consuming, and emotionally draining. Raising young children without the benefit of family close by also means that parents don't have people around to help them as they raise their kids, exacerbating the drain on resources even more.

The downstream effects of all these demands are grim. One study from the University of Michigan showed that folks in the sandwich generation were worse off emotionally and financially than their peers who only had to take care of a parent. For instance, 17% of those caring for a parent over sixty-five reported money troubles compared to 36% of those who were considered in the sandwich generation. Emotional strain clocked in at 44% for sandwiched mid-lifers, compared to 32% of their peers who were caring for just their parents.

The Adult Child

As parents are living longer, they often will need help in their later years. This can include assisting with transportation or shopping, going to doctor's appointments as an advocate, and making decisions about when a parent should stop driving or whether they can live on their own. Caring for a sick parent also may bring up sensitive issues of coordination with siblings, as John was able to eventually work out sharing the responsibilities of caring for his mom.

Lynn's sister, Sue, gave a lot of thought to the timing of when she would get married and have children. Sue married at twenty-five and had her first child at twenty-seven. She married her college sweetheart and they both had solid jobs, so when Sue took off some years after her first was born and when she was pregnant with her second a couple years later, the family was able to get by on just her husband's salary so Sue could stay home to take care of their toddler and new baby. Lynn, on the other hand, spent her late twenties and all through her thirties looking for "the one" to have a child with. She knew she wanted to have a child, but who "the one" might be was not so clear. Meanwhile, her career as a human rights attorney was as rewarding as it was all-consuming. She didn't have a lot of time for dating but, by chance, she met Paul, a human rights activist, at a conference when she was thirty-six. They had their first and only child when she was forty-one. Now Sue's children are all off at college or in their first job and Lynn is still raising her one child while managing her demanding career—both "jobs" she loves, but some days she will admit she is bone tired. Lynn and Sue's mother, who is seventy-nine, was recently diagnosed with dementia and, given that their father passed away eight years ago, is all on her own, so she needs help from her daughters. The fact that Sue's children are grown means she has more time to devote to their mother and this is something they are both grateful for as they share the many demands of caring for their aging mother.

One thing that is on the rise that adult children should be on the lookout for is scams against older adults. There has been a large increase in the number of financial losses due to older adults falling for phishing scams via emails and texts. And artificial intelligence, which can simulate photos and voices of family members and other acquaintances, has been applied to elaborate schemes to trick older adults into sending personal information for unlocking a prize or transferring money to rescue a grandchild supposedly in need. Older adults are targeted because they may have substantial financial resources, and they also are susceptible to scams because of cognitive changes with age. As executive functions decline with age, older adults may have more difficulty recognizing harm as they tend to filter out the negative with a preference toward the positive, and they may be more trusting of others who do not necessarily have their best interests in mind.

Older single men or women can be easy prey for others who know they are alone. Ralph was living on his own in his late seventies after a recent divorce. That meant the kids would need to step up, but he was living far away so they could not keep close tabs on him. He was afraid of living alone and didn't really know how to cook. A younger woman, Claire, spotted him at the neighborhood pool that he went to almost daily, and started being friendly toward him. He was excited that he found a younger woman who seemed interested in him and said she would take care of him. After she pressured him, he transferred the house deed to her and agreed to support her so she could quit her job and be with him. She asked him to make an investment in some property she was developing in South America. He was excited about the investment and gave her large sums of money but did not get anything in writing. She left him alone on weekends presumably to take care of an older woman who also needed her help. His children hired full-time home care to make sure he was well taken care of, suspecting that his friend did not have his best interests in mind. But Ralph did not want his kids to interfere in his so-called relationship. After his death his children discovered it was all a scam. Claire had made up everything. It turned out she was married (which she did not reveal) and did not invest in South America. And the job she said she had on weekends was made up as well.

Besides concerns about the day-to-day well-being of older parents, one of the most emotionally salient experiences of the adult child involves the loss of one's parents. Well over half of adults enter midlife with both parents living. During midlife, it is more likely than not that you will lose at least one parent, and this may be preceded by time caregiving for an ill parent. When one parent dies, the widowed parent living alone will typically need more attention from their adult children than those who are living with a spouse or partner. When adults leave midlife and cross the threshold to later adulthood, a majority will have had one parent die and about a third no longer have both parents living. Thus, an important transition point and emotional experience during the middle years is losing one or both parents and becoming the oldest generation in the family. Although this results in loss of the adult child role, it also brings on new roles and responsibilities as a senior member of the family. And it can make one's own mortality more salient.

While not everyone finds themselves in the sandwich generation, the dynamics of our social network shift in middle age no matter what. Part of what feels both good and difficult about this time of life is that we are in a new stage of development when it comes to our social selves. Research shows that one of the biggest gains we make in midlife is in the realm of *generativity*, the way we positively contribute to the world through care and concern for others. In this vein, even if the relationships we have stay the same, our roles and functions within those relationships change. We are generally more deeply connected to the people in our lives than ever before, and our engagement with our community changes as well. As mid-lifers seek to make their mark on the world by positively impacting others, they have the opportunity to be more connected and present in their relationships.

Taking on too much in this time of life is an easy trap to fall into, but if we can avoid it, and explore ways to cope with stress and minimize the negative impact of bearing our responsibilities, we reap huge rewards. This chapter is all about learning to find the social sweet spot by maximizing social *support* and minimizing social *strain* so we can enjoy all the psychological and physical health benefits of connecting with others during this time of life. But before we can understand how to balance the roles and responsibilities of midlife, it's important to understand how exactly our social lives have shifted in the first place.

Roles and Relationships

Compared to our twenties, when it feels like we have a zillion friends and not enough time on the social calendar, midlife might not seem all that full socially to those focused most intensely on their nuclear families. But by the data, it is the time when we have the largest number of roles and relationships. We might not have as many friends dominating that overall number as we did when we were younger, but we have connections galore: children, spouses, parents, siblings, grandparents, grandchildren, aunts, uncles, neighbors, coworkers, in-laws, parents of your kids' friends, friends from community organizations, friends from your fantasy football league, and mentees. And if you're lucky, you like a lot of them. But what determines the health of your social ecosystem isn't just numbers—it's the *roles* we play within those relationships and the strain they can cause.

The Many Roles We Play

The ballooning number of connections we have in midlife isn't a problem in and of itself—what really matters in terms of our challenge in juggling them is the resources we are putting into these connections. Time, money, and emotional energy all depend on what *role* we play in that relationship. Are we the giver, the taker, the organizer, the flake, or the initiator?

As we age, the roles we used to play in some of our oldest relationships can change drastically. In most cases, moving from the taker role to the giver requires a whole new level of engagement with others. One example of how roles can shift in midlife is "kinkeeping."

When we're young, someone in our family (usually a mother, aunt, or grandmother) was behind the scenes keeping family traditions, togetherness, and connections alive. The kinkeepers are the ones who organize holiday parties, assign dishes to be brought to Sunday and Thanksgiving dinners, decorate the house for the holidays, and are always there to help defuse family tensions. When the next generation of the family approaches midlife, the kinkeeping torch gets informally passed, usually to a female (why this is so gendered could be the topic of a whole other book!). Similarly, we see roles within the parent-child relationship evolve over time. When you are under eighteen, your parent is taking care of you. When you're in your twenties, you might forget they even exist outside of holidays (or move back in with them, as so-called boomerang children). When you're in your thirties, you might grow closer as they babysit your children or give you advice that you're finally ready to hear. But finally, at some point, as an adult child, the roles will drastically reverse, and you'll likely be looking after them—enter *parent*-keeping.

Toni Antonucci, a professor of psychology at the University of Michigan, has done research on what she calls the "social convoy," which recognizes that close relationships move with you throughout life even though the roles may change. She asks her research participants to fill in names in three concentric circles with those who are in their network. First is the innermost circle, which includes those individuals who "are so close that it's hard to imagine life without them," like your spouse, parents, and children, and a best friend or two. In the second circle are "those that are not quite as close but are still very important," like your siblings and cousins, and the third, outer circle are those that "are not quite as close, but still important," like in-laws, coworkers, and friends. Antonucci finds that the average convoy contains about seven to nine people. Having close relatives and friends as confidants and for support is particularly important to well-being in the hectic life of mid-lifers. When we are so busy with work and everyday needs of immediate family, we may neglect others in our network. It is important in midlife especially to continue to nurture close relationships. The members of your social convoy will change over time as people get divorced, die, move away, or change jobs. In later life it is more difficult to add members to your social convoy, so establishing and maintaining strong bonds in midlife can be a resource you draw on down the road.

Stress and Caregiving

In addition to friends and family already in our inner circle, we often take on new relationships and roles in midlife—becoming a spouse, parent, or boss. Most of the time, these roles are laden with more responsibility, not less. As we've seen in previous chapters, you're in a unique position in midlife to be of value to others—you're still healthy and mobile, you've got some wisdom under your belt, and you are likely close to the peak of your earning power. But the change from being in your twenties and early thirties, when your primary focus was likely on yourself, is profound. Suddenly, other people are depending on you in a more significant way. You can't just go MIA. Just like Joanie from *Doonesbury*, your disappearance will be noticed and felt. You are likely providing for not only yourself, but for others, whether that's your nuclear family or your chosen family. And you may be taking on leadership roles at work and in the community. It's a fact of life that when you're the one in charge, the responsibilities increase.

Nowhere is this truer than in the realm of parenting. While there are a lot of splashy headlines about the birth rate in the US declining, most Americans will at one point or another take on the role of parent. According to the CDC, in 2023, by the time they are in their forties, 86% of women and 76.5% of men have had children. Being a caregiver is considered one of the most stressful roles one can experience, especially if you are a single parent, have multiple children, or a child with an illness. In 2024 , the US Surgeon General released an advisory about the stress and mental health concerns of parents and caregivers. He cited results from a study by the American Psychological Association, which found that 48%—almost half the parents surveyed—were more likely to say they are experiencing overwhelming stress, whereas it was 26% for nonparents. Even more alarming, 41% of parents said that most days they are so stressed they cannot function. For parents of children with a disease or disability, Marsha Mailick, a researcher from the University of Wisconsin, found that stress levels are even higher than those of other parents. In fact, the stress can be so severe that Elissa Epel, a psychologist from the University of California, San Francisco, found that parents who were caring for a child with cancer had shorter telomeres—a sign of more rapid aging—than those who did not have a sick child.

While caregiving can take a toll on our physical health, often it is our mental health that takes the most obvious hit. I asked some of my friends who are clinical psychologists and psychiatrists (meaning they provide mental health treatment) about their midlife patients. I wanted to know what they hear from this group about what's most difficult for them. Right away each one said it was issues related to parenting. This includes the simple day-to-day stresses of child-rearing, plus conflicts with one's spouse or partner about how to raise children or discipline them. There are common arguments about what activities they should do or what to buy them or what not to buy them or how much freedom to give them or how much candy or soda they should have. And, of course, there are the digital-generation issues related to how much screen time kids should have or how late they can stay up scrolling on their devices. The inevitable comparisons with the "highlight reels" posted by other parents and kids on social media can also lead to distress.

Well-meaning parents can go overboard and become overprotective of their children in this world that seems to be more unsafe than when they were growing up. Parents of millennials were often called "helicopter parents" because of their tendency to hover over their children, watching their every move. Going beyond surveillance, the Gen X parents of Gen Z have often been called the "snowplow parents," meaning that they clear the way so that their children never have to face any adversity or obstacles. Perhaps this is helpful in the short run for the child, and well-intentioned, but what it does is take away the opportunities for children to learn from their mistakes and leads to an overdependence on adults for handling their day-to-day responsibilities. Unfortunately, I see evidence of this in today's Gen Z college students. More so than students in the past, they have difficulty meeting deadlines, and many more request various accommodations such as extra time on exams. One of my colleagues put it this way: If parents and teachers have served as the executive functioning for their children, when they get to college, they don't have the planning and organizing skills they should have developed by high school. In some ways, the seemingly closer relationships between parents and their children, facilitated by texting and email nowadays, can be a good thing. It may be somewhat comforting though for parents to keep in mind that when their children make mistakes it is not so bad; it can facilitate learning, growth, and a sense of mastery. And letting go can be good for parents too.

Even after children leave home, the parenting role is not over. When children go off to college or the armed forces, afterward they might return to the nest at least temporarily while they consider their next steps. This phenomenon of the "boomerang kid" has increased dramatically over the past decade in part due to economic pressures.

After learning all this, it might feel like the shifting landscape of social connections in midlife is pretty bleak—all give and no take, right? That is certainly how it can feel to people like John, who are crushingly caught in the middle, or people who are taking on new responsibilities at work and just feeling unready for the shift. Or the 48% of parents who are overwhelmed by stress.

But hidden within the tangled knot of the obligations, resource drain, and time scarcity, there is a silver lining—even though we may struggle to locate it.

The Paramount Importance
of Social Relationships

What we know from decades of research is that relationships in mid-life can either weaken you or strengthen you, make you or unmake you, depending on the level of awareness and intentionality you bring to them. So far, we've seen how the stress of new and shifting roles, including caregiving, can sap mid-lifers' resources. But counter-intuitively, the answer is not to cut all ties and divest of social connection. Instead, it is to focus on the quantity and quality of relationships that fortify and support you during midlife. While too much social obligation and connection can overwhelm your system, too little can leave you without the support and resources you need.

When There's Not Enough Connection

Researchers have been interested in how our social connections impact our health and happiness for a long time. One of the earliest studies on this was done by epidemiologists Lisa Berkman and S. Leonard Syme in 1979. In a longitudinal study they conducted in Alameda County in California they found that people who were socially isolated were more likely to die early than those who were more integrated into social networks. The relationship between social ties and mortality was found to be independent of self-reported physical health status at the time of the initial interview and health practices. They found that smoking, alcohol consumption, obesity, physical activity, and how much they used preventive health services didn't make as much a difference as who they were spending their time with (or not). Since this initial study, a mountain of research has replicated these general findings. In one of the more alarming reports from a review of many studies, Julianne Holt-Lunstad, a psychologist from Brigham Young University, and colleagues found that the health consequences of social isolation (or weak social relationships) is equivalent to smoking fifteen cigarettes a day.

In other words, social isolation can be deadly.

When you think about it from an evolutionary perspective, this makes a lot of sense. Thousands of years ago when we were still living in caves and the open desert, there was safety in numbers. A person wandering alone on the savannah was much more likely to be lion lunch than a person in a hunting party of half a dozen. Finding a water source was easier as a group than solo. Over millennia, our bodies became acutely attuned to the danger that solitude presented, developing physiological responses that encouraged healthy social connection.

Loneliness has gotten a good deal of attention in recent years after the US Surgeon General called it an epidemic in 2023. Indeed, being lonely or isolated increases the risk of accelerated aging and earlier death by as much as 26%. A study led by one of my former doctoral students, Eileen Graham at Northwestern University, found that loneliness follows a U-shaped curve over the life course, decreasing from young adulthood to midlife and increasing in older adulthood. It is not surprising that loneliness is lower in midlife given the large number of roles and relationships that middle-aged adults have. The study found that loneliness increased after age sixty, perhaps because some of the key roles (such as coworker or parent) from midlife were no longer as central or prominent.

Yet loneliness is not just tied to how many roles you have. Anyone who has been in a bad relationship knows that it's entirely possible to feel alone even while you're sitting next to someone. Likewise, you can be at a party, surrounded by people, and still feel isolated. Don't let numbers fool you—having poor or strained relationships can make you just as sick as having no relationships. They can increase cortisol, the stress hormone, as well as depress immune functioning and increase inflammation. Janice Kiecolt Glaser, a psychologist from Ohio State University College of Medicine, found that couples who had a lot of conflict and hostility were more likely to show spikes in stress hormones and were slower to heal wounds in the laboratory. Distressed couples also stored more fat, gained more weight, and had greater risk for heart disease. Given that we can have more stress and strain from relationships at midlife and that we need the support of those relationships more than ever, it's doubly important to maintain a balance of giving and receiving support.

When Relationships Are Dialed In

When we are engaged in healthy relationships, we know that they are a boon for health, happiness, and longevity. My colleague and friend Robert Waldinger, coauthor of *The Good Life*, has found that having supportive relationships is the best predictor of a long and happy life. He is director of the longest longitudinal study of happiness in history, which followed Harvard graduates from the classes of 1939 to 1944, and did extensive interviews with them throughout the years. Researchers on Waldinger's team collected information about many domains of life and the evidence was clear—having good relationships made the most difference for happiness. In other studies, researchers such as Sheldon Cohen at Carnegie Mellon have found that those who reported more supportive relationships were better able to fight off colds than those with stressful relationships. And we know that social support can lead to lowered inflammation and even faster healing of wounds.

Science aside, we all know from experience what a difference a caring, supportive, engaged social network can do for us. There is a reason that people have children, make friends, and kinkeep even when it temporarily stresses us out: It feels good to share our lives with others. Connection is a primary human need that we are constantly reaching for from the second we are born to the moment we take our last breath.

Midlife is a critical period for nurturing and strengthening the relationships that fill us up. The opportunity we have to positively impact others is one of the most pivotal aspects of midlife. We can have an impact on the mental health of our children, we can be valuable mentors to the next generation of workers, and we can add our wisdom and experience to community organizations that we are a part of. In midlife, we have the opportunity to be more connected and caring than ever as we raise our children, care for our parents, and attempt to leave our mark on the world. One of the best ways we can stave off loneliness, balance stress, maintain strong relationships, and bolster our social health is by leaning into the new developmental stage we have entered: generativity.

You Get What You Give

In his famous work on the eight stages of life, developmental psychologist and psychoanalyst Erik Erikson mapped out what he believed were the psychosocial struggles for each stage in the life cycle. In adolescence, he posited that we grapple with issues surrounding our identity. Then, once you have at least a preliminary sense of your own self-identity, it becomes possible to focus on forming intimate relationships with others. In midlife, the emphasis is a broader focus on making contributions to family and society—in other words: generativity.

This is *the* developmental task in our middle years. As we talked about earlier in the chapter, generativity involves reaching out to and supporting younger generations and leaving your mark on the world.

Several researchers have tested Erikson's ideas and developed ways to assess generativity across generations. What they found is that those in midlife, more than any other age period, agree with the type of statements developed by psychological researcher Dan McAdams from Northwestern University to assess generative qualities:

+ I have important skills that I try to teach others.

+ I feel as though I have made a difference to many people.

+ I try to pass along the knowledge I have gained through my experiences.

When participants responded to these items in the MIDUS study, those in middle age were more likely to describe themselves as generative compared to those under forty and over sixty. And we found that those who have higher generativity also had a higher sense of control. McAdams found that people in midlife who embrace generativity are interested in promoting the well-being of future generations. They see themselves as sensitive to the needs of others with a clear set of principles and goals along with a positive outlook and a can-do spirit. People with this description find more success in parenting and engaging positively with their communities.

But how do we do this? One of the best examples of generativity in action is mentoring.

Mentoring Magic

When Gary's second wife divorced him in his mid-fifties, it wasn't what you would call amicable. After all the papers were signed and the dust had settled, he didn't hear from his ex, which was fine. What was unexpectedly much harder was not being in touch with his step kids. He had adopted them and had been in their lives for over fifteen years and had loved watching them launch into adulthood, find their way in the world, and even have their own kids. Suddenly, now that he was divorced, there were no more loud family dinners, chaotic holidays, and updates on what was going on with them. His step kids had sided with their mother and were not interested in any more contact with Gary.

Gary missed having young people to connect with, and for a while he didn't do much about it but go on with his life, feeling a little emptier with each holiday that passed. One summer day he went golfing and got paired with a young man in his twenties who was just starting his own business. When he heard that Gary was a successful businessman who oversaw one hundred and fifty employees in three different regional offices, his eyes got wide with excitement. He peppered Gary with questions the entire round, and at the end the young man asked him if he wouldn't mind grabbing a coffee sometime to talk more. They exchanged business cards and got on with their days, but for Gary it was a lightbulb moment. When he climbed into his car, he felt lighter and happier than he had in months. Talking, telling stories, and listening to the young man's challenges had made him feel downright useful in a different way than he felt at work. He was helping someone, not because it boosted his bottom line, but because it just felt good. The reward was the act itself. This was how he had felt when his ex's son used to talk to him about how to handle a tricky situation with a professor in college, or when his daughter wanted to know how to negotiate a pay bump at her new job.

For months he had been missing those kinds of interactions with young people, and even mourning the loss. But that round of golf reminded him that his ex's kids weren't the only people around who might find him useful. From that day on, he not only helped the young man from the golf course, over the next several years Gary sought out every opportunity he could find to mentor the younger employees at his company, the kids of his friends, and anyone who might need it. Of course, they were all grateful to him for donating his time—they weren't family, after all. But Gary was always quick to tell them that their time together was just as important to him.

Mentoring is a key developmental task in midlife, which often gets pigeonholed as something you do formally in business or academia. But almost everyone has an opportunity to mentor someone, and it doesn't have to be formal at all. In midlife it can be as simple as sharing your gardening expertise with your twentysomething neighbor who has a black thumb or volunteering to coach your niece's soccer team. Like parenting, mentoring is all about helping others believe in themselves and develop the skills they need to handle challenges on their own. For the increasing number of people entering midlife without children of their own, mentoring can be a way to care for a new generation. People like Gary have found many ways to interact with and nurture children even if they don't have their own. Some have developed close relationships with their friends' kids, or their siblings' children. And many feel that this is the best of both worlds because you can enjoy the kids while you are with them but aren't as stressed out over day-to-day concerns as their parents are.

What Generativity Does for Us

I am reminded of the Beatles' lyrics "the love you take is equal to the love you make." Whether it's mentoring or being an engaged aunt or uncle, caring for others can be a great source of joy for many in midlife. Studies show that the quality of generativity, or the desire to care for others, is at a high point in our middle years, although it often continues well past midlife. In a longitudinal study, researcher Cindy Bergeman, a psychology professor at the University of Notre Dame, found that generativity peaked in the forties, and after a slight decline in the fifties remained fairly stable up to age seventy, after which it started to drop off.

Increased generativity is a good thing for those in midlife and it's also good for those around them. At the end of every semester, I ask the students in my Adult Development and Aging class to reflect on what they learned that could apply to themselves and another person, either a family member or a friend. One student remarked that learning about generativity helped her to understand that her parents' deep concern for her is a part of their own developmental journey, and not a reflection of their lack of trust in her decisions. This example nicely illustrates how understanding more about the nature of middle age could contribute to intergenerational harmony.

But it isn't only at home that our growing caregiving skills pay off. People in midlife also often take on more management and mentoring of younger generations at work and in community organizations, and their wisdom and experience can greatly benefit all involved. Given that we have more stress and strain from relationships at midlife, it might seem counterintuitive to take on *more*. However, sometimes giving more in strategic ways (like Gary did) can actually *improve* our well-being and our sense of control.

Now that we know how taxing social connections can be *and* how beneficial, it's time to look at how we can balance them so that the stress doesn't outweigh the joy.

Social Support vs. Social Strain

One night, right before John, who we met earlier in this chapter, was about to duck out for another cigarette, he looked at his wife. The sadness and disappointment in her eyes broke his heart. John couldn't take the discord at home or the sense of shame he felt about his new-old bad habit anymore. He realized that his desire to take care of his family and his mental health were at odds, and that something had to change. That night, he laid it all out for his wife: everything he had been keeping bottled up, all the stresses he felt overwhelmed by, and his deepening fear that he was losing his grip on the things in life that were truly important to him. And then he asked her for help. Over the next few weeks, they came up with a plan for how John could take care of the family and his mom, and most important, keep himself on an even keel. His first step was calling his siblings and letting them know what was really going on with their mom. Before, he had been trying to protect them from the sadness of it all, with the belief that he could just take care of it himself. That ship had sailed, and to his relief, his siblings were both happy to help. Instead of being the only one responsible for his mother's care, his brother and sister started taking turns shuttling her to appointments and bringing her meals.

Not having to go to his mom's every afternoon opened up some time for John to go grab a beer with a friend, attend a therapy appointment, or spend more time with his family. For the last few years, he had been completely MIA with his friend group, and as soon as he began engaging with them again, he couldn't believe what a difference it made. The truth was that when John opened up about what was going on in his life, he not only felt understood and seen, but his friends also began to talk about what they were going through. In other words, he felt both loved and useful. But by far the best decision he and his wife made that first night was to commit to a new habit: Every night after dinner, they would let their older boy babysit his younger brother and they would go for a quick walk around the neighborhood. It was during these walks when they downloaded their days that John felt the most connected to his wife. He began to look forward to getting the dishes done, not so he could go take a drive, but so he could play with his kids and walk with his wife. Between exercise, therapy, friends, and a renewed connection with the love of his life, John began to feel better. He also made another wise decision—he left his old job for a new one that he found much more compatible with his lifestyle. It wasn't an immediate or total solution—life was still relentless—but the improved balance he achieved allowed his body and mind opportunities for rest and renewal. Sort of like the difference between swimming with a life jacket and without one; every once in a while you can just float when you need to take a breather.

What John was able to accomplish with his new habits and commitments was some semblance of balance between giving and receiving social support. Taking on too much in midlife, and giving more support than we receive, is an especially easy trap to fall into. When relationships cause stress or grief for a whole host of reasons—interpersonal conflict, a high-maintenance friend, or just an interpersonal dynamic that is more negative than positive—that is what researchers refer to as *social strain*. That is what John was experiencing when things in his life felt out of control—his dynamic with his mother was fraught, and he was giving far too much to his family and work without counterbalancing it with what we call *social support*.

The definition of social support is simply a relationship (or relationships) that contributes to your well-being in a variety of ways. There are three general types of support: *informational* support, which involves sharing one's knowledge and experience; *emotional* support, which involves showing empathy, understanding, boosting someone's mood or their self-esteem; and finally, *instrumental* (or *tangible*) support, which involves physical help with things such as rides to appointments, childcare, making meals, doing errands, or providing financial assistance.

All of these are important components of supportive relationships. However, it is the emotional support that seems to be most closely related to health and well-being. In fact, research has shown that it's *the feeling* that you can count on someone to come through for you that is so important. You may never need them, but it is reassuring (and health boosting) to know that they would be there for you as someone you can call on without feeling afraid, guilty, or hesitant.

When we study emotional aspects of social support, these are the questions we ask about one's partner, friends, and family members: How much do they understand the way you feel about things? How much do they really care about you? How much can you rely on them for help if you have a serious problem? How much can you open up to them if you need to talk about your worries?

In contrast, to understand how much strain a relationship is causing, we ask: How often do they criticize you? How often do they make too many demands on you? How often do they get on your nerves? How often do they let you down when you were counting on them?

Interestingly, it may be the very people who cause you the most strain are also the ones who give you the most support. This probably isn't surprising if you've ever had a complex relationship with a parent/friend/sibling who is nonetheless unwavering in their support when things in your life really blow up. Those you are closest to are the ones who know you best, and who you likely spend the most time with. They may feel more comfortable giving you advice or feedback they think is helpful, but that you may not appreciate. On the other hand, if you get a lot of help and support from someone, you might be more reluctant to give them critical feedback about the things that really bother you. In other words, you don't want to lose the good, so you put up with the bad.

Giving and receiving support are both important for health, and where that give-and-take comes will evolve and change over a lifetime. Parents are the main ones who give support to their children, helping them navigate life challenges and make decisions. Later in life adult children often provide support for their older parents. At work we might turn toward a mentor to help us get established or become a mentor once we have more experience or take on a leadership role. In fact, a supportive supervisor has been found to be an important element of a healthy workplace for promoting good mental health for workers.

As we know from the data on both loneliness and the stress of caregiving, striking a balance between giving and receiving support is critical for our well-being. One study by my colleagues Edith Chen and Greg Miller at Northwestern University found that those who give more than they receive in terms of amount of time spent are at risk for earlier death than those who have more of a balance. Social relationships involve exchanges, and those who feel they give more than they receive are at risk for poor health. It is important to learn to accept support rather than being the one who always helps others.

How to Find Balance

So how do we do this at a time in our lives that feels chaotic and unbalanced by nature? It may not be easy, but it's an important goal to aim for. There are three main ways you can optimize your relationships and better balance strain and support.

Less Strain, More Gain

There is an art to making decisions about who to let into our inner circle. While you can't choose your family, you can choose your friendships. Friendships become particularly important in midlife because these are the relationships you can choose to nurture or abandon depending on whether they are serving up more strain than support. Luckily, in midlife there are opportunities to find friends in many different parts of your life, such as kids' sports and other activities, high school friends, college friends, neighbors, community or religious organizations, and work.

Research by Nicholas Christakis, a sociologist at Yale University, found that who you hang out with makes a difference for your health and well-being, confirming what your mother told you about picking friends who are a good influence. This research showed that the habits of your close relationships are related to your own obesity, happiness, smoking, and drinking. When a neighbor of mine, Jackie, started a new job at a newspaper, she and all her coworkers smoked. It wasn't until they covered a story about the increasing rates in several kinds of cancer among younger adults that they all decided to quit. Everyone in her circle remains smoke free. Humans are social animals, so it makes sense that we tend to mind-meld with those we hold dear.

In a review of thirty-eight studies by Rosemary Blieszner at Virginia Tech, she found that high-quality friendships can provide support and companionship that can lead to better well-being and less depression and anxiety. Friends can help us to deal effectively with stress, with one study showing that a person's blood pressure lowers just by talking with a supportive friend.

Doing a quick strain-versus-support check-in with current friendships is always a good idea when you're trying to lower your social stress overall. It can be as simple as reviewing the last year in your relationship with someone and asking yourself some tough questions about who has been there for you and who hasn't. Who makes your life more complicated and stressful? Who helps ease the burden? While deprioritizing relationships that aren't well balanced may be hard, it is important. This is the time in your life to maximize social relationships and generativity; it's natural and adaptive to prioritize meaningful and positive relationships. There isn't time for relationships that bring you grief and heartache. Lean into the relationships that will support you through the hard times and add joy to your life.

Solitude: Not the Same as Loneliness

As we've seen in midlife, people tend to give more than they receive. Knowing this, it's important to find some time for recharging and renewing your own mental health. In other words: me time. Considering we just read a whole lot of statistics about how loneliness is bad for you and social connection is good, this might seem paradoxical. But there is an important distinction between feeling alone and the value of seeking alone time and solitude—something that is often hard to come by in midlife with so many responsibilities and people depending on you. We've talked in previous chapters about the importance of carving out time for yourself, but it bears repeating. John's experience of being needed by so many people in his life and trying desperately to find time for himself is tragically common. Women in particular are socialized to give, give, give, and feel guilty for taking even a small amount of time away from caregiving. As we know from looking at baseline stress levels and health outcomes for caregivers, this is a crisis for many. Delegating responsibilities, hiring a babysitter, spending a little extra money on a personal trainer or therapist—these are all critically important steps you can take to help balance out the stress with something positive that you are doing only for you. To make space for alone time, you might have to do something that's surprisingly difficult to do when you're the one doing everything—ask for help. Those giving care need care too. And if you're someone who struggles to take time for themselves, if you won't do it for yourself, do it for your family. Your mental health affects others. After all, studies also show that the well-being of people in their middle years has a great impact on the mental health of their children.

Lean into Generativity

We saw from Gary's story that mentoring is one great way to help others and feel like you are making a difference in the world. For those in midlife who aren't as socially plugged in as they'd like to be, or don't have children and parents that they're caring for, what we call "social integration" is important. We know that supportive relationships (in whatever form they appear) are critical to ongoing health and well-being. Beyond mentoring, volunteering for community organizations is another way to feel a sense of purpose and connect with others. Whether it's volunteering to be on the board of the local library or spearheading a campaign to pick up trash on your local trails, getting involved opens you up to new relationships and connections, and it is good for your health.

For all the struggling young parents out there, remember that while you might be in the trenches now, giving support to children is generally rewarding and reaps benefits over time. I remember seeing on a morning news show a video of a father sitting next to his son when he opened an email saying that he was accepted at the college of his choice. The father screamed with excitement—"We did it!" Yes, it is a team effort to help kids navigate through childhood and their teenage years. But it doesn't end there. Parenting is a lifelong relationship, even though the nature of the roles differs over time. This is the same for many interpersonal relationships, which is why it's important not to let a "scarcity mindset" (i.e., believing there is never enough of something, in this case, time or energy) overwhelm you. Yes, this time of life is jam packed, but investing in other people and causes that you care about is a rewarding mechanism for balance.

One of the benefits of being in a very socially engaged moment of your life is the ability to fall back on those relationships when you need them. One of the facts of life at any age is that unexpected tragedies, challenges, and obstacles can pop up anytime. In midlife, there are a slew of potential curveballs and wake-up calls that can come at us seemingly out of nowhere: scary medical diagnoses, unexpected deaths, divorce, and so much more. Midlife brings us many gifts, but it can also throw us for a loop, and when it does, you'll be glad you have a social convoy of support, not strain, carrying you forward.

Chapter 7
Building Resilience When Life Throws You Curveballs

The last of the human freedoms is the ability to choose one's attitude in a given set of circumstances.

—VICTOR FRANKL, *MAN'S SEARCH FOR MEANING*

When Frank Bruni, journalist and contributing opinion writer for *The New York Times*, woke up one Saturday morning with impaired vision, he wasn't worried. Stumbling to his coffee maker that morning, he chalked the blurriness up to too many glasses of wine the evening before and the resulting crappy night's sleep. When he spilled coffee all over the counter, he saw it only as evidence that he needed that caffeine more than ever. Eventually, he sat down to start typing up transcripts for a story and noticed that the words jumped and tilted on the page. He cleaned his glasses, polished the computer screen, and even went to flush out his eyes. Nothing worked. It was as if someone had thrown a thin gauze over his eyes; he could still see, but it was compromised. Later that day he would go on a run and in the evening attend a dinner party, all without mentioning it to anyone, barely even worried about it himself.

The next day, nothing had changed, and eventually he discovered that it was his *right* eye that was the culprit because when he closed his left, the world became indecipherable. Everything looked the same, all blurry shapes with no sharp definitions. When he used both eyes, he sometimes felt a little off-balance, and he found working on the computer was impossible. It was only then that he told his partner, and they both agreed that it was time for him to get his eyes checked. In his memoir, *The Beauty of Dusk*, Bruni describes how he wasn't really worried about his vision because he assumed, as had been the case with his other midlife ailments, that there was an easy enough solution. At fifty-two he was on medications for cholesterol, depression, and even gout, so to his mind the vision problem was nothing that the medical establishment couldn't manage. As a guy who went for runs, climbed mountains, and still enjoyed a raucous dinner party, he had no reason to believe he could go to bed one night and wake up the next day blind in one eye. But after weeks of ophthalmology appointments and multiple visits, that's exactly what he discovered had happened.

It turns out the eye is incredibly resilient and good at recovering from injury, but it has an Achilles' heel: the optic nerve. When Bruni went to sleep that fateful night, at some point his blood pressure plummeted and starved his optic nerve of the blood it needed to survive. The damage this caused, as Bruni would discover, was irreversible. Try as he might (he endured two brutal clinical trials, one of which involved needles in his eye), the vision in his right eye didn't return. Worse still, he was told by his doctors that there was a 20–40%

chance that this rare stroke might take out his other eye sometime in the future. So not only did he have to live with the current curveball that had taken out half his vision, but he also had to live with the knowledge that at any minute another one could come out of nowhere, blinding him completely.

When a major sense organ is compromised or lost, it's deeply disruptive and destabilizing. How you go about your day, what work you can do, what level of activity you can handle, and what obligations you can fulfill all come into question. Everything that felt solid is now replete with cracks of uncertainty. The physical toll this reimagining of your life takes is immense, but the emotional toll even more so. Day by day you must choose an emotional path, and for Bruni it felt like he was zigzagging between two—one of defiance and one of resignation. As the clinical trials failed and Bruni became accustomed to navigating the world in an entirely new way, he realized that those who lose their senses like he did are involuntary pioneers of aging. "Ahead of schedule, these people took a crash course in limitations and uncertainty and compromises, and now I was enrolled in it."

Over the coming year, Bruni would cope with not one loss, but two. It turned out that his partner of ten years had begun an affair right before the stroke. Almost a year later the truth would come out, and they would say their painful goodbyes. Bruni had been struck by yet another curveball, this time coming from a different direction. In the aftermath of both, he did what anyone else would do in his situation. He had questions for God, he leaned into some dramatics, he reached out to friends and acquaintances who were vision-impaired, he worried, he felt lonely, he had to slow down, he felt sorry for himself, and he had embarrassing moments. It took some time, but remarkably quickly, he decided to change his relationship to gratitude and uncertainty. He began to ride the waves of his emotions and worked hard at pulling himself back to the glass-half-full perspective. Because it was true that he was lucky—he had the resources to get medical help, he had friends to buoy him when he needed it, and other than the eye, he was a relatively healthy guy.

As the days, weeks, and months passed he was amazed to realize how his other senses were starting to compensate for his loss of vision. He could hear the elevator clicking up the shaft in his building even while he was still in his apartment, when before he had never noticed it. But a pivotal point came when he realized he could run at dusk through a bumpy, treacherous part of the park with more confidence than ever before. Unexpectedly he is elated to realize that his senses and reflexes were now strangely *better* at dodging obstacles in the terrain. "The exhilaration wasn't about my vision but about my potential. Even in the later innings of our lives, we have unplumbed abilities, untaxed muscles, flexibility, growth. That made the prospect of further deterioration of my vision less scary. That made *everything* less scary."

In the years following Bruni's stroke, his life changed. He accepted a professorship at Duke University and moved to North Carolina. He stopped writing a regular column for the *Times*, but still occasionally contributes. Instead of fast days on the streets of New York City, he focused on long walks in the woods near his house and gazing up at the stars. Bruni admits that occasionally in his new reality the impact of his vision loss lays him low. Those moments are to be expected, but for him they aren't the whole story or even the most important part of the story. Determination is, and gratitude, and the understanding that while we can't control the curveball that knocks us down, there is plenty we can decide about what happens next.

Turning Lemons into Lemonade

I first heard Frank Bruni's story when he gave a keynote address at a conference on aging hosted by the Gerontological Society of America. One of the main reasons the society invited him was because of his unique, early experience of loss that in many ways has prepared him for dealing with aging-related losses that he and others might experience in the future. But what most struck me was the resilience he displayed when that loss came out of nowhere. Experiencing curveballs (unexpected events or changes) and wake-up calls (unexpected situations that act as a warning sign) is not uncommon in the middle years. Job loss, divorce, a health scare, a dear friend passing suddenly—all these events can spin us around and upend our expectations of the future. They can also challenge our sense of control over the course of our lives. While major changes can happen at any point throughout our lives—and often do—the impact and the consequences in midlife are unique. Just as we see a deepening of stakes when it comes to decision-making and social relationships, how we handle and recover from major life stressors in midlife is profoundly important. Not only to us, but to those around us as well. It's also a fact of life that as we age, our susceptibility to curveballs and wake-up calls around our health increase. For instance, the kind of stroke that Frank Bruni experienced happens almost exclusively in people over the age of fifty.

While emotionally and psychologically we may feel young as ever, wake-up calls can be a blessing in disguise, bringing our attention to preventative measures we need to take to maintain our health, hopefully avoiding something more serious. Unexpected life events that cause stress can also offer unique opportunities for growth in middle age. Studies show that one of the great gifts of midlife is that our capacity and skill when it comes to emotion regulation is greatly increased. This means that we can focus more on the positive versus negative aspects of experiences and find the silver linings more readily. It also means that emotions can be better controlled, so the highs and lows are less extreme. Paradoxically, dealing with sudden changes can boost your sense of mastery if you're able to get through it and make it to the other side. Since life is full of curveballs, this can help inoculate you against the new stressors that will inevitably find you in the future, giving you confidence that you can handle what comes, because hey, you've done it before.

Wake-up calls, whether or not they stem from a curveball, can be a real gift if you're willing to take a step back and look at them in a different light. Breaking your wrist and learning that you're in the early stages of osteoporosis can give you the information and motivation you need to start taking bone health more seriously. A spouse's infidelity can provide either an unexpected new beginning to an old relationship or a painful but necessary break from a stagnant one. The sudden loss of a longtime job could be the catalyst for pivoting to a new, more exciting field. Not everyone will change their behavior and their lives in the wake of these curveballs and wake-up calls, but everyone certainly has the chance.

With the right mindset and tools for coping and fostering resilience, studies show that these difficult midlife moments can lead to increases in key markers of well-being and growth. Such experiences can result in us moving closer to the people in our lives, inspire us to sift through what our values and goals are, and help us determine the things we want to hold close no matter what life throws at us. But all that relies on a mindset shift—seeing these curveballs or wake-up calls not as end points but as turning points. In this chapter we'll explore the factors that have led people in midlife to alchemize these challenging moments into new directions, perspectives, and inspiration. Before we talk about the inner resources mid-lifers need to make this magic happen, it's important to dive a little deeper into the nature of the curveballs and wake-up calls we might run into. We might not be able to see them coming, but we can do a better job of recognizing them when they arrive.

Expect the Unexpected

Both curveballs and wake-up calls have one major thing in common—they fly in unexpectedly, challenge our sense of stability, upend our plans, and send us on an unasked-for emotional journey. Typically, they both fall under the category of major life stressors that can erode our sense of control and bounce us back and forth between okay-ness and anxiety. The impact of these major life events can result in a positive shift or become something that impacts a person so dramatically they never fully recover. Of course, there are subtle differences between these potentially life-altering events. Let's take a look.

Curveballs. What I call a curveball is an event that has profound effects and can lead to major changes in your everyday life. It can happen to you or someone close to you. For instance, if your child is diagnosed with a serious illness—there's no doubt this is a curveball. It's something you didn't expect that has rocked your life to the core. A curveball can be something unfathomably traumatic like that, or it can be something that throws you off your game in a significant way, like getting laid off. Often curveballs can be unexpected situations that arise in relationships at home or at work, such as learning about a boss's bad behavior. This is a circumstance that is difficult to navigate and may require tough choices about whether to stay, leave, or report the situation. Disappointments or betrayals in romantic relationships or friendships also may surface, throwing a wrench in the status quo. When people you thought you could count on let you down it can be a big blow.

The list of potential curveballs in life is endless, but in midlife job loss, divorce, death of a loved one, illness, and other nonnormative events that influence your life course are the biggies. In pop culture, curveballs are the bread and butter of drama, but they also represent very real experiences that many of us encounter. When the cast of the late nineties hit show *Sex and the City* returned to debut a new series called *And Just Like That* . . . in 2021, the first episode ended with what networks might call a "bombshell" but what I would call a curveball. After many happy intervening years between the end of the old series and the start of the new, Sarah Jessica Parker's character Carrie suddenly loses her beloved husband "Big" to a heart attack. Becoming a widow or widower at any age is difficult, and in your forties or fifties it is likely an unexpected and singular life experience that can completely throw you off course. The remaining episodes in the first season show Carrie grieving and slowly navigating life without her husband. One of the biggest challenges she had was a return to dating, something she never anticipated or wanted to do again after finding the love of her life. But by the second season, we see that this tragic start to the series is also a new beginning, with SJP's character finding new relationships and reconnecting with old loves.

Wake-up calls. Wake-up calls are a different kind of unexpected situation, ones that sound an alarm or an early warning sign. Wake-up calls ideally can serve to prevent a curveball later in life. They are events that refocus your attention and awareness on something you may have taken for granted or not considered at all. This may be a friend or relative similar in age to you who has a heart attack or gets breast or colon cancer. It can be scary, highlighting your vulnerability and shaking you up. The startle can take you off autopilot and catalyze a more concerted effort to prevent or address similar issues you might have. It makes you aware of the things that can go wrong, which often leads to taking some action, such as eating a healthier diet, getting on high blood pressure medication, or getting a mammogram or colonoscopy. These are things you may have been putting off, but the wake-up call helps reality sink in. You know if it can happen to someone *just like you*, it can happen to you too.

Just as often, it is our own experiences that trip the alarm. When a friend of mine named Emma was in her mid-fifties, she began to experience extreme fatigue and was thirsty all the time. Nothing had changed in her diet, exercise, or routines, so for months she was flummoxed. Eventually, she went to her doctor, who ran some basic bloodwork and discovered that she was prediabetic, which could account for her symptoms. Naturally lean, Emma rarely ate sugar and had never dreamed that type 2 diabetes might be in her future, despite a strong family history. The unexpected diagnosis of prediabetes scared her. Her own father was on a continuous glucose monitor and relied on insulin to keep him alive. Seeing all the health complications that came from diabetes, Emma immediately went on the offensive, changing her diet and exercise routines to try to manage her blood sugar. It was a stressful six months until she was able to get it under control, but in the end, she felt grateful for the symptoms that tipped her off. Many people live with prediabetes for years without even knowing it—at least Emma still had time to reverse course and mitigate the likelihood of developing full-blown diabetes.

Whether you experience a curveball or a wake-up call, it can cause stress and demands a response. The response may be major, affecting daily life or something less severe that is a more gradual change. Your sense of control is likely to be challenged when something unexpected happens. It can be chalked up to bad luck or being in the wrong place at the wrong time. You may be thankful that you got a warning sign before something worse could materialize. Paradoxically, dealing with a stressful situation in a competent and successful way can help you deal with challenges in the future with more confidence.

Of course, the fallout from some curveballs and wake-up calls is more complicated than just dealing with what is in front of you. Sometimes, the journey we are on doesn't begin with the wake-up call—it began decades earlier.

The Long Reach of Childhood

One common result of curveballs and wake-up calls is that they might unexpectedly dig up the past and invite it into the present. Of course, the truth is that the past has been with us all along. Lifespan psychology tells us there is continuity throughout the life course—we never completely escape what happened earlier in our lives.

Triggering experiences. Around midlife, the unresolved residue of any adverse childhood experiences we carry can also get shaken loose when we get smacked with a curveball. Divorce, death, and illness are all destabilizing events that can trigger emotional reckonings. Likewise, the physical consequences of childhood trauma also begin to become more and more apparent with age as people start showing symptoms of conditions like prediabetes, autoimmune disorders, and cardiovascular disease, which studies have shown are more common in those with a history of childhood trauma.

Unexpected stressors that come in middle age may trigger strong memories of traumatic events or adverse experiences in childhood. Sometimes a revisiting of the difficult past can come as our parents begin to age and need help, making it impossible to avoid the family home that was a source of trauma, or forcing us back into a dysfunctional relationship pattern we thought we'd escaped. The death of a parent, the breakup of a marriage, or even the loss of a job can dredge up painful feelings, remind us of past failures, or cause someone to question their life path. When this happens it's a double whammy, because you're dealing with an emotionally difficult situation in the present *and* the past.

The effect of ACEs. Even if there is no conscious recollection of childhood trauma or obvious mental health challenges related to them, there may be a biological residue of past hardships that begins to show up in midlife. Whether it is growing up in a poor family without resources, being abused physically or emotionally by parents or other adults, serious health problems as a child, living with an alcoholic parent, parental divorce, or death, there are short-term and long-term physical and emotional consequences. These experiences can be assessed using a checklist of Adverse Childhood Experiences (ACEs), and having one or more of these ACEs can make a person vulnerable not only during their childhood years but well into adulthood. Ideally, children who experience ACEs are given special attention and services when they are young to help them deal with and overcome their adversities. However, not all children receive effective care, and there can be cumulative effects with long-term consequences that have been shown to surface in middle age.

We know that people with ACEs become more vulnerable in midlife as pressures mount and cumulative stresses take hold. They are more susceptible to mental health problems, substance abuse, and chronic disease. In one study with MIDUS participants that I conducted with colleagues Greg Miller and Edith Chen, we found that those who grew up in low socioeconomic circumstances were more likely than their more advantaged peers to have metabolic syndrome in midlife—a precursor to type 2 diabetes and heart disease—including abdominal obesity, elevated blood pressure, high triglycerides and fasting glucose, and low high-density lipoprotein levels. (Yet, we also found that if someone had a nurturing mother during childhood, the effects of the low socioeconomic environment were diminished.) Other studies have found childhood adversity can show up years later in terms of inflammation and multisystem dysregulation, which is related to conditions such as hypertension, obesity, diabetes, and cardiovascular disease.

How do these childhood experiences get under the skin to yield such long-term effects? There are many mechanisms by which trauma can turn into a propensity for disease, but one of the most fundamental is toxic chronic stress. Research has shown that ACEs can cause strain through chronic stress, which in turn leads to high levels of inflammation that can literally change the way the structures of the brain and tissues in the body grow and develop. For some, the effects of toxic stress are a lifelong struggle, while for others the impact is all but invisible until a curveball like a heart attack or stroke happens in midlife. This is why knowing about and dealing with ACEs and understanding the seriousness of a wake-up call is so critical—you might just have been gifted a second chance.

Mitigating the impact of ACEs. The good news is that those who had at least one supportive, loving adult in childhood were likely to have dampened the long-term health effects of challenging experiences. But even if you didn't have supportive relationships, research shows the promise of reversibility of those effects in midlife. For anyone who does get a curveball or wake-up call, there are plenty of resources, lifestyle adjustments, and treatment options that can be made to safeguard your health for the future. When it comes to your mental and emotional health, there are ways to buffer the effects of childhood difficulties, many of which we've already talked about: fostering a sense of control, having a purpose in life, and maintaining optimism. Lewina Lee, a clinical psychologist at the VA Boston, and her colleagues found that those who remained optimistic, had close relationships, or had high life satisfaction in midlife were able to overcome the deleterious effects of childhood stressors and break the cycle of stress.

What works for those with a history of ACEs also works for the rest of us. As much as we might hate that all these curveballs and wake-up calls are coming at us, there are ways to cope with them so we can move on and perhaps even find a new direction in life. In fact, for some people, even the most painful curveballs and wake-up calls can lead to looking at the world through the lens of positive change.

The Turning Point

The thing that Carol had been living in fear of had happened. Her beloved boss left for another company and a new person took over management of her division. In short order, Carol's new boss brought in people she'd worked with in her previous position and Carol was out. Carol had joined the company when she was twenty-four and she was now fifty-one. She couldn't help but notice that the new employees were younger and—she guessed—working for lower salaries than she had commanded after all her years with the company. Carol felt an odd mix of terror that she was too old and thus no other company would want her and excitement because she now had the opportunity to try something new. After much soul-searching and career counseling, Carol decided to go freelance. She started her own business and although not an easy transition, and initially finances were tight, in the end it worked out well. She loved being her own boss and not answering to anyone but her carefully selected clients. And she could set her own work hours so she had more time to go to her son's basketball games and have coffee with friends.

When Mary was forty-seven, her husband died of brain cancer. They had three beautiful children ages five, nine, and twelve, and she and the rest of the family were devastated. Life seemed to move by in a blur. It was at times unbearable and at other times numbing. More quickly than anyone expected, Mary got the kids back on their school schedules and went back to work herself. But only with the help of her parents, in-laws, and a whole network of friends who did everything from dropping off meals on her porch to taking her kids to the dentist. For her own part, Mary cooked meals, signed them up for swim lessons, and planned Christmas dinner. At times she was going through the motions, but at others when she and the kids would find themselves belly laughing at a TV show, she'd let herself hope they were on their way to healing.

A few years after her husband passed away, Mary began to feel she'd gotten her bearings back and was feeling it was time to move on. She started to push herself to do some of the things she used to love doing before this bomb went off in her life, including hiking. Feeling ambitious one New Year's Eve, Mary landed on a new goal of hiking all forty-six of the High Peaks in the Adirondacks. To try to make the hikes more fun, Mary signed up for a fifty-plus hiking group. She met Jack, a divorced man with three children of his own, hiking the fourth peak. Fast-forward two years and Mary and Jack began raising a close-knit, blended family of three boys and three girls.

Being widowed far too young was a tragedy. But years later, Mary was able to see it as a turning point as well. This "off-time" milestone of losing a spouse made her feel isolated and alone considering she didn't know anyone who had gone through something similar. But eventually, she began to see it as a superpower. Like Frank Bruni, she got an early crash course in loss, grief, and crucially, resilience. She learned how to be gentler with herself, to slow down and acknowledge what was out of her control. Some days it was enough just to put one foot in front of the other and allow small joys to seep into the giant cracks in her heart.

What Carol and Mary experienced is the biggest potential gift of curveballs and wake-up calls: a turning point. Turning points involve changes in your worldview, how you think or feel about something, and often lead to taking action and going in new directions. They can be obvious or subtle, negative or positive, with powerful effects. In the stories of our lives, these are the hinge points on which the action shifts. An early, near-miss heart attack in your fifties could lead to an abrupt change in diet and exercise, and maybe even a new passion for a group activity like CrossFit that leads to greater social connection and quality of life. The sudden estrangement of a sibling can result in grief, but also in a renewed and deepening relationship with chosen family members. Turning points are significant because the changes they bring tend to ripple out in different directions. What starts as a simple recovery from a painful divorce can quickly turn into an unexpected exploration of one's identity and travel that improves health, mood, and purpose. These are the silver linings of what can at first be harrowing, painful moments in our lives. The good news is that the acute pain of curveballs can be short-lived, while their tailwinds can blow us in a new and positive direction for a long time to come.

Not all turning points are triggered by a crisis. Turning points can happen in response to an event triggered by a curveball or wake-up call, but they can also come from deep self-reflection, or even something as simple as the betrayal of a friend. Not everything in midlife that triggers a turning point is necessarily traumatic or even dramatic; sometimes it's just an important realization about yourself or others.

In one MIDUS study, researchers looked at turning points to try to understand how they impact mid-lifers. In the study, participants were asked to identify whether they had experienced negative or positive psychological turning points in the past twelve months. This is how they were defined: "Psychological turning points (PTP) are *major changes* in the ways people feel or think about an important part of their life, such as work, family, and beliefs about themselves and about the world. Turning points involve people changing their feelings about how *important* or *meaningful* some aspect of life is or how much *commitment* they give it." Participants were then asked to identify seven specific types of turning points in the last twelve months:

1. *career*—a turning point that involves a job or career;

2. *upset for friend*—a turning point that involves learning that a close friend or relative is not the person one thought they were either for the better or the worse;

3. *happy for friend*—a turning point that involves discovering that a close friend or relative was a much better person than one thought they were;

4. *upset for self*—a turning point that involves learning upsetting things about oneself;

5. *happy for self*—a turning point that involves discovering important good things about oneself;

6. *give up dream*—a turning point that involves giving up an important dream; and

7. *fulfill dream*—a turning point that involves the fulfillment of a special dream.

The most common turning points for both men and women involved work-related accomplishments, although job or career turning points occurred later in midlife for women than for men. Work and/or family issues involving conflicts or trying to balance demands were more common for women than for men. The next most reported turning point was fulfilling a special dream, which is an example of a positive turning point. Special dreams included getting promotions at work, buying a home, or recognition in a person's various roles.

Many of the people we have surveyed in additional studies indicate that after an unexpected loss or change, what we could call curveballs, they experienced positive psychological turning points. Something they never imagined would happen happened—or maybe it was something they had lived in fear of for many years—but then they were able to turn things around, find meaning, and take control, using the situation as a moment to start anew, to grow. In a series of studies Carolyn Aldwin, a professor of human development at Oregon State University, and I asked adults to tell us about a low point in their lives. Many of the events happened in midlife and others had happened earlier. These low points included events such as unemployment or divorce, a house fire, or death of someone close. Most noted they drew on past experiences to help them through and they had developed better coping skills and confidence as well as new attitudes toward life. Many reported an increase in empathy or understanding of others, although some relayed negative lessons such as the unfairness in the world.

Studies like this show us that positive turning points can happen even in the most quotidian moments of our lives during middle age—stepping into a new role at work or taking the next step in a romantic relationship. But transforming a real low point in our lives into a positive turning point is a much heavier lift. It's an alchemy that hinges on personality, mindset, and agency—all aspects of midlife that we've touched on in this book, but that now come together to help form the raw materials of resilience.

The Power of Resilience

The best any of us could hope for when faced with curveballs and wake-up calls in midlife is a nice, juicy, positive turning point. Who doesn't want the hero's journey from conflict and pain to end in triumph? Naturally, life is a little trickier than all that. And yet, in the studies I conducted with Aldwin, we found that over 90% of the people surveyed were able to derive some meaning and learn from what they described as a "low point" in their lives, illustrating the resilience of the human spirit.

Despite being a big buzzword in the last decade, resilience has long been a defining feature of humanity. We typically define it as a successful adaptation to adversity. It can involve avoiding a negative outcome or it can focus on how people bounce back after a challenge and the ability to continue even in the face of adversity. The notion of resilience in human development was first discussed by developmental psychologist Michael Rutter regarding children whose parents had mental illness, yet the children did not develop problems. He formulated resilience as the positive component of an individual's response to stress and adversity. Unfortunately, not everyone experiences resilience. While many have low points and then rebound after adversity, others never recover. When researchers test for resilience, they often use a set of questions like the Nicholson McBride Resilience Questionnaire. Those who score high on resilience identify strongly with statements like: I don't take criticism personally; I generally manage to keep things in perspective; I am calm in a crisis; I'm good at finding solutions to problems.

There are a number of psychosocial resources that can help boost resilience, including positive emotions, flexibility, emotional intelligence, perseverance, spirituality, religion and faith, social support, emotion regulation, and a sense of mastery. Positive affect, personality factors such as conscientiousness and low neuroticism, and optimism are all protective factors that help us deal with adversity. While some people are born with personalities that grease the skids for resilience more readily (I'm looking at all the optimists out there), it's not all about the hand you're dealt at birth. You *can* develop resources such as coping skills or better emotional regulation in response to challenges. Having a supportive social network is one of the most well-established factors that helps one deal with adversity, and, as we learned in the last chapter, that is something we can actively cultivate in midlife.

Handling Stress Well

In midlife, the experience of a curveball or wake-up call is typically a stressful event. Getting a diagnosis of a disease in early midlife or losing your job is something that can require a total rewrite of life plans. Often, we are called to pivot after a curveball in a way that is not only unexpected but (often) initially unwanted. When this happens, a focus on how you perceive and respond to the situation is critical to boosting resilience and the likelihood of a positive turning point.

Sometimes it seems as if our feelings just bubble to the surface of our emotional lives, facts that we can't change. But the truth is that *how* you look at an event impacts the levels of stress you experience as the result of it. The same situation may be seen as a challenge to one person but a threat to someone else, and the stressful feelings that result will be very, very different. This isn't to say the feelings that crop up in response to a curveball aren't real, they are. But feelings are also malleable and manageable. Our initial mindset about a curveball is the first step toward resilience or despair. We do much better by acknowledging our own sense of agency than by throwing our hands up at the unfairness of it all. Two things can be true—you didn't choose this *and* you get to decide how you respond to it.

Naturally, people will vary in how they cope with stress. Richard Lazarus and Susan Folkman were faculty at the University of

California, Berkeley, when they postulated a theory of stress that is still widely applied today. They said that there are three aspects to the stress process. First is *primary appraisal,* which is whether you perceive the event or experience as a harm, a threat, a loss, a challenge, or something not stressful. Next is *secondary appraisal,* which involves thinking about how you might respond to the situation considering your assessment of your stress level. Third is the *coping process,* which involves taking action to respond to the event.

They found two broad approaches to coping. One is problem-focused, which involves doing something directly to alter the source of the stress. For instance, if you are diagnosed with high blood pressure, a warning sign in your early forties, taking medication and starting a new workout routine is a problem-focused approach to feeling less terrible and being more proactive about your new diagnosis. This action can help minimize the risk of a stroke. Problem-focused coping is considered more adaptive—meaning it's the first stop on the resilience train. The other approach to coping is emotion-focused, which is aimed at reducing or managing the emotional distress associated with the stressor. (You'll notice there's a parallel here between primary control and secondary control from earlier chapters.) Interestingly, problem-focused coping tends to be used more commonly in middle and later adulthood in contrast to younger adulthood, when emotion-focused coping is more prevalent. Some problem-focused coping strategies include planning, taking direct action, seeking assistance, looking for alternatives, and waiting for the right moment before acting.

If a stressor is uncontrollable, emotion-focused coping may be more appropriate to alleviate distress if the problem cannot be directly addressed. If the life event in question is the death of a loved one, there isn't anything we can do to control that stressor—you can plan all you want for the funeral and the aftermath, but the stress and grief resulting from an unfillable hole in your life doesn't just go away. These kinds of curveballs are arguably the most difficult to deal with precisely because of that lack of control and their major impact on one's life. When that happens, understand that managing your emotions around the stress is indeed a very healthy thing to do.

However, while emotion-focused coping can be positive, there are more opportunities for it to go in the wrong direction than problem-focused coping. For instance, denial, disassociation, and substance abuse are not *adaptive* strategies—meaning they're not helping us out—but they are emotional coping strategies. When in the position of dealing with a stressful curveball, we'd do better to lean into the healthier side of emotion-focused coping—positive reinterpretation of events and seeking out social support. Seeking social support can be considered problem-focused or emotion-focused depending on what is being sought, either assistance to solve the problem or emotional support.

The surprise and unexpected nature of curveballs and wake-up calls challenge our resilience because we can't plan for them. Yet, in response, we can develop skills for proactive coping that can help us in the direct aftermath *and* in the future.

The Upside of Stress

Growth and change can come from stressful experiences that are handled well, but that can be hard to appreciate when we are in the thick of it. We tend to think of stress as having only negative effects, but many studies have shown that when one is able to successfully cope with stressful life events it can lead to increases in mastery, self-confidence, and empathy. It can also improve health outcomes and spirituality. It can lead to closer social ties with others who are coping along with you. Such experiences can result in us moving closer to the people in our lives. They can also inspire us to sift through what our values are, to determine the things we want to hold tightly to no matter what life throws at us.

Stress inoculation theory tells us that if one can build confidence and strategies in response to a stressful event, it can be applied to future challenges. As exposure to a pathogen builds up immunity in the medical sense, experiencing stress can help build up resistance and adaptive responses to life's challenges. We'll be better prepared for what comes later if we have successfully navigated an earlier event. Although reacting to a stressor can negatively affect your health, there is also evidence that handling mild stressors builds up resistance and strength to deal with things to come. Research by Susan Charles at the University of California, Irvine, and David Almeida at the Pennsylvania State University has shown that people who experienced a moderate amount of stress had higher levels of well-being and better physiological responses to stress compared to people with either low or very high levels of exposure. They found that those who reported no daily stressors were less engaged in life, seemingly to protect themselves from adversity.

Experience dealing with difficult situations leads to developing a repertoire of skills to handle adverse experiences in the future. In this way it is like other realms of midlife in which we can draw on valuable experiences hard-won over time. Life provides the natural environment for learning what works and what doesn't. You can learn how to focus on what you can control, how to look on the bright side, and how to take your time before responding to a disturbing situation, or ask for help.

Some curveballs and wake-up calls are severe enough to cause extreme stress or trauma, although they are less common. They may result in post-traumatic stress disorder. This involves intense emotional or physical reactions when reminded of the event, including sweating, heart palpitations, anxiety, or panic. In such cases there is an extreme form of resilience called post-traumatic growth. It can lead to a new outlook or perspective on life, perhaps recognizing one has been given a second chance, a new appreciation for life, and a new connection to loved ones. Achieving such a positive outcome can take a lot of work, usually with help from a therapist or other professionals. How a person makes sense of life experiences is central—even in the most extreme, unimaginably traumatic moments.

Some of the most poignant curveballs and wake-up calls we can experience are the ones that speak directly to our future well-being, and how our health, happiness, and life trajectory will change. Reframing a curveball or wake-up call into a turning point is one way we can maintain control of the narrative of our lives. Another is making decisions that we feel good about in the wake of unexpected changes, as well as in everyday life. In the next chapter we'll look at the landscape of decision-making in midlife, and how we can make better decisions both big and small in the future.

Chapter 8
Choosing Wisely at the Crossroads of Life

May your choices reflect your hopes, not your fears.
—NELSON MANDELA

When Molly hopped on a Zoom call with her manager one Friday afternoon, she was expecting to give an update on her project and sail into the weekend. But about ten minutes into the meeting, her head was spinning. The nonprofit organization for whom she had tirelessly worked for over five years was "restructuring" and letting her go.

Her last day would be at the end of the month, which was only two weeks away. Don't worry, they said, we'll give you two weeks' severance pay! That was cold comfort considering it would barely cover the mortgage. As she walked down the stairs to tell her husband what happened, her eye snagged on the half-spackled Sheetrock on the ceiling and the piles of bathroom tiles on the hallway floor. They were two-thirds of the way through a massive home renovation, but all the way through their budget. Her three kids were in private school, and the tickets for their upcoming Alaskan cruise were sitting on their credit card collecting interest. Things were already tight, even with both adults working full time, so when Molly thought of a paycheck-shaped hole that would soon be in her bank account she felt like collapsing on the stairs.

After the initial shock and sadness waned, Molly found herself overwhelmed with something she hadn't had in about ten years: time. She went from spinning like a top while juggling, to having some semblance of balance in her life. It wasn't until she slowed down that she realized just how truly out of whack her life had become. Turns out, raising three kids, being a good (or at least acceptable) partner, working sixty hours a week, and living with a chronic illness is not a recipe for wellness. Molly realized her own health and well-being had been on the back burner for far too long, but before she lost her job she hadn't even realized it.

Dreaming of balance, Molly started thinking about getting out of nonprofit work altogether. Maybe pivoting to something that was less demanding. When she heard a story on the radio about a man who had worked all his life as a phone repair technician before starting a second career as a shoe designer, she thought, *Why not? I could have a second career!* She already knew what she was interested in—mind-body coaching. It was something she wanted to learn more about, and there was even a certification course—she would complete it and start her own business. For a few weeks she fantasized about working from home, designing a website, and helping people find their balance.

While she enjoyed taking the class and was grateful for the time that unemployment benefits had given her to think, she knew she needed to decide soon which direction to take. If she wanted to get back into her field and find a similar job to the one she had lost, she needed to start applying and networking now. Likewise, if she wanted to start her own mind-body coaching service, she needed to throw herself into the certification process completely and start rapidly building a business. But there were so many things to consider. All the contingencies and probabilities, all the pros and cons, raced through her head, her intuition rearranging itself completely from one minute to the next.

Somewhat bitterly, she thought about how if she were making this decision in her twenties, it would have been easier. She would have taken a shot at the mind-body coaching. If it hadn't worked out, she would have done an about-face and tagged back into the nonprofit game, no problem. If money was tight for a while, also no big deal—then she'd only had herself to worry about—she could eat ramen all day long. Now, at forty-nine, things looked very, very different. She had kids to feed and a mortgage to pay. The dangling unknowns of opening a business suddenly looked more like risk than adventure. It's one thing to try and fail when you are only letting yourself down, it's another to try and fail and have to tell your kids that you're selling the house. On the other hand, the idea of going back to the status quo was equally risky—she had been sacrificing her health for years, and that was just as much a problem for her family in the long run as taking a pay cut.

When she thought back to other decisions she had made in her life, none of them seemed this fraught, this complex, and it scared her. One evening over dinner her husband gently asked her which direction she was leaning.

Molly took a deep breath, looked at the kids, who were playing with their food, and said quietly through tears, "Honestly, I just don't know."

The Unique Landscape of Choice in Midlife

It is said that we make between thirty-three thousand and thirty-five thousand decisions each day. There are the thousands of small decisions we make, like what shirt to wear, what exercise to do (or not do), what doctor to see, or what food to feed your kids. Then there are the major life decisions, like whether to move across the country, have kids in the first place, or put an ailing parent in a nursing home. While the big decisions are splashy and obvious in their ability to alter your life, the little choices we make every day are just as consequential because they compound over time. The discrete choices we make about eating, moving our bodies, and spending time with loved ones are the daily decisions that stack up, impacting the rest of our lives both emotionally and physically.

At every stage of life, the context of our choices drastically changes. Over time, our priorities, our social responsibilities, our ability to emotionally regulate, and our capacity for wise reasoning evolves. Naturally, navigating the decision-making process at twenty versus forty or fifty is wildly different. Understanding how to make better decisions at any age is important and critical to one's well-being. On the subject of decision-making writ large, there are hundreds of books you can read to help make better choices. But none that I've come across look at how our *time of life* impacts that process and looks at evidence-based tools specifically shown to help folks in midlife. Here, there is still time for reinvention, awakenings, and big moves. But since there isn't *all* the time in the world left, decision-making at midlife needs to be more intentional than ever before. And what decisions we make in midlife affect not only us but the people around us, and even the people we will become as we enter older adulthood.

Over the last thirty years of studying midlife, I've discovered that no matter what the decision is—big or small—there are generally three main reasons why choices in midlife are uniquely challenging: the stakes, the complexity, and the pace of life. Obviously, they connect and overlap, but I find it useful to pull the threads apart a little bit so we can fully appreciate what we're dealing with.

The Stakes: More Pressure, Less Time

Given our many responsibilities in midlife, we can't do everything. Time is more limited than ever before—we must make the hard decisions. When we are younger, without children to raise and mortgages to pay, it's easier to experiment and follow one path for a while and then switch direction entirely and try out another. It's not so simple in our middle years. Molly knew this from the start, understanding intimately how risky it would be financially and emotionally to throw all her eggs in the mind-body coaching basket. Going all in on a second career works for some, but not for others—each person has to assess their appetite for risk, carefully considering the potential gains and losses. Of course,

Molly could have thrown caution to the wind and started a new business without considering all the angles, but with the well-being of her family on the line, the stakes felt far too high.

At this midpoint in our lives there is still plenty of time to do what we dream of, whether that's hiking the Appalachian Trail or writing a memoir. But usually, we recognize that some of our desires and goals need to happen *soon*. For instance, hiking the Appalachian Trail in your eighties is certainly possible, but it's going to be far more difficult and potentially dangerous than if you do it in your fifties. With an infinite number of desires and goals for one's precious life, limitations on exactly what we can shelve or put off start to sink in. For some of us, panic can set in as well as the pressure to "get it right" and stave off regret.

While most of us understand intellectually that we can't do everything we want, it's really at this age that it starts to hit us emotionally. In this way, when we make decisions at midlife, we must grapple with the emotional residue of not only what we do choose, but all the paths we can't choose. Either we need to factor in the needs of others, or we simply don't have time to go in another direction. Looking at the path we know we can't take, but want to, can be one of the most heartbreaking things about midlife. Even if your choice to forgo the second career or the move to Mexico seems like the right one, it doesn't mean it's the easy one.

While the big decisions tend to take up a lot of our time and attention, the small choices we make every day in the attempt to juggle our work and personal lives are equally profound (though far sneakier). These decisions might not seem like a big deal, but when kids leave home to go off to college, the military, or to explore the world, many parents find themselves wishing they'd spent more time with their children. Others find themselves in ill health and wish they had eaten fewer cheeseburgers and taken more walks. We may come to the later years of our lives and regret some of the choices or trade-offs we have made that seemed so small at the time. Remembering each day what our greatest priorities are as we make decisions big and small can make all the difference, but it's also far easier said than done. Especially with all the interlocking obligations, considerations, and relationships that we have to factor into every single choice.

Complexity Paralysis

Often, people in midlife are making decisions that not only impact them but other people as well—whether it's your kids, your spouse, your parents, or your friends. By midlife, people are more settled than ever before, which means their roots are deeper and their relationships more symbiotic. These kinds of personal entanglements amplify both the complexity and the stakes of each decision.

In Molly's case she had to take into consideration multiple layers of context that could potentially impact her family: their financial situation; her level of presence and engagement with her kids; the way her stress levels could damage her health and shift the domestic labor burden to her husband; and how she wants to model what it means to be a worker in the world for her kids. Then there are of course the ways that this decision also ripples out. It affects her parents, who would be asked to step up and provide more childcare if she went back to a high-intensity job. On a smaller but just as important level it would also impact how well she was able to be there for friends, volunteer at her kids' school, and say yes to community activism. Part of what Molly experienced when she described the stock ticker of contingencies in her head was what I call *complexity paralysis*. In midlife, the decision onion has so many layers, peeling it back can start to feel so daunting we could be forgiven for wanting to throw it at the wall.

The Pace: The Rush Hour of Life

Whether you have kids or not, a spouse or not, or are close with your family, the pace of midlife can feel unrelenting. People are often at the pinnacle of their careers with more responsibilities than ever, which often means putting in more time at work mentoring others or trying to expand a business. Folks with kids are acutely aware that this time of life is chock-full of orthodontist appointments, after-school sports, birthday parties, homework, school spirit days, family vacations, holidays, and a never-ending onslaught of viruses. For mid-lifers with aging parents, there are constant decisions to be made about care—coordinating with siblings, setting up in-home nursing care, or simply trying to decide when to fit another visit into an already packed schedule. The number of choices we need to make every day simply to check things off the to-do list and get dinner on the table is mind-blowing.

When big decisions do come up, we can be so overwhelmed by all the small ones that it can be really hard to slow down and get clarity. Molly herself noted the silver lining that she had in unemployment—she actually had *time* to think about her next move. But for most people, life doesn't stop while you're making a life-altering decision, it requires you to keep pace. Your dog died and your toddler has a fever? That's too bad, but you still have to decide whether to fail the student in your class who has been missing in action all semester because grades are due tomorrow.

Midlife has been referred to as the "rush hour" of life, and I can't think of a more apt description of the decision pileup. Not only is everything happening fast, it's also bumper-to-bumper choices, with each potential choice driven by conflicting demands. Every choice is competing for our attention, our money, and our time. In midlife people often have goals that are at odds with each other—like Molly's desire for life balance *and* a steady paycheck. Then of course there is the endless nature of midlife decisions big and small: Should we put an addition on the house we already own, or buy a new one with more room for the growing family? Should we buy a used car or splurge on a new one that's more reliable? Should we get a new puppy, or will that be too overwhelming? Should I keep showing up for a friendship that continues to take more than it gives? Should I focus on getting enough protein, or is fiber what's really important? Should we push our kid to try a sport, or just let them take the lead on finding their own passion? Should I volunteer at the local library or use that time to take up rock climbing? Should I put my savings in a Roth IRA or an account for the children's education?

It's no wonder that when faced with this kind of "choice overload" many people end up putting the smaller decisions in their lives on autopilot and the big ones on hold. While this is a good short-term solution, as we'll see later, it's not a winning approach for long-term health and happiness.

In these ways—and many more—the landscape of choice in middle age presents a unique challenge. Luckily, it's also a unique opportunity. Choosing wisely is always important, but in midlife, it is also a key mechanism for cultivating a healthy sense of control. We can't always anticipate how we will feel in the long run, so when we do have choices, we can try to make decisions that maximize opportunities and keep options open. If you are intentional and consider the different options carefully, it may help you avoid disappointments and regrets—making the most of the time you have left. During this period of life, there is still time to turn things around with well-thought-out decisions and the right plan.

Mid-Lifers Are Good Decision-Makers

Let's start off with a piece of good news—you already have what you need to make the best decisions of your life.

Research shows that people in midlife are well positioned cognitively, emotionally, and psychologically to make better choices than at any other time of life. This may come as a surprise considering how fast and furious the decision points are coming at us, but when we look a little closer, we see that we already have the "hardware" to make good decisions—we might just need to update our "software" to truly maximize our choices.

There is a robust research literature on decision-making and aging that focuses on both behavioral and neurological aspects of how we make decisions. Like so much research, the work typically compares young adults with older adults, with middle-aged adults left out of the conversation. While we know little *specifically* about how changes in the brain affect middle-aged decision-making skills, it's a safe bet that those in midlife likely fall somewhere in between what we already know about the decision-making skills of those younger and older.

What researchers have shown is that in older adults the aging brain can both help and hurt our ability to make good decisions. Because there are so many different components of the decision-making process, there are likewise many different parts of the brain that we use. There's no question that some of these brain structures experience neurodegeneration as we age, like the prefrontal cortex (the part of the brain responsible for executive functioning, the ability to plan and organize our lives), which is affected by hypertension and other vascular diseases more common as we age. Scientists use this information to infer that decision-making declines with age, but experts believe it to be pretty much intact in midlife. In fact, some researchers are even questioning the impact of neurodegeneration in older adults—suggesting that the changes in decision-making behavior might be the result of "active remodeling of neural circuits." In other words, as one part of the brain starts to slow down or fail, other parts swoop in to take over, which might mean that we see different decision-making strategies arise as we age.

Some research has shown that neurotransmitter and hormonal activity (dopamine, specifically) that drives our reward system changes as we age, influencing the way we reason. Older adults tend to think more about what they've learned from similar past decisions, whereas young adults privilege what they think will be the best choice for their future. This shows us the wisdom of evolution; thanks to neuroplasticity, we are able to shift and change how we make decisions to keep pace with our new constraints and changing contexts. It makes sense that a septuagenarian with decades of experience would weigh past experiences and outcomes more heavily than future hopes and dreams. On a less dramatic level, our brains are doing the same thing in midlife—they aren't making choices the same way our twenty-two-year-old self would have, but they also aren't lined up with how an eighty-two-year-old strategizes either.

To see more clearly how exactly mid-lifers fare when you stack them up against older and younger decision-makers, we have to turn away from neuroscience and toward behavioral economics where this question has been addressed. Economists have done some interesting work on financial decision-making across the adult years, including those in midlife who stood out with the best skills. David Laibson, a behavioral economist from Harvard, and his colleagues explored financial decisions across adulthood. They used large databases of information about credit cards and loans for borrowers with the best credit ratings. They found that middle-aged adults made fewer financial mistakes than either younger or older adults. The peak of good financial decisions was in middle age; in fact, the best cost-minimizing performance was found for adults specifically at age fifty-three. They found that middle-aged adults borrowed at lower interest rates and paid less in fees than did either younger or older adults. When they looked across ten different types of credit transactions, they concluded that fees and interest payments were lowest for those around age fifty-three.

The study investigators suggested that the findings were due to the experience and knowledge gained with age as well as learning from mistakes. This tracks with common sense, explaining why the middle-aged did better than the young, who don't have as much knowledge about financial plans and offers. On the other end of the lifespan, researchers believe that the middle-aged did better than older adults because their fluid intelligence and analytic abilities had not declined as much as they had for the older adults. The researchers concluded that "relatively young borrowers have low levels of experience and a high degree of analytical function, while older borrowers have high levels of experience but relatively lower analytical function."

Once again, it's good to be in the middle! Our neural hardware is still firing on most cylinders, and we have a bevy of hard-won life experiences to draw on. This is good news, because as we face the increasing stakes, complexity, and pace of decisions in midlife we can be confident in our capabilities. We have what it takes to make the best decisions of our life, but because we are making them under arguably the trickiest conditions in our lifespan, we just may need a little extra help.

How to Optimize Your Primetime Decisions

Knowing when to say no and choosing wisely are important mechanisms for cultivating a sense of control in our middle years, which we already know is correlated to better overall well-being. So how do we do that more effectively in the rush hour of life? We can pop the hood and look even more closely at what's tripping us up. We know that complexity, pace, and stakes make decisions emotionally difficult—but they also make things difficult from a practical standpoint.

The psychological research on decision-making shows that people get tripped up making decisions when there is a conflict between our goals or when we don't have the resources to reach the goal in the first place. Sometimes there is a conflict between our goals *and* we don't have the resources to reach the goal. Often our goals conflict in different domains of our life—maybe I want to refinish my basement, but I also want to take the kids to Disneyland. In this case, there are two goals—one is a homeowner goal and one is a parenting goal. They are in conflict precisely because there are not enough resources on hand to achieve them both (time and money). Sometimes, even if we only have one goal, or one decision to make, the demand on our resources is still too great. Then, instead of being successful in doing the thing we've chosen, we feel heightened anxiety and stress. A common thing for people to express in midlife is that they feel like they have multiple occupations (such as mother, partner, sister, worker, planner) and that they are doing a crappy job at all of them. This feeling of overload and dissatisfaction is rooted in a mismatch between goals and resources, and *this* is where we can improve our decision-making skills.

Selection, Optimization, Compensation Model (SOC)

Understanding where the conflicts exist, what the demands are on our resources, and *then* making decisions is actually the first step in a three-step model for improving decision-making, especially under conditions of competing demands or constraints of time and resources. It's called the Selection, Optimization, Compensation Model (SOC), which was developed by the husband-and-wife team of lifespan psychologists Paul and Margret Baltes. While it was not designed specifically for mid-lifers, research has shown that it's highly effective for this age group considering the rush hour of life and its pileup of conflicting demands.

Selection. When we're taking the first step to consider a decision, selection—meaning slowing down and figuring out goals and priorities—is the first stop. In Molly's case, at the beginning of the chapter, we saw that her conflicting goals were maintaining her health through work-life balance and financially supporting her family. Because Molly had time to consider her situation, she ran a thousand different scenarios to try to find her way out of this conflict. But this proved problematic, since her career opportunities were limited to a riskier pivot that might not pan out or to finding a similar job that might make work-life balance equally impossible. The decision point that she found herself at made it necessary to prioritize one goal over the other. Because of the demands on our resources (money, time, energy), we can't do it all—we have to choose.

This can be painful, and hard, but studies show there are two ways to deal with this and make our selection wisely. The first is using something we discussed in chapter 5, "goal shelving." Research shows that people fare better putting off one of their goals than simply giving up on it. The second option is to try to work it so that the goals "facilitate" each other or work together. An example of this would be if Molly could find a job that allowed her to work at home a few days a week and have a more flexible schedule so that she could take conference calls while walking the dog or making the kids lunch. Another way to facilitate both goals could be to work childcare duties out with her husband so she could build in time to meditate or exercise every morning. Maybe these facilitation moves would work, maybe they wouldn't. But if you can find a way to achieve both goals by getting them to support each other, that's one solution to resolving decision conflict.

The second way to make a wise selection is to *modify* your goal. This means looking at your reduced resources and abilities and then reordering your priorities accordingly. Maybe for Molly there is just not enough time at this stage in her life—the time constraint is simply too big for her to achieve her ideal work-life balance goal. Instead of finding a job that allows her to work from home, knock off early to go to Pilates, and doesn't ask her to work on weekends, she might have to lower her bar a little. Instead of either shelving her goal or discarding it, she could *modify* it and come up with a new goal. Maybe it isn't full work-life balance, but something more manageable within her constraints, like creating a new goal to attend a weekend meditation retreat every six months. This wouldn't conflict with her goal of financial security, and it would help her move in the direction of the balance she is looking for.

Ultimately, this is what Molly decided to do—she modified her high hopes for work-life balance and decided to look for a similar job to the one she had left. She'd aim to *facilitate* both goals as much as possible by gunning hard for a job with a flexible schedule, but she'd also make a commitment to getting up a half hour early every day to meditate. She knew it wouldn't be easy, but it felt a lot better than giving up on improving her health and happiness.

Optimization. Once we've made our selection (decision), the next step is to really make sure that we're doing everything we can to reach the goal successfully. The research defines optimization as "the process of acquiring, applying, and refining goal-relevant means to achieve selected goals." In other words, figuring out the best way to achieve the goal with the resources you have. This seems pretty obvious, almost like something we do naturally, but doing it successfully actually hinges on us being intentional. This is an important decision-making skill for two reasons:

1. It gives you good information for future decisions because you'll have a better sense of what you can handle and achieve, not to mention how best to get there, and

2. Because midlife is all about improving our sense of control, the degree to which we can have a hand in our own success is important. Just making decisions and hoping for the best isn't going to improve your stress levels or your life satisfaction. You made the decision for a reason—you want to achieve the goal. So how can you do that? Simply put—you've got to optimize wherever you can. Molly could just set her alarm for a half hour early, walk into the living room, and sit down on the floor to meditate. But, if she really wants to make her early meditation practice stick, she'd be wise to learn new strategies for habit formation, figure out the most comfortable setup, and maybe take a class beforehand so she doesn't get discouraged when meditation is (inevitably) harder than she'd imagined. This kind of commitment to the decision and the goal is necessary groundwork for success.

Compensation. Sometimes after a decision is made to pursue a goal, right in the middle of doing the darn thing, there is a curveball. Compensation is all about making the best out of a bad or unexpected situation. A constraint or a loss pops up and threatens the whole endeavor. Maybe Molly starts to meditate every day and gets really into it—so far, she's meeting her goal. But suddenly, her youngest son started waking up earlier too, and for days she is thrown off her meditation game. She tries to occupy him and meditate at the same time, but it doesn't work. A way she might compensate for this new constraint is by appealing to her husband to get up early and take care of the early bird. Or she might use her lunch break to meditate and eat at her desk afterward. Another option could be going to a meditation class in the evenings on certain days. None of these backup plans might be a perfect fit, but people who can do this successfully are much better off than those who get off track and throw up their hands. When there is control to be had in midlife, it's far better to take it.

The Art of Choosing Wisely

Many people lose their sense of control in midlife by either not making decisions or trying to do it all. When they do the latter, their stress skyrockets and their sense of well-being diminishes. We all know people who are spread so thin that they are never able to meet their deadlines or goals, and if they do, it's often a shoddy job. The antidote suggested by the SOC model is being selective in what we do so we can successfully manage the things that are most important to us in each area of our lives, whether it's caring for loved ones, mastering an art, or excelling in our profession. It involves acknowledging that you can't do everything at once. Sometimes it requires putting goals on hold until another time. This is relevant at the daily level and also with regard to longer-term goals. In midlife it helps to acknowledge that we can't do it all, at least if we want to do it well. There is time to select the highest priorities and come back to other goals later when time, energy, and money permit. The SOC model is the gold-standard for helping us manage our lives by making those decisions wisely and following through successfully on our goals. So much of conflict during this time of life is between internal desires and external pressures. The SOC model helps us recognize the conflict in our decision points, assess constraints and resources, make a call, and then succeed even in the face of all the demands and losses that can throw us off track.

SOC strategies are found to be most often used by those in middle age and indeed are most beneficial for those overloaded by what's on their plate. In one study my former student Salom Teshale and I showed that those middle-aged and older participants who used SOC strategies most frequently in daily life reported greater happiness.

How do you use SOC in daily life?

Michelle is a forty-five-year-old teacher who wants to go back to school to get her master's degree so she can get a higher salary. She is also considering going for additional training so she can be a principal. She has three kids who are five, eight, and eleven. They are all doing multiple activities. So, she spends hours after work and on weekends driving them to their practices, games, and other events.

She barely has time for herself, but she is good about getting up early every morning so she can exercise on the treadmill in her basement. Her husband can't help during the week, but he is available on weekends to pitch in with the carpooling and they often have to split up to go to different games. Michelle is using selection as she realizes she cannot do it all and has to make a choice. She decides to focus on her parenting role, keeping the kids in their activities, and puts off her extra schooling until they are older and more independent. If she had more resources she could hire someone to transport the kids, but she decides she wants to be involved anyway, realizing they are only young once and that there is plenty of time when the kids are older for her to focus on her goals. She decides that when the kids are a little more independent, she can start taking some online courses in the evenings toward her degree and administration training.

At age fifty Jane is excited to change careers. She has been a social worker for the past twenty-five years and has enjoyed it. But now she's decided she wants to pursue what has always been a hobby. She has a talent for design and has decorated her own house and advised her friends. Yet, she knows she will need training in order to get licensed and open a legitimate business as an interior decorator. She also has to keep her social work job to bring in money. She left the social work job at the agency and opened a practice in her home to gain flexibility. This way she has more control over her hours and less travel time. She can then spend the time to take interior design courses and work toward her credentials. She starts to take courses on weekends and some evenings and cuts back somewhat on her social work clients. She is optimizing her skills by taking courses and studying. She builds her portfolio by doing some design work for her friends. Ultimately, she gets all the coursework she needs and quits her practice to start her new profession as an interior designer.

Hannah is a fifty-six-year-old lawyer who specializes in injury litigation. She has built up a lucrative practice and is in great demand. She has been having some health problems of late and has been having trouble keeping up with her work. She especially has difficulty standing for long stretches in court and making forceful and cogent arguments. After many tests her doctor informs her she has multiple sclerosis. It turns out to be the mild form but nevertheless, she now understands why her stamina is not what it used to be. Hannah wants to keep working but she needs to compensate for her symptoms. And she needs to reduce her stress so the symptoms do not flare up. She decides to work as a consultant advising other lawyers. She can use her vast experience to help them prepare their cases and she can work from home. This allows her to continue the work she loves while finding a way to reduce the stress and accept the fact that she is not as able to stand on her feet and argue cases in a high-pressure court environment. Hannah has figured out how to use compensation strategies to maintain her goals.

The irony is that while all the winnowing down of choices we must do in midlife might technically give us fewer choices, it actually allows us to focus more on what we really, really want. It turns out that when we can draw on all that we have learned thus far in our lives, weighing what it is we feel truly passionate about and what gives us purpose and meaning, the best choices for ourselves and the people we love become clear.

How to Turn Off Autopilot

In midlife we are often on autopilot given all the responsibilities and tasks there are to accomplish on a regular basis. You may feel like you don't have time to think. At this time of life, routines and habits can be a lifeline. They help us save time and can reduce stress. One serious drawback is that when we're on autopilot, we do things mindlessly. You can't remember if you locked the front door or turned on the alarm because you did it without thinking. As useful and efficient as it is to do things without much thought, when it comes to the everyday decisions that compound over time, autopilot can be dangerous. Why? Because as the years tick by, our circumstances and contexts change. The same breakfast of bacon, eggs, and toast you have made every day for the last fifteen years might not be the best choice for you as your cholesterol starts to climb. Likewise, as we get older, maintaining muscle mass becomes hugely important. If you're still slogging it out on the elliptical machine every day out of habit, you're missing out on some important gains that could be had with strength training. Being on autopilot in midlife means that we're often avoiding decisions altogether, and in the process, giving up the chance to make things better. Remember that it's normal for things to change, and in fact, we will be much happier and healthier if we embrace these changes instead of ignoring them. Not to mention, expanding our horizons and developing new routines is both rewarding and cognitively beneficial.

One way to take ourselves off autopilot is to be more present with ourselves and the world. Ellen Langer, a famous social psychologist at Harvard University, has been investigating mindfulness for many years. What she's found is that those who are mindful when making decisions are less likely to regret what they have done because presumably they have been thoughtful and purposeful in making their choices. It may seem obvious but using mindfulness—which is simply the process of being aware and actively noticing things around us—can help pull us out of our routine by connecting us with the feelings and thoughts we are having in the present. What feels good now? What does my body need *now*? If you slow down and tune in to what your body and heart are telling you, you'll be making decisions with updated information instead of living in the past. Decisions we made years ago to craft our days in a thousand tiny ways need to be updated now and again to make sure they are still serving the person we are now and hope to be in the future.

It's a wildly successful trick for pulling yourself off autopilot. But it doesn't only help us with making a thoughtful choice—mindfulness encourages novelty seeking, creativity, and flexibility in thinking and behavior. This is exactly what we need to optimize getting to our goal and to compensate for any losses that pop up. Langer's research shows that if we pay attention to what we are doing and what is happening in our environment, we can reduce stress and improve performance and health.

Another way to use mindfulness effectively is to pay attention and recognize opportunities for happiness when they arise unexpectedly. Not all events in life are based on purposeful decisions or planned actions. The renowned psychologist Albert Bandura, who wrote a lot about mastery and control, also had something to say about the role of chance occurrences in one's life path. He talks about serendipitous events and how they can lead people in new directions. If you are open to chance occurrences it can lead to interesting and exciting new opportunities. Although they are unpredictable, Bandura says there are ways to increase the likelihood that good things may come to pass. This entails pursuing an active lifestyle that increases the chances of fortuitous encounters. Put yourself out there, pay attention, think outside the box, and look for golden opportunities. Bandura tells the story of when he was a graduate student, he and a friend took a break from an uninspiring reading assignment and decided to play golf. And that is where he met his future wife, on the golf course. She was ahead of him on the course and her twosome was very slow. His twosome caught up with them and they started to talk and eventually joined together as a foursome. They would never have met otherwise, and the rest is history.

Go with the Flow

Making decisions we feel good about is one of the best ways we can minimize regret and maximize presence in midlife. By understanding the changing context of gains and losses at this time of life, and remaining flexible in how we approach our decisions, we can go with the flow of midlife instead of fighting against it. It might feel like you've been thrown out of a boat going down a Class 5 rapid, but using what you have for resources and moving with the river instead of against it is still a good choice!

Paradoxically, sometimes a way to gain a sense of control is by letting go of it. We've talked a lot in this chapter about how good decision-making skills can improve your sense of control in midlife (and they do!). It's also important to know when to take a deep breath and remember that not everything is in your control. You can make the best possible choices and do everything right and *still* find yourself unable to reach your goal. With all the external factors pressing in on us during this time of life, this is truer than ever. But if you follow SOC and are mindful, intentional, and present when making your choices in midlife, you can rest more easily. You've done what you can. Despite the ticking of the lifespan clock, we would also do well to take a deep breath on the precipice of major life decisions and remember that few decisions are irrevocable. Though midlife decisions might be more consequential, remember to hang on to that expansive view of time.

Chapter 9
Beyond Midlife: Reaping the Rewards

It is not by muscle, speed, or physical dexterity that great things are achieved, but by reflection, force of character, and judgment; in these qualities old age is usually not only not poorer but is even richer.

—CICERO, "ON OLD AGE"

Sue may be turning sixty in a few months, but in her mind, she is still in her early forties. While she still feels middle-aged, she knows that the shift to retirement and later life is coming soon, and she's nervous. It's the kind of life transition that no one really talks about, a faint buzzing noise that you can tune out most of the time, but in some moments, it becomes very apparent. Long telomeres appear to run in the family, with her grandmother living until 103 and her great-aunt living until 105, both in pretty good health up until the very end. If she's lucky to live so long, that means she has a huge chunk of her life left to live and explore. This is both exciting and a little terrifying.

One of the more nervous-making aspects of this thought experiment is the fact that Sue doesn't have a partner, or children. She knows that aging alone is difficult, and she worries about her ability to remain independent and happy. Luckily, she has strong bonds with her siblings and niece who live nearby and has cultivated a deep network of friends that she knows will be there for her in whatever way they can. Whenever she brings up her fear of being a lonely old woman, her friends remind her that there are plenty of people who are married now who will be widowed in ten years, and whose kids live across the country. That's usually when they go into *Golden Girls* mode and start fantasizing about how they will all live with each other somewhere warm as they age, continuing to have adventures and late-night cheesecake.

Whenever she starts to mentally spin about the future, she reminds herself how lucky she is. While many of her friends are sick of their jobs and readying themselves for retirement, Sue just started a new job as a manager at a healthcare company. If all goes well, she'd like to work another ten years. In her early fifties she received sizeable insurance policy benefits when her father and mother died. Not enough to make her a millionaire, but certainly enough to make up for spotty retirement savings in her thirties and forties. Recently, she even bought her first home, which felt like a huge victory after decades of job-hopping and not being able to save enough for a down payment.

For Sue there isn't a specific number that marks the end of midlife—it's more about how healthy she feels. In that regard, so far, she's been lucky. Her health is good. Throughout her life she has exercised and eaten a wholesome diet. In her early fifties she started taking hormone replacement therapy to treat her menopause symptoms and continues to take them today, noticing a huge difference in how much more energy she has and how drastically it improves her mood. Right now, the only disappointment on the health front is an upcoming knee replacement surgery, but she knows plenty of people who have had those and resumed their active lives. Sue is still picking up new hobbies and making new friends, and she recently signed up for a dating app. Ideally, after she retires, she wants to travel, maybe with friends or even going through a solo travel company to finally visit Japan. She'd also like to spend more time photographing beautiful scenery, maybe even getting to the point where she could turn a hobby into a small business.

When she looks back at the bulk of her own Primetime Sue has few regrets. She feels happy where she is in her life, so when she looks at the future it is mostly with optimism. While there are plenty of small, persistent worries, she also expects there are plenty of good surprises in store.

If you make it to age sixty-five, there is a good chance you'll be gifted another twenty years of life, on average. If you're someone with good genes and good health, like Sue, add another decade or more to that and you have a lot of time left. For many people at the end of their midlife journey, the transition into old age can feel daunting. What does the next phase look like? Will I be healthy enough to do the things I want to do in the world? Am I financially secure enough to do them? What will others in my life expect of me? Will I be happy, or are things about to get worse?

These are all important questions as we reach the end of midlife, and they are particularly important questions to ponder before you reach your mid-sixties. While none of us has a crystal ball, we know that the years ahead depend substantially on genetics, luck, attitude, and the effects of what we have done (or not done) in midlife. After sixty-five, we all hit a time in life when the losses start to pile up. The spectrum of health and happiness begins to broaden, and you see a wider gap between individuals. This occurs because the cumulative impact of lifestyle decisions starts to become more apparent, and our biological resilience begins to decline. This goes for all parts of our lives as we age, not just physical health. The variation between us becomes more obvious in terms of social network, financial stability, and cognitive health, the older we get.

In this book we have looked at aging from a lifespan perspective, which views growing older as an ever-evolving process. While the tendency in our culture is to put firm demarcations between "youth" and "middle age," between "middle age" and "old age," the truth is that it is a continuous process; we are always growing, taking our experiences and what we learned from one period of our lives and bringing it into the next. Our brains really are plastic, and our lives are flexible too, changing and bending to accommodate the gains and losses that are inevitable in life.

As you move from the middle years into what many have called "the Third Act," you can make changes today that will help you be the best version of yourself at sixty-five and beyond. If you come through the middle with a strong sense of being in control, intact, and on top of your game, the transition to old age can be relatively smooth.

However, in every phase of life there are challenges. Our research shows that after peaking in midlife, our sense of control declines in later life. Personal mastery decreases and perceived constraints increase. This may, in part, reflect circumstances related to losses of relationships with close friends and relatives due to illness or death. It is also tied to increases in health problems and difficulties with everyday physical and cognitive functioning. But it's not all bad news—if you look at specific domains of life in the later years, there are some areas where we feel an increase in control. Yes, perceived control over health declines as does control over children and sex life. In contrast, perceived control over work, finances, and relationships with significant others increases in later life. It turns out all the nurturing of our relationships during middle age (like Sue did) reaps rich benefits in later life, helping us lessen the loneliness commonly associated with old age.

Midlife lasts for about twenty to twenty-five years, and because it is such a frantic and busy time, it can feel like it's gone by quickly. When adults turn sixty or sixty-five, they discover their eligibility for senior discounts or social security and other perks and wonder, how did I get here so fast? They also may come to realize maybe midlife wasn't so bad after all—research shows life satisfaction continues to increase well into the sixties. And many look back at midlife as the best of times. In an interview about her podcast *Wiser Than Me*, actress Julia Louis-Dreyfus was asked by Jancee Dunn of *The New York Times* what her favorite age decade has been so far. Dreyfus said, "I'm really enjoying my 60s, but I would say my 50s. And by the way, you know how much I loved it? I got breast cancer in my 50s and I still loved it. I just generally felt more confident about who I was as a human being."

How we live our lives in midlife doesn't stay in midlife, it sets the course for the next phase of life. Investment in a healthy lifestyle and good habits in the middle years pays off with big returns and benefits, making it more likely the later years will be successful. But even if you are someone who has woken up at the age of sixty pondering these questions of health and happiness in old age for the very first time, there is still time to improve the quality of your life moving forward.

The Third Act has also been called the "third age," or even "late adulthood." In any case, these terms describe the time of life after many people have stopped or cut back on working and their children have left home, when they can pursue creativity, personal fulfillment, and new opportunities. It is relatively recent that people have had so many years and so much extra time for new pursuits after they complete child-rearing and work. Since the turn of the last (twentieth) century, about twenty-five to thirty years have been added to the lifespan. It is mainly because of longer lifespans that there is a long period of life that is typically unplanned with the potential for time to engage in new pursuits and to find new sources of meaning.

Next, we'll look at what impacts our perception of late adulthood, and what we can expect from role transitions and retirement. By understanding how midlife impacts our experience of later life, we can get a better sense of which direction we're headed and, if needed, adjust. Understanding the trajectory we're on can help us stop, take stock, and really harness these middle years in service of our future selves.

The In-Between Stage

Similar to how people think about the beginning and end points of midlife, there is a great deal of variation in when people start to think of themselves as old rather than middle-aged. In one of the MIDUS study questionnaires we asked people when they thought midlife ended and we found that most people saw sixty-five as the exit point, although there were some thinking middle age ends at seventy-five. And studies have found that conceptions of when old age begins have increased to the mid-seventies and beyond. Perhaps the fault of helpful delusion, the definition of midlife creeps up as you age. The older you are the later you think midlife starts and ends. What we've found is that views on the transition from middle age to old age are largely dependent on health status. If you've developed health problems, especially those that lead to limitations in mobility or hinder your ability to carry out everyday tasks, this usually results in self-acknowledgment and the perception by others that you're no longer middle-aged. In addition to health as a determinant, your subjective age is also tied to how active you are and whether you're still working or have children at home.

Those in their late sixties or early seventies who are in good health will typically report feeling about twelve to fifteen years younger than their actual age, so it is no wonder they don't consider themselves old. Yet, those who have health problems are more likely to say they feel their age or even older. *Subjective age is an important indicator* of one's stamina and energy. Yet, how old you feel can fluctuate from day to day. Some days are better than others. If you're feeling tired or experiencing pain it makes you feel older. If you have a lot of energy and feel rested and in control, you may feel younger.

Ultimately, subjective age comes down to how you perceive the gains relative to losses. Perhaps the most important driver of how you feel and how you are seen in terms of your age is about how quickly and noticeably the losses are tipping the scales in their favor. In midlife, gains and losses are still balanced, but in later life, losses start weighing us down. This doesn't mean there aren't still gains to be had, but they are fewer and farther between. Manfred Diehl, emeritus professor of human development and family studies at Colorado State University, examined views of gains and losses in later life. He found that people expect their mental capacity and energy to decline. They expect they may need to limit their activities and will be more dependent on others for help. On the other hand, they also say they have more experience and knowledge than in the past and more freedom to live as they wish, as well as a better perspective or sense of what is important in life. At the same time, older adults pay more attention to their health and appreciate relationships more than they have in the past. Diehl and Shevaun Neupert, a former postdoc in my lab and a psychology professor at North Carolina State University, found that these views about gains and losses associated with aging are related to one's health. In other words, the better your health, the rosier your view of gains and losses, and the more likely you are to feel good.

When midlife ends and old age begins may be subjective and a little fuzzy depending on who you are talking to, what their health is like, and what losses they are contending with, but one thing is for sure: Life changes as we grow older. But beyond our aches and pains and the stereotypes of retirement, what can we really expect? What's in store for us that no one is talking about that might help us contextualize our own transition into our third act?

What to Expect: Role Transitions

In the same way that the transition into midlife brings sweeping changes in some areas of our lives, so too does the exit. Many will go from intense child-rearing to empty-nesting. And some will take on new caregiving responsibilities for parents. Others will be winding down their work lives as they look forward to retirement, travel, or even moving across the country to be closer to their children. Some may be charging full steam ahead with their careers, blasting through their sixties into their seventies with continued success and important contributions like Oprah Winfrey and Meryl Streep. In chapter 4 we talked about the physical changes that you can expect in midlife, and as we venture into our sixties and beyond, we can expect more of the same. Some of the biggest changes we can expect during the after-party in later life revolve around our shifting roles at work and home.

Parenting

Of the 69% of Americans with children, most will find themselves moving from an active parenting role to a more passive one as adult kids leave home and begin their own lives. For some, the nest may have emptied out during the latter part of middle age, but either way this transition can be a long process as children navigate their own work lives and intimate relationships. When exactly your nest empties depends on how old you were when you had your last child. If you had your last child at age forty, then your nest will likely empty in your sixties. If you had your last child when you were thirty-five, your nest will likely empty in your mid-to-late fifties. And it also depends on how independent your children are. Those mid-lifers who are remarried with blended families may have a variety of family constellations moving well beyond midlife. Children with intellectual or developmental disabilities might leave much later, or not at all. Others might move back home after they finish college so they can save money while they look for work or try to claw their way out of a low-paying job. Given the high costs of housing and uncertainty of entry-level jobs, this is becoming more common.

Some parents enjoy having their adult children back home and others . . . not so much. Many people struggle with this role change—moving from an authoritative parenting role to more of a roommate role where they ask their children to pay rent or contribute to expenses. The role confusion and adjustment period can cause some butting of heads around lifestyle and schedules, straining relationships. If you find yourself in this position, it may be useful to keep in mind that one day the tables may very well be turned, and you will be depending on your children to help *you* out. In most situations, though, children never return home except to visit. But, even if they have moved out, parents still have a central role until their children establish their own nuclear family, move long distance, or become financially independent. As you move into later life the dynamics of the relationship may shift to children concerned about you rather than the other way around. And adult children may come to appreciate their parents more as they realize they won't be around forever.

Regardless of where our children land and whether we even have children, those in long-term relationships can also expect a shift. Catherine, from chapter 3, experienced this shift when her children left home and she and her husband found each other moving into a completely new phase of their relationship. In their case, they were able to reconnect after years of caregiving and professional distractions, finding new tenderness in their marriage. For relationships both in the middle and in the Third Act, decades of being with the same person can become stale as the excitement and novelty associated with beginnings has long since faded. One of the challenges is to keep the same old things fresh and interesting. Humans naturally habituate to long-term partners, jobs, and other all-too-familiar routines. We may not have the time to think or plan let alone enjoy the middle years. And then as the later years approach, many find themselves wishing they had done things differently.

Divorce

In fact, there is a growing trend toward what is called "gray divorce," which is divorce that occurs after age fifty after a long-term marriage. This is increasing with one in ten divorces today among those over fifty and one in four divorces among those over sixty-five. In some cases, the marriage was in trouble for a long time, but the couple wanted to wait until the children were launched before splitting. For others, the specter of retirement with someone you have grown apart from is enough to cause a rift. Older couples tend to split for reasons that have to do with diverging visions of their remaining decades, conflict about how to spend money in retirement, and infidelity. Although people often think of marriage after sixty-five as golden years, divorce at this age can wreak havoc on finances and retirement plans. Yet another reason not to put your relationship on autopilot during the middle years, and pay attention to whether your connection is solid, and if it isn't, do something about it.

Grandparenting

Beyond children moving out and divorce, many older adults find themselves in the new role of grandparent. Some love becoming grandparents, hailing it as "the dessert course of life," as Lesley Stahl wrote in her book *Becoming Grandma*. Grandparenthood may become a central focus and bonding mechanism for adult children and their parents, even reconnecting them after years of living more separate lives. Others, especially those who may have had their own children spaced far apart in years, may not be ready to become a grandparent with all its attendant joys and responsibilities during a part of their life when they are finally feeling a bit more free.

Once upon a time the role of grandparent may have had a more consistent form, but now we see huge variation in how older adults engage with their grandchildren. In some cases, grandparents fill a critical need for caregiving if the parents are unable to do so for health or financial reasons. If the adult child is divorced or sick, cannot afford day care, or just prefers to have a close family member around, the grandparent can fill that role. Sometimes the grandchild lives with the grandparent, called a custodial grandparent. This can happen in extreme circumstances where the parents are struggling with drug addiction or mental illness. Other times, the grandparent role is more informal, yet it can be a highly satisfying relationship. It is often said that the benefits of grandparenting are the opportunity to enjoy the positive side of interacting with children without all the responsibilities. After spending a lovely day with grandchildren, you are free to leave and go about your business while the parents deal with the tantrums and boundary-setting.

For some people in their sixties and beyond, the most notable thing about the grandparent role is that it hasn't happened for them yet. In the same way people in their thirties have the desire to marry or have children but can't seem to find the right partner, people in the third age can feel the deep longing for grandchildren. With climate change and financial precarity on their minds, these days more and more adults are choosing to live child-free, which has the knock-on effect of leaving their parents without grandchildren. For some this is fine, for others it is a great grief they must process. It's important to remember that many people without grandchildren (or children) of their own find other ways in older adulthood to be deeply involved in the lives of the youngest generation. Luckily, for most, there is plenty of love and time to give to grandnieces and grandnephews, babysitting for your friends' grandkids, or volunteering in schools and day cares.

What to Expect: Retirement

Retirement is one of the most important and critical shifts we make in our lives: when to retire, how to retire, what to do when we retire. These are all big questions with voluminous answers that have been the subject of countless great books. For our purposes, we'll take a quick look at the basics of retirement so that you know what to expect, but more importantly, so you understand the importance of thinking about this while you're still in midlife. There is so much that we can do to ready ourselves physically, financially, socially, and emotionally for the Third Act.

Many people have been working for thirty years or more when they reach the transition from midlife to older age. That's a long time, and it's the reason work is often so integral to our identity and everyday lives. Maybe you've had the same job your entire adult life or maybe you've held multiple jobs in different professions. Maybe your job for the last two decades was a stay-at-home parent, but since the kids have left you are trying to pivot to a new career. Either way, work of all types provides many of us with purpose. For those of us who enjoy our jobs, the decision to retire can be difficult and emotionally draining. For others, retirement can't come soon enough. And of course, there are plenty of people in the middle who would love to be done working but worry about who they will be and what they will do in retirement. For those who have saved enough money for retirement, the transition is easier and comes ready-made with opportunities to do all the activities and traveling they've dreamed of for years. For those without substantial savings, retirement may be a dream to be deferred.

When Does Retirement Happen?

What we know for sure is that retirement is a pivot point in people's lives, and it's different for everyone. But with that variation in mind, what *can* we expect? When do most people retire?

Sixty-two is the earliest you can collect Social Security in the US (although you can't get full benefits until age sixty-seven), which many people rely on to fund their retirement. Keep in mind, if you wait until age seventy, you can collect the maximum amount of Social Security, an additional 24%. While there is no formal age of retirement, many companies have policies for leadership, requiring their employees to retire by age seventy-two. The American College of Surgeons recommends surgeons retire between sixty-five and seventy, while airline pilots must retire by age sixty-five (although pilot shortages are putting pressure on this limit). Firefighters and police officers have an age limit that ranges from fifty-seven to sixty-five depending on their organization or state, while teachers typically can retire with benefits after working for thirty years. But most experts say that age-based retirement requirements aren't particularly useful considering how health and abilities vary greatly in people of the same age.

When retirement makes sense also really depends on the job, which is why it's critical to start thinking about this when you're in midlife so you can plan accordingly. Given your job, how long will you be healthy enough to work? Those jobs that demand physical strength may require earlier retirement than those that are more sedentary. For example, my hairdresser is in his early fifties but struggles with leg pain due to vascular problems that make it difficult to stand for long periods of time. He knows that he won't be able to do his job much longer and is scrambling to come up with a retirement plan and an alternative career. For others whose jobs may be sedentary but are based on technology, obsolescence is a major factor when thinking about retirement. With the rapidly changing world of technology and the AI wave, many workers need to be willing to learn new skills if they want to avoid becoming obsolete. If you're being forced to learn new techniques involving complicated new software or hardware, that may hasten your desire to leave. But keep in mind you can learn new things after midlife even if it takes a little longer and extra effort.

Financial Considerations

Regardless of what type of job you have, one of the reasons it's so critical to think about retirement in midlife is financial. How much money do you need to retire and how does your financial reality match up with your retirement goals? Fifty-seven percent of American workers think they're behind where they should be in terms of retirement savings. They are right to be concerned. According to recent data, 19% of Americans ages sixty-five and older are still in the labor force, many because of financial pressure. A Pew research study reported that the *fastest*-growing age demographic in the workforce are people who are seventy-five or older: The study found that 9% of all Americans ages seventy-five and up are employed today—about double the share working in 1987 (4%). While that might seem like an immediate reflection of economic strain, it's important to note that not all older adults are forgoing or delaying retirement for financial reasons; some (such as myself) really love their jobs and consider themselves lucky they can still work.

For most people, Social Security is an important piece of financing retirement, but it's also usually not enough income to support their preretirement lifestyle. With a clear-eyed view of when you want to retire, you can make better decisions in midlife about saving and downsizing your lifestyle or home to reduce financial strain after retirement. These are big scary things to consider in midlife, and you'd be forgiven for wanting to put your head in the sand about all of it, but the fact remains that it's coming. Why not set yourself up for success?

Most people have difficulty thinking long term, especially when it comes to making choices about financial trade-offs. Hal Hershfield, professor of marketing, behavioral decision-making, and psychology at UCLA's Anderson School of Management, and colleagues did a study about saving for retirement with younger adults. Those who saw an image of their future older selves using software to produce older images of themselves were more likely than those who just saw a current photo to say they would donate the money to their retirement fund rather than other options such as buying something special for someone else or putting it in their savings account. The reality of one's own aging process seemed to be the motivation to focus on a long-term investment.

The Transition to Retirement

There is plenty beyond the timing and finances of retirement to consider. For instance, what does the actual retirement process look like? For those who haven't given it much thought, it's easy to see it as a very black-and-white, "cold turkey" process—one day you leave your workplace and that is the end. While many people do this, most agree it's hard, and it's certainly not the only option. Many retirees engage in a slow disengagement process that involves cutting back time and commitments over a period of a year or more before fully leaving the workplace. Retirement could also involve taking on a different job, or part-time work, or even serving in an advisory role. Mo Wang, a professor of business at the University of Florida, described three different paths to retirement:

1. decreasing the number of work hours gradually in the same job,

2. bridge employment, which involves transitioning to retirement by working in a less demanding role or part time with the same or a new organization or self-employment as a career change, and

3. early retirement, which is sometimes done by those who have enough financial resources or have health problems.

   He also described three retirement options:

1. Full retirement

Example: Monica spent thirty years as a marketing executive and was ready to be fully done with her job, so she picked a date and that was that. Now she spends her time watching her grandchildren, working out with a personal trainer, and traveling.

2. Officially retired but still working

Example: Sid was a history teacher at a local high school for twenty-five years. He was sick of being in the classroom full time, but knew he didn't want to stop teaching completely. So, he retired from the school district and started collecting his state pension but decided to teach two history classes at a local community college.

3. Back-and-forth transition from working and retirement

Example: Martha spent most of her life waiting tables, but when she hit her mid-sixties, she decided to stop punishing her feet. After about six months of being retired she felt too pinched financially and decided to take a part-time job answering phones at a law office. A couple of years into that job, the firm downsized, and she is retired again, but not at all sure she'll stay that way.

Whichever route you choose, it's good to know that your options go beyond cold turkey and a golden parachute.

Given that retirement—regardless of form—involves a major role change that upends your everyday life, it's not surprising that studies have found negative consequences for retirement. In some cases, health is affected by the change, but more often the person retired because of health problems that already existed. Other studies have found that people may experience cognitive decline and an increase in loneliness. For this reason, it's critical to prepare for retirement and navigate ways to make up for the losses besides the paycheck that accompany retirement.

Dealing with Work-Related Losses

Although you may gain more free time for leisure activities and have less stress, there are three things that you typically lose with retirement that are important to find substitutes for postretirement: cognitive stimulation, social contact, and physical activity.

At work, you are stimulating your brain not only with the tasks you do but also by using memory and executive functioning to remember what you need to do and when you need to do it. Your cognitive skills are used at work in keeping to a schedule, making sure you get to work on time, and fulfilling your responsibilities. Then there are the social aspects of work. You have coworkers you meet with, collaborate with on projects, and share your lunch hours with, and possibly customers to talk to. Whether or not your job is remote, you likely have conversations with others virtually and you have meetings and support from your supervisor and need to negotiate with others. The last aspect is physical activity. Even if your job is a sedentary one, you must move to get to the job. Whether you are walking to the bus stop or walking from the parking lot, or walking up stairs to get to your office, you are out there moving. When you retire, it is important to find substitutes for the cognitive, social, and physical engagement that you no longer have from your work life. This can go a long way to making sure you remain healthy and happy in retirement.

Volunteer work is one excellent way to meet these goals. It has some of the same features of work with regard to cognitive, social, and physical stimulation. There is a famous intervention study called the Experience Corps, a program that originated in Baltimore, where older adults went to work in inner-city classrooms. The intergenerational program started by Linda Fried, director of the Robert N. Butler Aging Center at Columbia University, benefited the children in many ways (reading achievement and better behavior) and it had health and cognitive benefits, including changes in brain volume, for the older volunteers. The older adults increased their physical activity in getting to the school and walking the kids to their different activities, they were stimulated cognitively helping the kids with their work, and they had social contact with each other and the teachers and children. This program was so successful that now it has been expanded to many other locations across the United States sponsored by AARP. Adults fifty and older are recruited for the program to help make a difference in children's learning. It also gives the volunteers a meaningful sense of purpose in life as well as other benefits.

Asking people about their plans for retirement in their forties and even fifties can feel like asking a kid what they want to be when they grow up—a nebulous, open-ended question that invites a dreamy response. It can be scary to think about the final third of our life and what might be in store, but it can also be exciting if we get a little more grounded. Dreaming is great, but as the years tick by it can turn into anxiety. Much better to have a solid plan that lays the groundwork and options for what you really want to do in your third act.

What Happens in Midlife Doesn't Stay in Midlife

In earlier chapters we talked about the critical moves you can make to feel better in midlife, like eating well, exercising, and managing stress. As we look ahead to old age, we can't ignore that how we live our lives and treat our bodies in midlife has a huge impact on where we find ourselves in the last decades of our lives. Responsibly shepherding our physical selves through middle age is one of the biggest opportunities we have at this time in our life, and it's one of the biggest gifts we can give to our future selves. What you can do in retirement is determined in large part by your health, mobility, and strength. If you dream of playing soccer in the backyard with the grandkids or finally hiking Machu Picchu, those require that you maintain your health span. While many of the physical problems that can befall us in later life are out of our control, there is always a certain amount we can control.

It's Never Too Late

For those readers still in midlife who are wondering what sixty-five or seventy might look like, you can get some clues from your current health. From recent research we know:

- Inflammation and sleep in midlife are important predictors of later-life cognitive and physical health;

- Poor physical fitness in middle age is linked to a smaller brain size twenty years later;

+ Those most satisfied with their life at age fifty were the healthiest physically and mentally at age eighty;

+ Those who had higher reports of personal growth at midlife had better cognition in later adulthood;

+ A higher BMI and waist size in midlife is linked to greater risk of frailty in later life;

+ Pulmonary function in midlife is related to later-life cognitive declines;

+ Participating in leisure-time physical activity at least twice a week in midlife was associated with lower odds of dementia later in life compared to a sedentary lifestyle;

+ Blood pressure in midlife is a better predictor of late-life health than late-life blood pressure;

+ Midlife hypertension has a stronger association with dementia than late-life blood pressure levels;

+ Being overweight in midlife (BMI 25 to 29.9) is associated with a twofold increased risk for Alzheimer's disease; and

+ Midlife obesity (BMI ≥ 30) is associated with over a threefold increased risk for Alzheimer's disease.

If you've already identified some less-than-ideal health metrics, just remember it's never too late to start turning things around. We already talked about what you can do in midlife to feel better now and ensure that you're ready to take retirement by storm, but here's a brief refresher: eat and sleep well, move your body, maintain a strong social network, and keep your brain stimulated.

Author and longevity expert Dan Buettner identified areas in the US and around the world, called "Blue Zones," where people live in good health with the longest life expectancy. What he has learned in places like Okinawa, Japan; Ikaria, Greece; and Loma Linda, California, is that there are some common lifestyle features in these locations that may hold the secret to their citizens' long lives. People in Blue Zones primarily eat a plant-based diet, exercise regularly, drink moderate amounts of alcohol, get enough sleep, and have good spiritual, family, and social networks. One of the biggest aspects of living in these areas is the multigenerational connections. Many of the centenarians studied lived with family and took an active part in caring for their grandchildren and great-grandchildren, lending a strong sense of purpose to their lives. They are deeply connected to their communities and continue to walk, garden, and participate in civic life well into their nineties.

What this means for us is that while getting a handle on our health and well-being in midlife is critical, even if you find yourself in your sixties wishing you had done things differently, it's never too late. You can make like a Blue Zone resident and find connection in community, take up an active hobby, and find a purpose in volunteering. Those who quit smoking at sixty-five can expect to live five years more than those who don't quit at all. Starting to save for retirement at thirty means your savings will grow exponentially due to compound interest, but starting at age sixty is certainly better than nothing. And we know from research on sarcopenia (muscle loss) that older adults gain benefits from strength training, including increased muscle mass and bone density, and greater vitality and independence.

Super Activities

We used to have an image of older retired adults sitting on their laurels on their porch in a rocking chair after a life of hard work. For those who are no longer working or are working part time, it is reasonable to enjoy some leisure time relaxing, whether at home or through travel. But sedentary behavior is dangerous for your health at every age. In the US, the number of sedentary hours is larger than in other countries. In European countries (and ALL the Blue Zones), people walk more to do their daily errands, and they hike or ride their bikes to get places. In the US, we are more dependent on our cars. Even for those who exercise regularly, it is harmful to spend too much time sedentary. Sitting is bad for our health. If you sit more than seven to ten hours a day it can lead to health problems and premature mortality.

We discussed the value of both aerobic and strength exercises in chapter 4. But it is not just exercise that is valuable. Being active in general is advantageous. A study with the MIDUS participants showed that it is not just how much activity you engage in, but the diversity of activities is also important for psychological well-being and volume of the hippocampal region of the brain, which is tied to memory functioning. There are many activities that have been found to be helpful to older adults or even those younger: Engaging in a variety of activities like tai chi, meditation, swimming, gardening, card games, and dancing can go a long way toward maintaining good health.

The good news is that many in retirement will have more time than they did in midlife to engage in what I call "super activities," which will help you maintain your health and well-being. These activities are super because they can fulfill multiple goals at once. These goals include learning something new, doing something with others, and doing what you enjoy. If you enjoy doing an activity, you are more likely to do it on a regular basis and make it part of your lifestyle. These super activities target brain health, physical health, and social well-being. Learning something new and engaging in challenging tasks leads to new pathways in the brain. Denise Park, a professor at the University of Texas at Dallas, found that learning how to use a digital camera or how to quilt led to more connections in the brain and better performance on cognitive tests when compared to a comparison group who did activities together but did not learn something new.

Travel and volunteer work are other great ways to do something with others. A nonprofit called Road Scholar (formerly Elderhostel) arranges trips with older adults that include a learning component. Some trips are intergenerational or include families, which can be a great opportunity for learning and traveling along with loved ones. There are other lifelong learning opportunities at universities and senior centers in towns that offer programs for learning and teaching others. Seniors Helping Seniors is an organization that hires older adults to help other older adults who need help and companionship.

There are many national and local volunteer programs that provide a way for older adults to volunteer to help others in need. AARP is a resource with lots of useful financial and health information, and tips for active living and learning.

The Staircase

Ageism, which is based on stereotypes and misconceptions about aging, is widespread and has health-damaging effects. Stereotypes about aging typically involve negative or pessimistic attitudes and beliefs, for example, that declines in physical and cognitive health are inevitable and irreversible (that is, out of our control) or that older adults have little value or purpose. The worst part about these stereotypes is not that others use them against us, it's that we can use them against ourselves. Internalized ageism is one of the biggest battles we have to fight as we transition from midlife to old age, and it's reminiscent of the mindset shift many must make in early midlife as they transition out of young adulthood. As such, we know it's possible to revise images and views of aging to be more positive, that is, seeing people in later life as being active and capable as opposed to helpless and senile.

Mick Jagger famously wails "What a drag it is getting old" in the opening line of a 1966 Rolling Stones hit. You could say: He was only twenty-three, what did he know? But Jagger got this notion from somewhere. It was an idea running through the culture at the time— and it's an idea that still runs through our culture to this day. Given that in his eighties Jagger is still going strong performing and releasing an album with the Rolling Stones, he may well have changed his thinking on whether aging is a drag. Yet, as Yale psychologist Becca Levy's work shows, cultural notions do have a real-time impact on our perception of our actual health and well-being in our middle years and beyond, and if the "information" is more myth than reality, it can have deleterious effects.

You might remember from earlier in the book that Levy's research found that "older individuals with more positive self-perceptions of aging, measured up to 23 years earlier, lived 7.5 years longer than those with less positive self-perceptions of aging." That is a significant number of years up for grabs if we can change our mindset.

One of Jane Fonda's, who is now in her late eighties, great contributions to the culture, aside from her iconic IMDb credits, activism, and trailblazing workout videos, is popularizing a metaphor for aging that arms us for battle against ageism and provides a much more hopeful look at the future. In an interview at age seventy-three about aging gracefully in what she calls "Life's Third Act," she said, "We need to revise how we think of aging. The old paradigm was: You're born, you peak at midlife, and then you decline into decrepitude. Looking at aging as ascending a staircase, you gain well-being, spirit, soul, wisdom, the ability to be truly intimate and a life with intention." In her talk, she further described how as we age we learn more, grow more, teach more, give more—finding greater and greater meaning and emotional fulfillment along the way.

To me this is a much more fitting view of aging than the arch or the "hill" that we see in pop culture and artists' depictions of the life course, with a downhill slope beyond the midpoint. Fonda's vision of the staircase reflects key psychosocial factors that are important for healthy aging: positive affect, optimism, social connections, purpose, and a sense of control.

As the transition from midlife to later life unfolds there are choices and decisions to make in dealing with the expected and the unexpected. The key is how you view and think about your life and the actions you take to stay in alignment with those beliefs. We can remember that a smooth passage from the middle years to the later years is in our hands.

Conclusion
Life Begins Now

On my mother's fortieth birthday she received a present that I'll never forget. It was a hardcover book with a deep red cover that was gold embossed with the title: *Life Begins at Forty* by Walter Pitkin. I can't remember who gave it to her, but I do recall her sweet, rueful laugh as she unwrapped it. While I was only fourteen at the time, later I would learn that it was a bestseller Pitkin had written years earlier, during the Great Depression. It was an upbeat book released during a time of expanding life expectancy, a gift that was supposed to dampen the trepidation my mother had about turning forty that many people still share today.

If only it was truly the beginning of my mother's life rather than so close to the end. Three years after she received the book, at forty-three, she died of breast cancer.

Unfortunately, I didn't have the privilege of watching my mother navigate the middle years of her life. Decades later, as I entered midlife, I would catch myself wanting to ask her a question about menopause or aging. Sadly, I realized she probably wouldn't have had the answers anyway.

When I turned forty-three, I thought a lot about how devastating it must have been for my mother knowing her life would be cut short at such a young age. Right before she fell ill, she had just jumped back into the workforce, earning a master's degree (unusual for a woman to do back in the day) and working at the local high school teaching calculus. She was in the prime of life with a loving family and so many more joys, sorrows, and adventures ahead of her. Even the little experiences that she missed still break my heart. A few years before she died, she had taken a cruise to the Caribbean and bought beautiful English bone china cups and saucers. After her funeral, family and friends came to our home to mourn with us and we used the china for the very first time. I remember thinking how sad it was that she never got to drink from those delicate cups.

In my early forties I deeply related to the title of Pitkin's book. I was just starting to get cooking with my career, I had two young children, and there was so much more I wanted to do—to dream, to taste, to feel, to experience. It really did feel like I had so much life in front of me, and I felt little of the dread or anxiety that my peers were feeling about getting older. If I had to guess, I'd say my outlier status in this regard has a lot to do with losing my mother when I did. Because of my loss—*her* loss—I have come to appreciate most things about aging. I find myself focusing on the opportunities and good fortune of living a long life and taking the challenges as part of the territory.

I see middle age as a privilege. But in both my personal and professional life, I have heard so much angst and fear from people about midlife and aging in general. My kids, who at this point are about to enter middle age themselves, are dreading it. They don't think of themselves as middle-aged and are horrified at the prospect; to say they enter with trepidation is an understatement. Although I no longer consider myself middle-aged, I do look back fondly on my forties and fifties as a fantastic, meaningful period of my life. This experience of midlife and the decades of insights I've gleaned from studying the life course have given me a nuanced and positive perspective. Not only do I know from personal experience that this time of life can be important and pivotal, even if demanding and stressful, I can see it in the research findings as well. No one period of our lives has a monopoly on being the best or worst. Yet, the middle years are so central and so misunderstood and undervalued that I wanted to write this book, if not to correct the record, at least to offer a different, more hopeful perspective.

One of the benefits of starting to research midlife when you're still in your thirties is that you can't ignore it. All the reading, interviewing, surveys, and research I did throughout my thirties and beyond meant that every day I went to work and was confronted with the realities of aging. Even though I started this journey when I was relatively young, my future, older self was always very close. This was a gift, because I never went completely on autopilot. It led me to contemplate what this time of life might be like for me, and it prepared me for it. As I entered middle age while researching it, I saw the hidden potential for this time of life that few were talking about, and that insight perhaps has helped me to navigate, embrace, and enjoy midlife much more than I would have otherwise.

While I have written and published scores of articles in peer-reviewed journals and edited books, only a modest circle of academics has read this work.

The MacArthur Foundation, which funded the initial work we did on midlife, emphasized the importance of sharing our research findings with a broad audience in order to contribute to the greater good. I came to realize that many of the positive, exciting, and fascinating parts of midlife were hidden, as it takes a long time for some of the most helpful scientific insights to make their way out of the ivory tower. So about fourteen years ago I decided to try to write a book for a general audience while I was on sabbatical at the Stanford Center for Advanced Study in the Behavioral Sciences. For most of the year, I was focused on my funded research grants and did a good deal of thinking and writing. But toward the end of the year, I started to draft a proposal for a book on midlife I called *MidPoints*. Time ran out and I was not able to accomplish my book goal then. In my next sabbatical I thought about returning to the idea, but again the more immediate needs of my grants and graduate students took precedence.

Around that time, I was in the thick of midlife and characteristically had so much going on I could just barely meet all my work and family responsibilities. The book was a dream, not a priority. But I never gave up on it; instead I "goal shelved" it for later when the time was finally right. With a great deal more knowledge and experience on board to share with readers, the time was right. Proof positive that it's almost never too late to write a book, or for that matter to find love, achieve success, learn a new art, visit an exciting place, or do just about anything you want—and the earlier in your life you can embrace that, the better.

If you walk away with one message from this book, I hope it's this: Mindset is powerful, and if you can adjust yours as you enter midlife, your body, mind, and soul will be the better for it. How we look at time, decision-making, losses, regrets, relationships, our bodies, and ourselves during midlife (and beyond) *matters*, deeply. We can't stop the clock or the curveballs that midlife will throw at us, but we can both prepare for the inevitable and greet it with grace when it comes. Yes, midlife is hard in new and scary ways, but so is every new epoch of our lives. Once upon a time the teenage you was terrified of starting high school or your first job, and twentysomething you was sure you'd never find your calling. Each age comes with its own challenges and opportunities, so beware the cultural narratives that mischaracterize midlife as the one time of life we should all dread. Imbibing this junk will only eat away at your confidence, positivity, and the very mindset you need to cultivate to live your life to the fullest in midlife.

So give yourself grace—yes, midlife is challenging in so many new ways, but there are also hidden gifts if you only remember to look for them. By managing your own anxiety about midlife and becoming happier and more confident, you can help those around you regulate their emotions (I'm rooting for you, parents of the "anxious generation"). With a glass half-full, you have more to share with those you love and are charged with caring for. You can make the time to bolster the relationships that refill that energy when it gets too low. And most importantly, you can see with greater clarity the insights, wisdom, and confidence that you've earned and can now deploy to make the second half of your life even sweeter than the first.

In an effort to keep things interesting and fun at holiday time in my lab at Brandeis, a couple of years ago we had a contest for a T-shirt illustration. While there were plenty of good designs floating around, one lab member's drawing in particular captured the beauty and science of the full life course, from birth through middle age, on to our later years. Like Jane Fonda's concept, it employs the idea of the life course as an ascending staircase. On the first step is a tree, just beginning to leaf out, with its crown in the shape of a brain. To me, the leaves, flowers, and fruit that grow with each step represent what we gain each year on this planet, living, loving, and learning. We gain more and more, and just like a tree, have more fruit to give to others as we approach midlife and older age.

Should you be so lucky to ascend the stairs into midlife, I hope you marvel at the blooms and relish the fruit.

Original Design by Luna Li

Acknowledgments

This book would not have come to fruition without the contributions of many talented and dedicated people. I am very grateful to my colleagues, friends, and family members for their support and encouragement.

I first would like to thank Nathaniel Jacks, my extraordinary literary agent at Inkwell Management. Nat served as an exceptional guide with his insights, wisdom, and patience. He was a source of inspiration and support throughout the process. His reassurance and pep talks kept me going and helped me to see the book project through to the end. I also want to thank Lyndsey Blessing and Jessie Thorsted at Inkwell for all their help.

I am fortunate to have worked with Lauren Hamlin, who is a gifted and highly talented writer. She worked magic on my manuscript, helping me to turn jargon into meaningful and accessible prose. I am so grateful that she helped me to convey the implications of the research. I also thank her partners at Splash Literary: Aaron Schulman for his creative feedback, and Elisa Ortega Montilla for her help with formatting.

At Simon Element it has been my privilege to work with executive editor Lauren Marino and her all-star team. Lauren is a brilliant and dedicated editor whose feedback helped to improve the book in many ways. I appreciate her insightful comments and suggestions for crafting the final product. I also thank Katie McClimon at Element for answering all of my questions and helping me navigate the publication process.

Sara Carder was instrumental in helping me to develop the book proposal. I thank her for her creative vision and passion for the project. I thank Leah Miller for her interest and inspiration in acquiring the book. Her enthusiasm stuck with me throughout the writing process even after she moved to another position.

I could not have carried out the research presented in this book without the contributions of many current and past graduate students and postdocs in the Lifespan Lab at Brandeis University. I especially wish to thank Stefan Agrigoroaei, Carrie Andreoletti, Alycia Bisson, Eileen Graham, Taylor Lazzari, Xin Yao Lin, Yujun Liu, Elizabeth Mahon, Shevaun Neupert, Ann Pearman, Elizabeth Rickenbach, Stephanie Robinson, Christina Röcke, Kylie Schiloski, Mirjam Stieger, Morgan Taylor, Salom Teshale, and Stacey Whitbourne.

My work on midlife would not have been possible without an incredible group of collaborators. I am grateful to my MIDUS collaborators for their valuable contributions to the science of midlife. I especially appreciate David Almeida, Dan Mroczek, and Carol Ryff for their dedication to the MIDUS longitudinal study for over thirty years.

I am fortunate that my mentors, Paul Baltes and John Nesselroade, set me on a fruitful path to study adult development and aging from a lifespan perspective. And I thank Orville Gilbert Brim for initiating the study of midlife and inviting me to participate in the John D. and Catherine T. MacArthur Research Network on Successful Midlife Development.

When I was on sabbatical as a fellow at the Center for Advanced

Study in the Behavioral Sciences at Stanford University, I began to think about writing a book on midlife. Thank you to Laura Carstensen for making that year possible and for including me in the working group she organized with an inspiring group of scholars: Ulman Lindenberger, Daniel McFadden, and John Rowe.

My colleagues and collaborators at Brandeis over the years have contributed in many ways to the insights and content that is included in the book. I have benefited from the ongoing interactions and opportunities to share ideas with my Brandeis family: Teresa Amabile, Anne Berry, Evelyn Caira, Joe Cunningham, Phil Gnatowski, Angela Gutchess, Winnie Huie, Derek Isaacowitz, Xiaodong Liu, Patricia McDonough, Hannah Snyder, Pat Tun, Mick Watson, Ellen Wright, and Leslie Zebrowitz.

I am privileged to have a number of colleagues and collaborators with whom I have worked over the years to conduct and publish research on midlife: Eric Cerino, Edith Chen, Roger Dixon, Nancy Galambos, Dennis Gerstorf, Jeremy Hamm, Jutta Heckhausen, Frank Infurna, Arun Karlamangla, Erik Kim, Adam Jaffe, Mary Kaltenberg, Hazel Markus, Greg Miller, Teresa Seeman, and Carsten Wrosch.

I thank Dee Spiro, who provided helpful feedback on chapter drafts. Her enthusiasm for the book was reassuring and a source of motivation.

My dearest friends have helped me to find balance in my life and have kept my social convoy filled with support: Elaine Anderson, Rosemary Bliezner, Steve Gerus, Mark Ginsberg, Susan Golbeck, Caryn Harding, Debbie Heilbrunn, Lorraine Heilbrunn, Elisa Klein, Karen Mondell, Barbara Reichle, Tom Rudel, Manfred Schmitt, Lori

Solon, Jennifer Stone, Robert Waldinger, Eileen Weisel, Harriet Worobey, and John Worobey. I appreciate their wisdom and guidance.

I wish to acknowledge the support provided for my research program by the John D. and Catherine T. MacArthur Foundation, the National Institute on Aging, and the Alfred P. Sloan Foundation.

I am grateful to the many research participants from MIDUS and other studies who contributed to our knowledge about midlife. A heartfelt thank-you to those who shared their personal stories about midlife for this book, most of whom remain anonymous. Their rich experiences have made the research come alive, helping readers to appreciate the varied nature of midlife.

I am blessed with a wonderful family who supported me throughout my career and while I was writing this book. I thank my husband, Ron Spiro, for keeping me centered and finding humor and passion in our everyday lives, and for all the helpful discussions and feedback on the book. I found inspiration for this book from my children and their spouses—Julia, Neil, Peter, and Lynley—and from my grandchildren—Ella, Gavin, Drew, and Miller. I thank them for their love and the tremendous joy they bring me. I hope their developmental journeys will always be filled with delightful experiences, happiness, and good health.

Notes

Introduction

4   *Studies have shown that many people in midlife*: Eric S. Cerino et al., "Perceived Control Across the Adult Lifespan: Longitudinal Changes in Global Control and Daily Stressor Control," *Developmental Psychology* 60, no. 1 (2024): 45–58, https://doi.org/10.1037/dev0001618; and Margie E. Lachman, Salom Teshale, and Stefan Agrigoroaei, "Midlife as a Pivotal Period in the Life Course: Balancing Growth and Decline at the Crossroads of Youth and Old Age," *International Journal of Behavioral Development* 39, no. 1 (2015): 20–31, https://doi.org/10.1177/0165025414533223.

4   *Positive affect (psychology-speak for pleasant feelings)*: Gabrielle N. Pfund et al., "Lifespan Trajectories of Negative and Positive Affect: A Coordinated Analysis of 14 Longitudinal Studies," *European Journal of Personality* 39, no. 5 (2024): 747-69, https://doi.org/10.1177/08902070241293967.

4   *It can even* shave years off our lives: Becca Levy, *Breaking the Age Code: How Your Beliefs About Aging Determine How Long and Well You Live* (William Morrow, 2022).

11   *We can glean wisdom and meaning*: Tristen K. Inagaki and Edward Orehek, "On the Benefits of Giving Social Support: When, Why, and How Support Providers Gain by Caring for Others," *Current Directions in Psychological Science* 26, no. 2 (2017): 109–13, https://doi.org/10.1177/0963721416686212.

14   *Recent research findings regarding deaths*: Anne Case and Angus Deaton, *Deaths of Despair and the Future of Capitalism* (Princeton University Press, 2020).

15   *I decided I wanted to learn more*: Paul B. Baltes and L. R. Goulet, eds., *Life-Span Developmental Psychology* (Academic Press, 1970).

16   *Which means it compared people*: Robert J. Waldinger and Avron Spiro, "Studying Adult Development and Aging the Long Way: 100 Years of US Longitudinal Studies of Aging," in *APA Handbook of Adult Development and Aging*, ed. Margie E. Lachman and Avron Spiro (American Psychological Association, 2026), 81–99.

Notes

17 *This would require longitudinal studies*: Spiro and Waldinger, "Studying Adult Development and Aging the Long Way."

18 *However, the balance of increases and decreases*: Paul B. Baltes, "Theoretical Propositions of Life-Span Developmental Psychology: On the Dynamics Between Growth and Decline," *Developmental Psychology* 23, no. 5 (1987): 611–26, https://doi.org/10.1037/0012-1649.23.5.611.

18 *As physical and mental abilities start to wane*: Lea Moersdorf, Moritz M. Daum, and Alexandra M. Freund, "For Whom Is the Path the Goal? A Lifespan Perspective on the Development of Goal Focus," *Collabra: Psychology* 8, no. 1 (2022): 31603, https://doi.org/10.1525/collabra.31603.

18 *While the framework of gains and losses*: Natalie C. Ebner, Alexandra M. Freund, and Paul Baltes, "Developmental Changes in Personal Goal Orientation from Young to Late Adulthood: From Striving for Gains to Maintenance and Prevention of Losses," *Psychology and Aging* 21, no. 4 (2006): 664–78, https://doi.org/10.1037/0882-7974.21.4.664; and Baltes, "Theoretical Propositions of Life-Span Developmental Psychology."

20 *It's called the SOC model*: Paul B. Baltes and Margret M. Baltes, "Psychological Perspectives on Successful Aging: The Model of Selective Optimization with Compensation," in *Successful Aging: Perspectives from the Behavioral Sciences*, ed. P. B. Baltes and M. M. Baltes (Cambridge University Press, 1990), 1–34.

Chapter 1: The Myth of the Midlife Crisis

32 *"Up till now life has seemed an endless upward slope"*: Kieran Setiya, *Midlife: A Philosophical Guide* (Princeton University Press, 2017).

33 *Enter, the U-shape of Happiness*: "The U-Bend of Life: Why, Beyond Middle Age, People Get Happier as They Get Older," *The Economist*, December 16, 2010, https://www.economist.com/christmas-specials/2010/12/16/the-u-bend-of-life.

33 *In 2008, economists David Blanchflower*: David G. Blanchflower and Andrew J. Oswald, "Is Well-Being U-Shaped over the Life Cycle?," *Social Science and Medicine* 66, no. 8 (2008): 1733–49, 10.1016/j.socscimed.2008.01.030.

33 *In 2012, Oswald*: Alexander Weiss et al., "Evidence for a Midlife Crisis in Great Apes Consistent with the U-Shape in Human Well-Being," *Proceedings of the National Academy of Sciences* 109, no. 49 (2012): 19949–52, https://doi.org/10.1073/pnas.1212592109.

33 The Atlantic *even published a story*: Jonathan Rauch, "The Real Roots of Midlife Crisis," *The Atlantic*, December 2014, https://www.theatlantic.com/magazine /archive/2014/12/the-real-roots-of-midlife-crisis/382235/.

34 *In our MIDUS surveys*: Elaine Wethington, "Expecting Stress: Americans and the 'Midlife Crisis,'" *Motivation and Emotion* 24, no. 2 (2000): 85–103, https:// doi.org/10.1023/A:1005611230993; and Margie E. Lachman et al., "Images of Midlife Development Among Young, Middle-Aged, and Older Adults," *Journal of Adult Development* 1 (1994): 201–11, https://doi.org/10.1007/BF02277581.

34 *Other studies have backed up our central findings*: Wethington, "Expecting Stress."

35 *Only about 10% of people*: Wethington, "Expecting Stress."

35 *Others who reported having a midlife crisis*: Alexandra M. Freund and Johannes O. Ritter, "Midlife Crisis: A Debate," *Gerontology* 55, no. 5 (2009): 582–91, https://doi.org/10.1159/000227322.

35 *Feeling the need to correct the record*: Nancy L. Galambos et al., "The U Shape of Happiness Across the Life Course: Expanding the Discussion," *Perspectives on Psychological Science* 15, no. 4 (2020): 898–912, https://doi.org/10.1177 /1745691620902428.

36 *This worsening of mental health*: Frank J. Infurna et al., "Loneliness in Midlife: Historical Increases and Elevated Levels in the United States Compared with Europe," *American Psychologist* 80, no. 5 (2024): 744-56, https://doi.org/10.1037 /amp0001322; and Frank J. Infurna et al., "Historical Change in Midlife Health, Well-Being, and Despair: Cross-Cultural and Socioeconomic Comparisons," *American Psychologist* 76, no. 6 (2021): 870–87, https://doi.org/10.1037/amp0000817.

36 *Many speculate*: Sara Pequeño, "US Plummeted in World Happiness Ranking Because of Young People Like Me. I'll Tell You Why," *USA Today*, March 21, 2024, https://eu.usatoday.com/story/opinion/columnists/2024/03/25 /world-happiness-report-us-millennials-gen-z-unhappy/73056887007/.

37 *He now says he was wrong*: David G. Blanchflower, Alex Bryson, and Xiaowei Xu, "The Declining Mental Health of the Young and the Global Disappearance of the Hump Shape in Age in Unhappiness," Working Paper 32337, National Bureau of Economic Research, http://www.nber.org/papers/w32337.

37 The Anxious Generation: Jonathan Haidt, *The Anxious Generation: How the Great Rewiring of Childhood Is Causing an Epidemic of Mental Illness* (Penguin, 2024).

38 *I'd argue that the single U-shape curve*: Paul B. Baltes, Ursula M. Staudinger, and Ulman Lindenberger, "Lifespan Psychology: Theory and Application to Intellectual Functioning," *Annual Review of Psychology* 50 (1999): 471–507, https://pubmed.ncbi.nlm.nih.gov/15012462/.

Notes

38 *This phenomenon is called "hedonic adaptation"*: Daniel Gilbert, *Stumbling on Happiness* (Vintage Canada, 2007).

39 *People who were the happiest*: Margie E. Lachman et al., "Realism and Illusion in Americans' Temporal Views of Their Life Satisfaction: Age Differences in Reconstructing the Past and Anticipating the Future," *Psychological Science* 19, no. 9 (2008): 889–97, https://doi.org/10.1111/j.1467-9280.2008.02173.x.

39 *It's far more nuanced*: Sujata Gupta, "The 'Midlife Crisis' Is Too Simple a Story, Scientists Say," *Science News*, November 4, 2024, https://www.sciencenews.org/article/midlife-crisis-mental-health-happiness.

40 *He believed that humans*: Gabriel A. Orenstein and Lindsay Lewis, "Erikson's Stages of Psychosocial Development," *StatPearls*, 2022, https://www.ncbi.nlm.nih.gov/books/NBK556096/.

40 *In 1963, Erikson postulated*: Erik Homburger Erikson, *Childhood and Society 2000 Edition* (Norton, 1963).

41 *Psychologists Daniel Levinson and Roger Gould*: Roger Gould, *Transformations: Growth and Change in Adult Life* (Simon & Schuster, 1978); and Daniel Levinson, "A Conception of Adult Development," *American Psychologist* 41, no. 1 (1986): 3–13, https://doi.org/10.1037/0003-066X.41.1.3.

41 *"The primary tasks of every transitional period"*: Levinson, "A Conception of Adult Development."

41 *A series of six studies*: Adam L. Alter and Hal E. Hershfield, "People Search for Meaning When They Approach a New Decade in Chronological Age," *Proceedings of the National Academy of Sciences* 111, no. 48 (2014): 17066–70, https://doi.org/10.1073/pnas.1415086111.

42 *During the so-called quarter-life crisis*: Alexandra Robbins and Abby Wilner, *Quarterlife Crisis: The Unique Challenges of Life in Your Twenties* (TarcherPerigee, 2001).

43 *In a survey of over a thousand millennials*: "Millennials in Crisis: Survey Finds 81% Can't Afford a Midlife Crisis," *Thriving Center of Psychology* (blog), April 16, 2024, https://thrivingcenterofpsych.com/blog/millennial-midlife-crisis/.

43 *Research done by Becca Levy*: Becca Levy, *Breaking the Age Code: How Your Beliefs About Aging Determine How Long and Well You Live* (William Morrow, 2022).

44 *Older Japanese are both revered and* expected: Levy, *Breaking the Age Code*, 4.

44 *What she discovered in her lab*: Levy, *Breaking the Age Code*, 5.

45 *"health through psychological"*: Levy, *Breaking the Age Code*, 15.

45 *Those who had a more positive outlook*: Emily F. Hittner et al., "Positive Affect Is Associated with Less Memory Decline: Evidence from a 9-Year Longitudinal Study," *Psychological Science* 31, no. 11 (2020): 1386–95, https://doi.org /10.1177/0956797620953883.

46 *"deaths of despair" have increased*: Anne Case and Angus Deaton, *Deaths of Despair and the Future of Capitalism* (Princeton University Press, 2020).

49 *The life review was first introduced*: Robert N. Butler, "The Life Review: An Interpretation of Reminiscence in the Aged," *Psychiatry* 26, no. 1 (1963): 65–76, https://doi.org/10.1080/00332747.1963.11023339.

49 *But a life review*: Abigail Stewart and Elizabeth A. Vandewater, "'If I Had It to Do Over Again . . . '": Midlife Review, Midcourse Corrections, and Women's Well-Being in Midlife," *Journal of Personality and Social Psychology* 76, no. 2 (1999): 270–83, https://doi.org/10.1037/0022-3514.76.2.270.

49 *Unlike at older ages, in midlife the goal*: Gerben J. Westerhof and Ernst T. Bohlmeijer, "Celebrating Fifty Years of Research and Applications in Reminiscence and Life Review: State of the Art and New Directions," *Journal of Aging Studies* 29 (2014): 107–14, https://doi.org/10.1016/j.jaging.2014.02.003.

50 *These are the periods*: Daniel J. Levinson, *The Seasons of a Man's Life* (Ballantine Books, 1986), and *The Seasons of a Woman's Life: A Fascinating Exploration of the Events, Thoughts, and Life Experiences That All Women Share* (Ballantine Books, 1997).

Chapter 2: The Myth of Stability: Can People Really Change in Midlife?

56 *These are often called the Big Five*: "Big 5 Personality Traits," *Psychology Today*, https://www.psychologytoday.com/basics/big-5-personality-traits.

57 *This is backed up by twin studies*: Igor Zwir et al., "Uncovering the Complex Genetics of Human Character," *Molecular Psychiatry* 25, no. 10 (2020): 2295–2312, https://doi.org/10.1038/s41380-018-0263-6.

58 *This dimension of who we are*: Susan Krauss Whitbourne, Joel R. Sneed, and Karyn M. Skultety, "Identity Processes in Adulthood: Theoretical and Methodological Challenges," *Identity* 2, no. 1 (2002): 29–45, https://doi.org /10.1207/S1532706XID0201_03.

59 *Research shows that identity exploration*: James E. Marcia, "Identity and Psychosocial Development in Adulthood," *Identity* 2, no. 1 (2002): 7–28, https://doi.org/10.1207/S1532706XID0201_02.

59 *"set like plaster"*: Paul T. Costa and Robert R. McCrae, "Still Stable After All These Years: Personality as a Key to Some Issues in Adulthood and Old Age," in *Life Span Development and Behavior* 3, ed. P. B. Baltes and O. G. Brim (Academic Press, 1980), 65–102.

59 *How much someone's personality changes*: Mirjam Stieger et al., "Personality Change Profiles and Changes in Cognition Among Middle-Aged and Older Adults," *Journal of Research in Personality* 95 (2021): 104157, https://doi.org /10.1016/j.jrp.2021.104157.

59 *Psychologist Brent Roberts used longitudinal data*: Brent Roberts, Kate E. Walton, and Wolfgang Viechtbauer, "Patterns of Mean-Level Change in Personality Traits Across the Life Course: A Meta-Analysis of Longitudinal Studies," *Psychological Bulletin* 132, no. 1 (2006): 1–25, https://doi.org/10.1037 /0033-2909.132.1.1.

60 *Likewise, Bernice Neugarten*: Bernice L. Neugarten, *Middle Age and Aging* (University of Chicago Press, 1968).

60 *A study of identity in the adult years*: Päivi Fadjukoff, Lea Pulkkinen, and Katja Kokko, "Identity Formation in Adulthood: A Longitudinal Study from Age 27 to 50," *Identity* 16, no. 1 (2016): 8–23, https://doi.org/10.1080 /15283488.2015.1121820.

61 *Well, a study highlighted in* The Atlantic: Scott Barry Kaufman, "Would You Be Happier with a Different Personality?," *The Atlantic*, August 5, 2016, https:// www.theatlantic.com/health/archive/2016/08/would-you-be-happier-with-a -different-personality/494720/.

61 *If you increased your openness*: Christopher J. Boyce, Alex M. Wood, and Nattavudh Powdthavee, "Is Personality Fixed? Personality Changes as Much as 'Variable' Economic Factors and More Strongly Predicts Changes to Life Satisfaction," *Social Indicators Research* 111 (2013): 287–305, https://doi.org /10.1007/s11205-012-0006-z.

62 *You're also more likely*: Thomas A. Widiger and Joshua R. Oltmanns, "Neuroticism Is a Fundamental Domain of Personality with Enormous Public Health Implications," *World Psychiatry* 16, no. 2 (2017): 144–45, https://www .ncbi.nlm.nih.gov/pmc/articles/PMC5428182/.

63 *In addition, higher openness and conscientiousness*: Angelina R. Sutin et al., "Five-Factor Model Personality Domains and Facets Associated with Markers of Cognitive Health," *Journal of Individual Differences* 44, no. 2 (2023): 97–108, https://doi.org/10.1027/1614-0001/a000383.

63   *In another study, MIDUS participants*: Stieger et al., "Personality Change Profiles and Changes in Cognition Among Middle-Aged and Older Adults."

64   *Earlier research had already made it clear*: Brent W. Roberts et al., "A Systematic Review of Personality Trait Change Through Intervention," *Psychological Bulletin* 143, no. 2 (2017): 117–41, https://doi.org/10.1037/bul0000088.

64   *For instance, in one meta-analysis*: Roberts et al., "A Systematic Review of Personality Trait Change Through Intervention."

65   *Across all types of interventions*: Roberts et al., "A Systematic Review of Personality Trait Change Through Intervention."

65   *So, in a randomized controlled trial*: Mirjam Stieger et al., "Changing Personality Traits with the Help of a Digital Personality Change Intervention," *Proceedings of the National Academy of Sciences* 118, no. 8 (2021): e2017548118, https://doi .org/10.1073/pnas.2017548118.

66   *To see if these results would stick*: Mirjam Stieger, Christoph Flückiger, and Mathias Allemand, "One Year Later: Longer-Term Maintenance Effects of a Digital Intervention to Change Personality Traits," *Journal of Personality* 92, no. 5 (2023): 1424–37, https://api.semanticscholar.org/CorpusID:265729186.

67   *Both within and beyond academia*: Peter Haehner, Amanda Jo Wright, and Wiebke Bleidorn, "A Systematic Review of Volitional Personality Change Research," *Communications Psychology* 2, no.1 (2024): 115, https://pmc.ncbi.nlm.nih.gov /articles/PMC11608366/.

67   *Psychologist Shannon Sauer-Zavala suggests*: Shannon Sauer-Zavala, "Can You Change Your Personality? Psychology Research Says Yes by Tweaking What You Think and Do," *The Conversation*, September 25, 2024, https://theconversation .com/can-you-change-your-personality-psychology-research-says-yes-by-tweaking -what-you-think-and-do-237190.

67   *In several studies I have used cognitive restructuring*: Shevaun D. Neupert, Margie E. Lachman, and Stacey Whitbourne, "Exercise Self-Efficacy and Control Beliefs: Effects on Exercise Behavior After an Exercise Intervention for Older Adults," *Journal of Aging and Physical Activity* 17, no. 1 (2009): 1–16, https://doi.org /10.1123/japa.17.1.1.

67   *This can include providing strategies*: Margie E. Lachman, "Perceived Control over Aging-Related Declines: Adaptive Beliefs and Behaviors," *Current Directions in Psychological Science* 15, no. 6 (2006): 282–86, https://doi.org/10.1111 /j.1467-8721.2006.00453.x.

68 *So, we conducted a seven-week trial*: Mirjam Stieger, Mathias Allemand, and Margie E. Lachman, "Effects of a Digital Self-Control Intervention to Increase Physical Activity in Middle-Aged Adults," *Journal of Health Psychology* 28, no. 10 (2023): 984–96, https://doi.org/10.1177/13591053231166756.

Chapter 3: Mastering Midlife: Balancing the Gains and Losses

78 *In the MIDUS study we found that*: Elizabeth Hahn Rickenbach, Stefan Agrigoroaei, and Margie E. Lachman, "Awareness of Memory Ability and Change: (In)Accuracy of Memory Self-Assessments in Relation to Performance," *Journal of Population Ageing* 8 (2015): 71–99, https://doi.org/10.1007/s12062-014-9108-5.

78 *In another longitudinal study*: Rickenbach, Agrigoroaei, and Lachman, "Awareness of Memory Ability and Change."

79 *When Lauren's daughter*: "Fluid and Crystallized Intelligence," *ScienceDirect*, https://www.sciencedirect.com/topics/neuroscience/fluid-and-crystallized-intelligence.

80 *These two dimensions of intelligence*: Timothy A. Salthouse, "What and When of Cognitive Aging," *Current Directions in Psychological Science* 13, no. 4 (2004): 140–44, https://doi.org/10.1111/j.0963-7214.2004.00293.x.

81 *Poor performance or declines*: Timothy Salthouse, "Consequences of Age-Related Cognitive Declines," *Annual Review of Psychology* 63 (2012): 201–26, https://doi.org/10.1146/annurev-psych-120710-100328.

81 *Still more promising*: "Seattle Longitudinal Study," UW Medicine, Department of Psychiatry and Behavioral Sciences, https://sls.psychiatry.uw.edu/.

82 *Researcher Timothy Salthouse*: Timothy A. Salthouse, "The Processing-Speed Theory of Adult Age Differences in Cognition," *Psychological Review* 103, no. 3 (1996): 403–28, https://uva.theopenscholar.com/files/vcap/files/the_processing-speed_8.pdf.

83 *Over a ten-year period*: Matthew L. Hughes et al., "Change in Cognitive Performance from Midlife into Old Age: Findings from the Midlife in the United States (MIDUS) Study," *Journal of the International Neuropsychological Society* 24, no. 8 (2018): 805–20, https://doi.org/10.1017/s1355617718000425; and Audrey Hamilton, "Self-Esteem Declines Sharply Among Older Adults While Middle-Aged Are Most Confident," *American Psychological Association*, April 1, 2010, https://www.apa.org/news/press/releases/2010/04/self-esteem.

84 *What accounts for all this confusion*: Cheryl L. Grady and Fergus Craik, "Changes in Memory Processing with Age," *Current Opinion in Neurobiology* 10, no. 2 (2000): 224–31, https://doi.org/10.1016/S0959-4388(00)00073-8.

86 *In one of my studies*: Orah R. Burack and Margie E. Lachman, "The Effects of List-Making on Recall in Young and Elderly Adults," *The Journals of Gerontology: Series B* 51B, no. 4 (1996): 226–33, https://doi.org/10.1093/geronb/51B.4.P226.

87 *An article by Melissa Lee Phillips*: Melissa L. Phillips, "The Mind at Midlife," *Monitor on Psychology* 42, no. 4 (2011): 38, https://www.apa.org/monitor/2011/04/mind-midlife.

88 *A lot has been written about the effect*: Arthur Brooks, *From Strength to Strength: Finding Success, Happiness, and Deep Purpose in the Second Half of Life* (Portfolio, 2022).

89 *Whereas younger adults might use one side of the brain*: Patricia A. Reuter-Lorenz and Denise C. Park, "Human Neuroscience and the Aging Mind: A New Look at Old Problems," *The Journals of Gerontology: Series B* 65B, no. 4 (2010): 405–15, https://doi.org/10.1093/geronb/gbq035.

89 *There is also evidence that as we age*: Shelley H. Carson, "Creativity and the Aging Brain," *Psychology Today*, March 30, 2009, https://www.psychologytoday.com/us/blog/life-art/200903/creativity-and-the-aging-brain.

89 *We all have the potential*: "What Is Cognitive Reserve?" *Harvard Health Publishing*, February 1, 2024, https://www.health.harvard.edu/mind-and-mood/what-is-cognitive-reserve.

90 *One study she often cites shows*: Dennis Chan et al., "Lifestyle Activities in Mid-Life Contribute to Cognitive Reserve in Late-Life, Independent of Education, Occupation, and Late-Life Activities," *Neurobiology of Aging* 70 (2018): 180–83, https://doi.org/10.1016/j.neurobiolaging.2018.06.012.

91 *We found that just as many career inventors*: Mary Kaltenberg, Adam B. Jaffe, and Margie E. Lachman, "Invention and the Life Course: Age Differences in Patenting," *Research Policy* 52, no. 1 (2023): 104629, https://doi.org/10.1016/j.respol.2022.104629.

94 *For instance, studies show*: Joanna H. Hong et al., "The Positive Influence of Sense of Control on Physical, Behavioral, and Psychosocial Health in Older Adults: An Outcome-Wide Approach," *Preventive Medicine* 149 (2021): 106612, https://doi.org/10.1016/j.ypmed.2021.106612.

95 *My colleagues and I have identified two important factors*: Margie E. Lachman, Shevaun D. Neupert, and Stefan Agrigoroaei, "The Relevance of Control Beliefs for Health and Aging," in *Handbook of the Psychology of Aging* (Seventh Edition), ed. K. Warner Schaie and Sherry L. Willis (Academic Press, 2011), 175–90, https://doi.org/10.1016/B978-0-12-380882-0.00011-5.

96 *But the research on sense of control*: Lachman, Neupert, and Agrigoroaei, "The Relevance of Control Beliefs for Health and Aging."

97 *A recent MIDUS study*: Eric S. Cerino et al., "Perceived Control Across the Adult Lifespan: Longitudinal Changes in Global Control and Daily Stressor Control," *Developmental Psychology* 60, no. 1 (2024): 45–58, https://doi.org/10.1037/dev0001618.

97 *In our research we have found*: Kimberly M. Prenda and Margie E. Lachman, "Planning for the Future: A Life Management Strategy for Increasing Control and Life Satisfaction in Adulthood," *Psychology and Aging* 16, no. 2 (2001): 206–16, https://doi.org/10.1037/0882-7974.16.2.206.

101 *Research and theory on aging*: Alexandra M. Freund and Natalie C. Ebner, "The Aging Self: Shifting from Promoting Gains to Balancing Losses," in *The Adaptive Self: Personal Continuity and Intentional Self-Development*, ed. Werner Greve, Klaus Rothermund, and Dirk Wentura (Hogrefe, 2005), 185–202.

101 *The loss viewpoint*: Freund and Ebner, "The Aging Self."

102 *Those who believe they are in control of their lives*: Lachman, Neupert, and Agrigoroaei, "The Relevance of Control Beliefs for Health and Aging."

Chapter 4: Healthy in Midlife

113 *As ob/gyn and author Mary Claire Haver*: Mary Claire Haver, "Aging Is Normal, Suffering Is Not," YouTube, November 24, 2023, https://www.youtube.com/watch?v=aCi3-JYIBSs.

113 *Probably the most important message*: Lisbeth Nielsen et al., "The NIH Science of Behavior Change Program: Transforming the Science Through a Focus on Mechanisms of Change," *Behaviour Research and Therapy* 101 (2018): 3–11, https://doi.org/10.1016/j.brat.2017.07.002.

113 *"[r]ecent estimates suggest that human behavior"*: National Research Council Panel on Understanding Divergent Trends in Longevity in High-Income Countries, "International Differences in Mortality at Older Ages: Dimensions and Sources," ed. Eileen M. Crimmins, Samuel H. Preston, and Barney Cohen (National Academies Press, 2010), https://pubmed.ncbi.nlm.nih.gov/21977541/; and Nielsen et al., "The NIH Science of Behavior Change Program."

114 *The seen (and felt) hallmarks*: Richard G. Stefanacci, "Changes in the Body with Aging," *Merck Manual*, https://www.merckmanuals.com/home/older-people%E2%80%99s-health-issues/the-aging-body/changes-in-the-body-with-aging.

116 *You might not be able to stop decreases in brain volume*: Anum Saeed et al., "Cardiovascular Disease and Alzheimer's Disease: The Heart-Brain Axis," *Journal of the American Heart Association* 12, no. 21 (2023): e030780, https://www.ahajournals.org/doi/10.1161/JAHA.123.030780.

117 *The average age of menopause is*: "Menopause Basics," Office on Women's Health, U.S. Department of Health and Human Services, https://womenshealth.gov/menopause/menopause-basics.

117 *While 75% of women experience hot flashes*: Angela Haupt, "8 Signs You're in Perimenopause," *Time*, September 17, 2024, https://time.com/7019600/perimenopause-signs-symptoms/.

118 *Perimenopause may be having a cultural moment*: Mary Claire Haver, *The New Menopause* (Rodale, 2024), 3.

118 *A 2024 editorial published*: Jennifer Allen, "Effective Menopause Education Methods: Addressing the Needs of Current Medical Trainees," *Menopause* 31, no. 2 (February 2024): 89–90, https://doi.org/10.1097/GME.0000000000002308.

118 *While many doctors*: Haver, *The New Menopause*, 6–7.

119 *It was so influential*: Marie N. Stagnitti and Doris Lefkowitz, "Statistical Brief 347: Trends in Hormone Replacement Therapy Drugs Utilization and Expenditures for Adult Women in the U.S. Civilian Noninstitutionalized Population, 2001–2008," Agency for Healthcare Research and Quality, November 2011, https://meps.ahrq.gov/data_files/publications/st347/stat347.shtml.

119 *But just as importantly*: Haver, *The New Menopause*, 76.

120 *There's no reason that*: "Let's Talk Menopause!," https://www.letstalkmenopause.org/.

120 *Especially since one Mayo Clinic study*: Stephanie S. Faubion et al., "Impact of Menopause Symptoms on Women in the Workplace," *Mayo Clinic Proceedings* 98, no. 6 (2023): 833–45, https://www.mayoclinicproceedings.org/pb-assets/Health%20Advance/journals/jmcp/JMCP4097_proof.pdf.

120 *It is statistics like these*: "Menopause in the Workplace," *Carrot Fertility*, 2022, https://content.get-carrot.com/rs/418-PQJ-171/images/Carrot%20-%20Menopause%20in%20the%20workplace.pdf.

120 *After all, women are 51%*: "QuickFacts," U.S. Census Bureau, https://www
.census.gov/quickfacts/; https://www.dol.gov/agencies/wb/data/widget.

120 *"systemic inflammatory phase"*: Micheline McCarthy and Ami P. Raval, "The
Peri-Menopause in a Woman's Life: A Systemic Inflammatory Phase That Enables
Later Neurodegenerative Disease," *Journal of Neuroinflammation* 17, no. 317
(2020), https://doi.org/10.1186/s12974-020-01998-9.

121 *The immune system triggers*: Roma Pahwa, Amandeep Goyal, and Ishwarlal Jialal,
"Chronic Inflammation," *StatPearls*, August 7, 2023, https://www.ncbi.nlm.nih
.gov/books/NBK493173/.

121 *Whatever the cause, chronic inflammation*: Claudio Franceschi and Judith Campisi,
"Chronic Inflammation (Inflammaging) and Its Potential Contribution to Age-
Associated Diseases," *The Journals of Gerontology: Series A* 69, Suppl. 1 (2014):
S4–S9, https://doi.org/10.1093/gerona/glu057.

121 *The idea behind inflammaging*: Tamas Fulop et al., "Immunology of Aging:
The Birth of Inflammaging," *Clinical Reviews in Allergy and Immunology*
64, no. 2 (2023): 109–22, https://pmc.ncbi.nlm.nih.gov/articles/PMC844
9217/.

122 *In one study, for example*: Carolin V. Schneider, Kai Schneider, Alexander Teumer,
et al., "Association of Telomere Length With Risk of Disease and Mortality,"
JAMA Internal Medicine 182, no.3 (2022): 291-300, https://doi.org/10.1001
/jamainternmed.2021.7804.

122 *Stress shortens telomeres*: Agus Surachman, Elissa Hamlat, and Elissa Epel,
"Stress and Biological Aging," in *Handbook of Adult Development and Aging*,
ed. Margie E. Lachman and Avron Spiro (American Psychological Association,
2026).

122 *There are more unstable molecules*: "Oxidative Stress: Causes, Symptoms and
Treatment," Cleveland Clinic, last reviewed February 29, 2024, https://
my.clevelandclinic.org/health/articles/oxidative-stress.

123 *A study of parents who were caregivers of children with cancer*: Elissa S. Epel et al.,
"Accelerated Telomere Shortening in Response to Life Stress," *Proceedings of the
National Academy of Sciences* 101, no. 49 (2004): 17312–15, https://doi
.org/10.1073/pnas.0407162101.

123 *Negative interactions with family*: Karen D. Lincoln, Donald A. Lloyd, and
Ann W. Nguyen, "Social Relationships and Salivary Telomere Length Among
Middle-Aged and Older African American and White Adults," *The Journals of
Gerontology: Series B* 74, no. 6 (2019): 1053–61, https://doi.org/10.1093
/geronb/gbx049.

123 *Other studies have found*: Nicola Schutte and John M. Malouff, "The Association Between Optimism and Telomere Length: A Meta-Analysis," *The Journal of Positive Psychology* 17, no. 1 (2022): 82–88, https://doi.org/10.1080/17439760.2020.1832249.

123 *what I call the psychosocial anti-inflammatories*: Margie E. Lachman and Kylie A. Schiloski, "The Psychosocial Anti-Inflammatories: Sense of Control, Purpose in Life, and Social Support in Relation to Inflammation, Functional Health and Chronic Conditions in Adulthood," *Journal of Psychosomatic Research* 187 (2024): 111957, https://doi.org/10.1016/j.jpsychores.2024.111957.

124 *this is called health span*: Eileen M. Crimmins, "Lifespan and Healthspan: Past, Present, and Promise," *The Gerontologist* 55, no. 6 (2015): 901–11, https://doi.org/10.1093/geront/gnv130; Stuart J. Olshansky, "From Lifespan to Healthspan," *JAMA* 320, no. 13 (2018): 1323–24, https://pubmed.ncbi.nlm.nih.gov/30242384/; and Peter Attia, *Outlive: The Science and Art of Longevity* (Harmony, 2023).

124 *To beat back inflammation*: Lachman and Schiloski, "The Psychosocial Anti-Inflammatories."

124 *These include having positive beliefs*: Margie E. Lachman and Shevaun D. Neupert, "Psychosocial Factors and Health: Toward a Psychosocial Prescription for Healthy Aging," in *Handbook of Adult Development and Aging*, ed. Margie E. Lachman and Avron Spiro (American Psychological Association, 2026).

125 *Those who have a higher sense of control*: Kylie A. Schiloski and Margie E. Lachman, "The Relationship Between 10-Year Changes in Cognitive Control Beliefs and Cognitive Performance in Middle and Later Adulthood," *The Journals of Gerontology Series B* 79, no. 11 (2024): gbae155, https://doi.org/10.1093/geronb/gbae155; and Carol D. Ryff, Burton H. Singer, and Gayle Dienberg Love, "Positive Health: Connecting Well-Being with Biology," *Philosophical Transactions of the Royal Society B: Biological Sciences* 359, no. 1449 (2004): 1383–94, https://doi.org/10.1098/rstb.2004.1521.

125 *A narrative review of twenty-eight studies*: Dusti R. Jones and Jennifer E. Graham-Engeland, "Positive Affect and Peripheral Inflammatory Markers Among Adults: A Narrative Review," *Psychoneuroendocrinology* 123 (2021): 104892, https://doi.org/10.1016/j.psyneuen.2020.104892.

125 *Several studies have found*: Margaret Gough and Kanya Godde, "A Multifaceted Analysis of Social Stressors and Chronic Inflammation," *SSM - Population Health* 6 (2018): 136–40, https://doi.org/10.1016/j.ssmph.2018.09.005; and

Jasmin Guevara and Kyle Murdock, "High Social Strain and Physical Health: Examining the Roles of Anxious Arousal, Body Mass Index, and Inflammation," *Psychoneuroendocrinology* 106 (2019): 155–60, https://doi.org/10.1016 /j.psyneuen.2019.04.005.

125   *In contrast, social support*: Bert N. Uchino et al., "Social Support, Social Integration, and Inflammatory Cytokines: A Meta-Analysis," *Health Psychology* 37, no. 5 (2018): 462–71, https://doi.org/10.1037 /hea0000594.

126   *Exercise is the one thing*: Margie E. Lachman et al., "When Adults Don't Exercise: Behavioral Strategies to Increase Physical Activity in Sedentary Middle-Aged and Older Adults," *Innovation in Aging* 2, no. 1 (2018): igy007, https://doi.org /10.1093/geroni/igy007.

126   *Last but not least, physical activity*: Massod A. Shammas, "Telomeres, Lifestyle, Cancer, and Aging," *Current Opinion in Clinical Nutrition and Metabolic Care* 14, no. 1 (2011): 28–34, https://www.ncbi.nlm.nih.gov/pmc/articles/PMC 3370421/; Seonghyeok Song, Eunsang Lee, and Hyunjoong Kim, "Does Exercise Affect Telomere Length? A Systematic Review and Meta-Analysis of Randomized Controlled Trials," *Medicina (Kaunas)* 58, no. 2 (2022): 242, https://pmc.ncbi.nlm.nih.gov/articles/PMC8879766/; and Joshua Denham and Maha Sellami, "Exercise Training Increases Telomerase Reverse Transcriptase Gene Expression and Telomerase Activity: A Systematic Review and Meta-Analysis," *Ageing Research Reviews* 70 (2021): 101411, https://doi.org/10.1016 /j.arr.2021.101411.

126   *Of course, despite the widespread knowledge*: Nazik Elgaddal, Ellen A. Kramarow, and Cynthia Reuben, "Physical Activity Among Adults Aged 18 and Over: United States, 2020," NCHS Data Brief 443 (2022): 1–8, https://www.cdc.gov/nchs /products/databriefs/db443.htm.

127   *One of our interventions used Implementation Intentions*: Peter M. Gollwitzer, "Implementation Intentions Strong Effects of Simple Plans," *The American Psychologist* 54, no. 7 (1999): 493–503, https://doi.org/10.1037 /0003-066X.54.7.493.

127   *In a study with*: Stephanie A. Robinson et al., "Time for Change: Using Implementation Intentions to Promote Physical Activity in a Randomised Pilot Trial," *Psychology and Health* 34, no. 2 (2019): 232–54, https://doi.org/10.1080 /08870446.2018.1539487.

128   *Compared to the control condition*: Robinson et al., "Time for Change: Using Implementation Intentions to Promote Physical Activity in a Randomised Pilot Trial."

Chapter 5: Time Is on Your Side

139   *Researchers have studied*: Laura L. Carstensen, "The Influence of a Sense of Time on Human Development," *Science* 312, no. 5782 (2006): 1913–15, https://doi .org/10.1126/science.1127488.

140   *what is called a "positivity effect"*: Laura L. Carstensen, "Socioemotional Selectivity Theory: The Role of Perceived Endings in Human Motivation," *The Gerontologist* 61, no. 8 (2021): 1188–96, https://doi.org/10.1093 /geront/gnab116.

140   *They reach more intensely for*: Frieder R. Lang and Laura L. Carstensen, "Time Counts: Future Time Perspective, Goals, and Social Relationships," *Psychology and Aging* 17, no. 1 (2002): 125–39, https://doi.org/10.1037 /0882-7974.17.1.125.

140   *Folks in their forties and fifties*: Laura L. Carstensen et al., "What's Time Got to Do with It? Appreciation of Time Influences Social Goals and Emotional Well-Being," *Psychology and Aging* 39, no. 8 (2024): 833–53, https://doi.org /10.1037/pag0000856.

141   *When he and his wife*: Mitch Albom, "What We Choose to Carry Is Actually What Ends Up Defining Us," *Making Space with Hoda Kotb*, October 11, 2021, https://podcasts.musixmatch.com/podcast/making -space-with-hoda-kotb-01h1ngdz40x4acpqbz0zw5v0wb/episode/mitch -albom-what-we-choose-to-carry-is-actually-what-1h1ngdz40h1jbjfx464 wgnwmq.

141   *While the author might be best known*: "Mitch Albom," *Wikipedia*, last modified April 7, 2025, https://en.wikipedia.org/wiki/Mitch_Albom.

141   *"I happened to ask the guy who"*: Albom, "What We Choose to Carry Is Actually What Ends Up Defining Us."

143   *Dan Pink's survey of regret found*: Daniel H. Pink, "Summary of Our Mini-Survey on Regret," Daniel H. Pink (website), https://www.danpink.com/summary-of -our-mini-survey-on-regret/.

144   *It has even been shown*: Eimear O'Connor, Teresa McCormack, and Aidan Feeney, "Do Children Who Experience Regret Make Better Decisions? A Developmental Study of the Behavioral Consequences of Regret," *Child Development* 85, no. 5 (2014): 1995–2010, https://doi.org/10.1111/cdev.12253.

144   *For adults, feelings like regret and guilt*: Robert L. Leahy, "Is Regret Ever Useful?," *Psychology Today*, June 7, 2022, https://www.psychologytoday.com/us /blog/anxiety-files/202206/is-regret-ever-useful.

144   *Those who continued to ruminate*: Francine Russo, "The Best New Year's Resolution Might Be to Just Let Go of an Unfulfilled Life Goal," *Scientific American*, December 28, 2022, https://www.scientificamerican.com/article/the-best-new-years-resolution-might-be-to-just-let-go-of-an-unfulfilled-life-goal/.

144   *From this work*: Carsten Wrosch and Jutta Heckhausen, "Perceived Control of Life Regrets: Good for Young and Bad for Old Adults," *Psychology and Aging* 17, no. 2 (2002): 340–50, https://doi.org/10.1037/0882-7974.17.2.340.

146   *For situations like these, Heckhausen*: Wrosch and Heckhausen, "Perceived Control of Life Regrets."

146   *In contrast, people who find it difficult*: Russo, "The Best New Year's Resolution Might Be to Just Let Go of an Unfulfilled Life Goal."

148   *"It's not just other people"*: Albom, "What We Choose to Carry Is Actually What Ends Up Defining Us."

149   *Life course sociologist Glen Elder*: Glen H. Elder, *Children of the Great Depression, 25th Anniversary Edition* (Routledge, 1999).

149   *Lifespan psychologists Frank Infurna*: Frank J. Infurna et al., "Historical Change in Midlife Health, Well-Being, and Despair: Cross-Cultural and Socioeconomic Comparisons," *American Psychologist* 76, no. 6 (2021): 870–87, https://doi.org/10.1037/amp0000817.

150   *The findings are striking*: Frank J. Infurna et al., "Loneliness in Midlife: Historical Increases and Elevated Levels in the United States Compared with Europe," *American Psychologist* 80, no. 5 (2024): 744–56, https://doi.org/10.1037/amp0001322.

151   *In the US it is now age*: "Figure MS-2 Median Age at First Marriage: 1890 to Present," U.S. Census Bureau, https://www.census.gov/content/dam/Census/library/visualizations/time-series/demo/families-and-households/ms-2.pdf.

151   *The median age of having a first child*: Anne Morse, "Fertility Rates Declined for Younger Women, Increased for Older Women: Stable Fertility Rates 1990–2019 Mask Distinct Variations by Age," U.S. Census Bureau, April 6, 2022, https://www.census.gov/library/stories/2022/04/fertility-rates-declined-for-younger-women-increased-for-older-women.html.

152   *Bernice Neugarten wrote about being "on time" or "off time"*: Bernice L. Neugarten, *Middle Age and Aging* (University of Chicago Press, 1968).

155   *And yet, changing norms*: Suzanne M. Bianchi, John P. Robinson, and Melissa A. Milkie, *Changing Rhythms of American Family Life* (Russell Sage Foundation, 2006); Ruth Grace Wong, "Working Moms Today Spend as Much Time on Childcare as Stay-at-Home Moms 40 Years Ago," *Joyful Parenting SF*,

September 7, 2023, https://joyfulparentingsf.com/p/working-moms-today
-spend-as-much; and Bryan Caplan, *Selfish Reasons to Have More Kids: Why Being
a Great Parent Is Less Work and More Fun than You Think* (Basic Books, 2011).

155 *A recent Gallup poll*: Kristin Barry, Kate Den Houter, and Karen Guggenheim,
"More Than a Program: A Culture of Women's Wellbeing at Work," Gallup
Workplace, December 4, 2024, https://www.gallup.com/workplace/653843
/program-culture-women-wellbeing-work.aspx.

155 *[And] women with children*: Barry, Den Houter, and Guggenheim, "More Than a
Program: A Culture of Women's Wellbeing at Work."

157 *The solution that Chris and Kyle*: Katy Milkman, *How to Change: The Science of
Getting from Where You Are to Where You Want to Be* (Portfolio, 2021).

158 *It is important to recognize*: Christina Kamis, "The Long-Term Impact of
Parental Mental Health on Children's Distress Trajectories in Adulthood,"
Society and Mental Health 11, no. 1 (2020): 54–68, https://doi.org/10.1177
/2156869320912520.

158 *For example*: Myrna M. Weissman et al., "Offspring of Depressed Parents: 30
Years Later," *American Journal of Psychiatry* 173, no. 10 (2016): 1024–32,
https://doi.org/10.1176/appi.ajp.2016.15101327.

158 *And poor physical health in a parent*: Poppert Cordts et al., "More Than Mental
Health: Parent Physical Health and Early Childhood Behavior Problems," *Journal
of Developmental & Behavioral Pediatrics* 41, no. 4 (2020): 265–71, https://doi
.org/10.1097/DBP.0000000000000755.

159 *In fact, today's mid-lifers*: Anna Medaris, "Gen Z Adults and Younger Millennials
Are 'Completely Overwhelmed' by Stress," *American Psychological Association*,
November 1, 2023, https://www.apa.org/topics/stress/generation-z-millennials
-young-adults-worries.

159 *In midlife, despite the realization*: Tianyuan Li, "In Control of Future Time: Sense
of Control Weakens the Negative Association Between Age and Future Time
Perspective," *Current Psychology* 41 (2022): 5127–33, https://doi.org/10.1007
/s12144-020-01019-1.

Chapter 6: The Age of Generativity: The Dynamic Social Network

163 *According to Pew Research*: Juliana Menasce Horowitz, "More than Half of
Americans in Their 40s Are 'Sandwiched' Between an Aging Parent and Their
Own Children," Pew Research Center, April 8, 2022, https://www.pewresearch
.org/short-reads/2022/04/08/more-than-half-of-americans-in-their-40s-are
-sandwiched-between-an-aging-parent-and-their-own-children/.

164 *Emotional strain clocked*: Lianlian Lei, Amanda N. Leggett, and Donovan T. Maust, "A National Profile of Sandwich Generation Caregivers Providing Care to Both Older Adults and Children," *Journal of the American Geriatrics Society* 71, no. 3 (2023): 799–809, https://doi.org/10.1111/jgs.18138.

166 *One thing that is on the rise*: "FBI Highlights Growing Number of Reported Elder Fraud Cases Ahead of World Elder Abuse Awareness Day," Federal Bureau of Investigation, June 14, 2024, https://www.fbi.gov/news/press-releases /fbi-highlights-growing-number-of-reported-elder-fraud-cases-ahead-of-world -elder-abuse-awareness-day.

166 *As executive functions decline*: Matthew D. Grilli et al., "Is This Phishing? Older Age Is Associated with Greater Difficulty Discriminating Between Safe and Malicious Emails," *The Journals of Gerontology: Series B* 76, no. 9 (2021): 1711–15, https://doi.org/10.1093/geronb/gbaa228.

167 *Well over half of adults enter midlife*: George M. Hayward, "Losing Our Parents: New 2021 Data Visualization Shows Parent Mortality: 44.2% Had Lost at Least One Parent," U.S. Census Bureau, March 21, 2023, https://www.census.gov /library/stories/2023/03/losing-our-parents.html.

167 *When adults leave midlife*: Hayward, "Losing Our Parents: New 2021 Data Visualization Shows Parent Mortality: 44.2% Had Lost at Least One Parent."

167 *Thus, an important transition point*: Margie E. Lachman, "Development in Midlife," *Annual Review of Psychology* 55 (2004): 305–31, https://doi.org /10.1146/annurev.psych.55.090902.141521.

170 *The kinkeepers are the ones*: Danielle Friedman, "The Constant Work to Keep a Family Connected Has a Name," *The New York Times*, May 8, 2024, https:// www.nytimes.com/2024/05/08/well/family/kinkeeping-families.html.

170 *what she calls the "social convoy"*: Toni C. Antonucci, Kristine J. Ajrouch, and Kira S. Birditt, "The Convoy Model: Explaining Social Relations from a Multidisciplinary Perspective," *The Gerontologist* 54, no. 1 (2014): 82–92, https://doi.org/10.1093/geront/gnt118.

170 *She asks her research participants*: Noah J. Webster, Toni C. Antonucci, and Kristine J. Ajrouch, "Linked Lives and Convoys of Social Relations," *Advances in Life Course Research* 54 (2022): 100502, https://doi.org/10.1016/j .alcr.2022.100502.

171 *Antonucci finds*: Toni C. Antonucci, Hiroko Akiyama, and Keiko Takahashi, "Attachment and Close Relationships Across the Life Span," *Attachment and Human Development* 6, no. 4 (2005): 353–70, https://doi.org/10.1080/14616 73042000303136.

172 *According to the CDC*: Gladys M. Martinez and Kimberly Daniels, "Fertility of Men and Women Aged 15–49 in the United States: National Survey of Family Growth, 2015–2019," *National Health Statistics Reports* 179, January 10, 2023, https://www.cdc.gov/nchs/data/nhsr/nhsr179.pdf; and Gretchen Livingston, "They're Waiting Longer, but U.S. Women Today More Likely to Have Children Than a Decade Ago," Pew Research Center, January 18, 2018, https://www.pewresearch.org/social-trends/2018/01/18/theyre-waiting-longer-but-u-s-women-today-more-likely-to-have-children-than-a-decade-ago/.

172 *In 2024, the US Surgeon General*: U.S. Department of Health and Human Services, *Parents Under Pressure: The U.S. Surgeon General's Advisory on the Mental Health and Well-Being of Parents*, 2024, https://www.hhs.gov/surgeongeneral/priorities/parents/index.html.

172 *For parents of children with a disease*: Jieun Song, Marsha R. Mailick, and Jan S. Greenberg, "Health of Parents of Individuals with Developmental Disorders or Mental Health Problems: Impacts of Stigma," *Social Science and Medicine* 217 (2018): 152–58, https://doi.org/10.1016/j.socscimed.2018.09.044.

172 *In fact, the stress can be*: Elissa S. Epel et al., "Accelerated Telomere Shortening in Response to Life Stress," *Proceedings of the National Academy of Sciences* 101, no. 49 (2004): 17312–15, https://doi.org/10.1073/pnas.0407162101.

175 *One of the earliest studies*: Lisa F. Berkman and Leonard Syme, "Social Networks, Host Resistance, and Mortality: A Nine-Year Follow-up Study of Alameda County Residents," *American Journal of Epidemiology* 109, no. 2 (1979): 186–204, https://doi.org/10.1093/oxfordjournals.aje.a112674.

176 *In one of the more alarming reports*: Julianne Holt-Lunstad, Timothy Smith, and Bradley Layton, "Social Relationships and Mortality Risk: A Meta-Analytic Review," *PLoS Medicine* 7, no. 7 (2010): e1000316, https://doi.org/10.1371/journal.pmed.1000316.

176 *Loneliness has gotten a good deal*: U.S. Department of Health and Human Services, *Our Epidemic of Loneliness and Isolation: The U.S. Surgeon General's Advisory on the Healing Effects of Social Connection and Community*, 2023, https://www.hhs.gov/sites/default/files/surgeon-general-social-connection-advisory.pdf.

176 *Indeed, being lonely or isolated*: Colin Freilich et al., "Loneliness, Epigenetic Age Acceleration, and Chronic Health Conditions," *Psychology and Aging* 39, no. 4 (2024): 337–49, https://doi.org/10.1037/pag0000822.

176 *and earlier death*: Julianne Holt-Lunstad et al., "Loneliness and Social Isolation as Risk Factors for Mortality: A Meta-Analytic Review," *Perspectives on Psychological Science* 10, no. 2 (2015): 227–37, https://doi.org/10.1177/1745691614568352.

176 *A study led by*: Eileen K. Graham et al., "Do We Become More Lonely with Age? A Coordinated Data Analysis of Nine Longitudinal Studies," *Psychological Science* 35, no. 6 (2024): 579–96, https://doi.org/10.1177/09567976241242037.

177 *My colleague and friend*: Robert Waldinger and Marc Schulz, *The Good Life: Lessons from the World's Longest Scientific Study of Happiness* (Simon & Schuster, 2023).

178 *In other studies*: Sheldon Cohen, "Keynote Presentation at the Eight International Congress of Behavioral Medicine Mainz, Germany August 25–28, 2004," *International Journal of Behavioral Medicine* 12 (2005): 123–31, https://doi.org/10.1207/s15327558ijbm1203_1.

178 *And we know that social support*: "Do Social Ties Affect Our Health? Exploring the Biology of Relationships," *News in Health*, National Institutes of Health, February 2017, https://newsinhealth.nih.gov/2017/02/do-social-ties-affect-our-health.

179 *In his famous work on the eight stages of life*: Erik Homburger Erikson, *Childhood and Society 2000 Edition* (Norton, 1963).

179 *What they found is that those in midlife*: Dan McAdams and Ed de St. Aubin, "A Theory of Generativity and Its Assessment Through Self-Report, Behavioral Acts, and Narrative Themes in Autobiography," *Journal of Personality and Social Psychology* 62, no. 6 (1992): 1003–15, https://doi.org/10.1037/0022 -3514.62.6.1003; and Dan McAdams, Ed de St. Aubin, and Regina Logan, "Generativity Among Young, Midlife, and Older Adults," *Psychology and Aging* 8, no. 2 (1993): 221–30, https://doi.org/10.1037/0882-7974.8.2.221.

180 *They see themselves as sensitive*: Dan McAdams and Jen Guo, "Narrating the Generative Life," *Psychological Science* 26, no. 4 (2015): 475–83, https://doi.org/10.1177/0956797614568318.

182 *In a longitudinal study*: Niccole A. Nelson and Cindy S. Bergeman, "Development of Generative Concern Across Mid- to Later Life," *The Gerontologist* 61, no. 3 (2021): 430–38. https://doi.org/10.1093/geront/gnaa115.

185 *The definition of social support*: Karen S. Rook, "Social Networks in Later Life: Weighing Positive and Negative Effects on Health and Well-Being," *Current Directions in Psychological Science* 24, no. 1 (2015): 45–51, https://doi.org/10.1177/0963721414551364.

186 *How much can you open up*: Heather R. Walen and Margie E. Lachman, "Social Support and Strain from Partner, Family, and Friends: Costs and Benefits for Men and Women in Adulthood," *Journal of Social and Personal Relationships* 17, no. 1 (2000): 5–30, https://doi.org/10.1177/0265407500171001.

Notes

187   *In fact, a supportive supervisor*: Oliver Hämmig, "Health and Well-Being at Work: The Key Role of Supervisor Support," *SSM - Population Health* 3 (2017): 393–402, https://doi.org/10.1016/j.ssmph.2017.04.002.

187   *As we know from the data*: Holt-Lunstad et al., "Loneliness and Social Isolation as Risk Factors for Mortality: A Meta-Analytic Review."

187   *One study by my colleagues Edith Chen*: Edith Chen et al., "The Balance of Giving Versus Receiving Social Support and All-Cause Mortality in a US National Sample," *Proceedings of the National Academy of Sciences* 118, no. 24 (2021): e2024770118, https://doi.org/10.1073/pnas.2024770118.

188   *Research by Nicholas Christakis*: Nicholas A. Christakis and James Fowler, *Connected: The Surprising Power of Our Social Networks and How They Shape Our Lives* (Little, Brown Spark, 2009).

189   *In a review of thirty-eight studies by Rosemary Blieszner*: Rosemary Blieszner, Aaron M. Ogletree, and Rebecca G. Adams, "Friendship in Later Life: A Research Agenda," *Innovation in Aging* 3, no. 1 (2019): igz005, https://doi.org/10.1093/geroni/igz005.

189   *Friends can help us to deal*: Julianne Holt-Lunstad et al., "On the Importance of Relationship Quality: The Impact of Ambivalence in Friendships on Cardiovascular Functioning," *Annals of Behavioral Medicine* 33, no. 3 (2007): 278–90, https://doi.org/10.1007/BF02879910.

189   *But there is an important distinction*: Christiane A. Hoppmann and Theresa Pauly, "A Lifespan Psychological Perspective on Solitude," *International Journal of Behavioral Development* 46, no. 6 (2022): 473–80, https://doi.org/10.1177/01650254221130279.

Chapter 7: Building Resilience When Life Throws You Curveballs

193   *Later that day*: Frank Bruni, *The Beauty of Dusk: On Vision Lost and Found* (Avid Reader Press, 2022), 4.

195   *"Ahead of schedule, these people"*: Bruni, *The Beauty of Dusk*, 22.

196   *He could hear the elevator*: Terry Gross, host, *Fresh Air*, "After a Stroke Blinded One Eye, Frank Bruni Focused on the Future," *NPR*, May 17, 2022, https://www.npr.org/2022/05/17/1099465610/after-a-stroke-blinded-one-eye-frank-bruni-focused-on-the-future.

196   *"The exhilaration wasn't about my vision"*: Bruni, *The Beauty of Dusk*, 152.

197   *For instance, the kind of stroke*: Bruni, *The Beauty of Dusk*, 26.

204 *These experiences can be assessed using*: "Adverse Childhood Experience Questionnaire for Adults," California Surgeon General's Clinical Advisory Committee, May 5, 2020, https://www.acesaware.org/wp-content/uploads /2022/07/ACE-Questionnaire-for-Adults-Identified-English-rev.7.26.22.pdf.

204 *Yet, we also found that if someone*: Gregory E. Miller, Margie E. Lachman, Edith Chen, Tara Gruenewald, Arun Karlamangla, and T. E. Seeman, "Pathways to Resilience: Maternal Nurturance as a Buffer Against the Effects of Childhood Poverty on Metabolic Syndrome at Midlife," *Psychological Science* 22, no. 12 (2011): 1591–1599. https://doi.org/10.1177/0956797611419170; and Gregory E. Miller, Edith Chen, and Karen J. Parker, "Psychological Stress in Childhood and Susceptibility to the Chronic Diseases of Aging: Moving Toward a Model of Behavioral and Biological Mechanisms," *Psychological Bulletin* 137, no. 6 (2011): 959–97, https://doi.org/10.1037/a0024768.

205 *Research has shown that ACEs*: Maureen Sanderson et al., "Adverse Childhood Experiences and Chronic Disease Risk in the Southern Community Cohort Study," *Journal of Health Care for the Poor and Underserved* 32, no. 3 (2021): 1384–1402, https://dx.doi.org/10.1353/hpu.2021.0139.

206 *Lewina Lee, a clinical psychologist*: Lewina O. Lee et al., "The Long Arm of Childhood Experiences on Longevity: Testing Midlife Vulnerability and Resilience Pathways," *Psychology and Aging* 34, no. 7 (2019): 884–99, https:// pubmed.ncbi.nlm.nih.gov/31524422/; and Lewina O. Lee et al., "Optimism Is Associated with Exceptional Longevity in 2 Epidemiologic Cohorts of Men and Women," *Proceedings of the National Academy of Sciences* 116, no. 37 (2019): 18357–62, https://doi.org/10.1073/pnas.1900712116.

210 *In a series of studies*: Carolyn M. Aldwin, Karen J. Sutton, and Margie E. Lachman, "The Development of Coping Resources in Adulthood," *Journal of Personality* 64, no. 4 (1996): 837–71. https://doi.org/10.1111 /j.1467-6494.1996.tb00946.x.

211 *And yet, in the studies I conducted*: Aldwin, Sutton, and Lachman, "The Development of Coping Resources in Adulthood."

212 *He formulated resilience*: Michael Rutter, "Psychosocial Resilience and Protective Mechanisms," *American Journal of Orthopsychiatry* 57, no. 3 (1987): 316–31, https://doi.org/10.1111/j.1939-0025.1987.tb03541.x.

212 *While many have low points*: Frank J. Infurna et al., "Historical Change in Midlife Health, Well-Being, and Despair: Cross-Cultural and Socioeconomic Comparisons," *American Psychologist* 76, no. 6 (2021): 870–87, https://doi.org /10.1037/amp0000817.

212 *When researchers test for resilience*: "Nicholson McBride Resilience Questionnaire," BlockSurvey, https://blocksurvey.io/templates/resilience-scales/nicholson -mcbride-resilience-questionnaire.

212 *There are a number of psychosocial resources*: Carol Ryff et al., "Varieties of Resilience in MIDUS," *Social and Personality Psychology Compass* 6, no. 11 (2012): 792–806, https://doi.org/10.1111/j.1751-9004.2012.00462.x; and Alex J. Zautra, Anne Arewasikporn, and Mary C. Davis, "Resilience: Promoting Well-Being Through Recovery, Sustainability, and Growth," *Research in Human Development* 7, no. 3 (2010): 221–38, https://doi.org/10.1080/15427609.2010.504431.

213 *Richard Lazarus and Susan Folkman*: Susan Folkman and Richard S. Lazarus, "An Analysis of Coping in a Middle-Aged Community Sample," *Journal of Health and Social Behavior* 21, no. 3 (1980): 219–39, https://doi.org/10.2307 /2136617.

214 *If a stressor is uncontrollable*: Folkman and Lazarus, "An Analysis of Coping in a Middle-Aged Community Sample."

216 *Although reacting to a stressor*: David Almeida et al., "Charting Adult Development Through (Historically Changing) Daily Stress Processes," *American Psychologist* 75, no. 4 (2020): 511–24, https://doi.org/10.1037/amp0000597.

216 *Research by Susan Charles*: Susan T. Charles et al., "The Mixed Benefits of a Stressor-Free Life," *Emotion* 21, no. 5 (2021): 962–71, https://doi.org/10.1037 /emo0000958.

217 *In such cases there is an extreme form*: Richard G. Tedeschi and Lawrence G. Calhoun, "The Posttraumatic Growth Inventory: Measuring the Positive Legacy of Trauma," *Journal of Traumatic Stress* 9, no. 3 (1996): 455–71, https://doi.org /10.1002/jts.2490090305.

Chapter 8: Choosing Wisely at the Crossroads of Life

222 *It is said that we make*: Amanda Reill, "A Simple Way to Make Better Decisions," *Harvard Business Review*, December 5, 2023, https://hbr.org/2023/12 /a-simple-way-to-make-better-decisions.

227 *Midlife has been referred*: Victoria Schüttengruber, Franciska Krings, and Alexandra M. Freund, "Positive and Negative Spillover Effects: Managing Multiple Goals in Middle Adulthood," in *Withstanding Vulnerability Throughout Adult Life*, ed. Dario Spini and Eric Widmer (Palgrave Macmillan, 2023), 31–47.

229 *While we know little specifically about*: JoNell Strough, Corinna E. Löckenhoff, and Thomas M. Hess, "The Present, Past, and Future of Research on Aging and Decision Making," in *Aging and Decision Making: Empirical and Applied*

Perspectives, ed. T. M. Hess, J. Strough, and C. E. Löckenhoff (Academic Press, 2015), 1–14.

229 *What researchers have shown*: Emily Sohn, "How Decision-Making Changes with Age," Simons Foundation, March 2, 2022, https://www.simonsfoundation.org /2022/03/02/how-decision-making-changes-with-age/.

229 *There's no question that*: Gregory R. Samanez-Larkin and Brian Knutson, "Decision Making in the Ageing Brain: Changes in Affective and Motivational Circuits," *Nature Reviews Neuroscience* 16 (2015): 278–89, https://doi.org /10.1038/nrn3917.

229 *"active remodeling of neural circuits"*: Sohn, "How Decision-Making Changes with Age."

229 *Older adults tend to think*: Sohn, "How Decision-Making Changes with Age."

230 *David Laibson*: Sumit Agarwal et al., "The Age of Reason: Financial Decisions over the Lifecycle," National Bureau of Economic Research 13191 (2007), http://www.nber.org/papers/w13191.

230 *They found that middle-aged adults*: Agarwal et al., "The Age of Reason."

231 *"relatively young borrowers"*: Agarwal et al., "The Age of Reason."

233 *It's called the Selection, Optimization, Compensation Model*: Paul B. Baltes and Margret M. Baltes, "Psychological Perspectives on Successful Aging: The Model of Selective Optimization with Compensation," in *Successful Aging: Perspectives from the Behavioral Sciences*, ed. P. B. Baltes and M. M. Baltes (Cambridge University Press, 1990), 1–34.

237 *SOC strategies are found*: Salom M. Teshale and Margie E. Lachman, "Managing Daily Happiness: The Relationship Between Selection, Optimization, and Compensation Strategies and Well-Being in Adulthood," *Psychology and Aging* 31, no. 7 (2016): 687–92, https://doi.org/10.1037/pag0000132.

237 *In one study my former student*: Teshale and Lachman, "Managing Daily Happiness."

240 *Ellen Langer, a famous social psychologist*: Ellen J. Langer, *Mindfulness* (Balance, 2014).

241 *Langer's research*: Ellen J. Langer, *The Mindful Body: Thinking Our Way to Chronic Health* (Ballantine Books, 2023).

241 *The renowned psychologist Albert Bandura*: Albert Bandura, "The Psychology of Chance Encounters and Life Paths," *American Psychologist* 37, no. 7 (1982): 747–55, https://doi.org/10.1037/0003-066X.37.7.747.

Chapter 9: Beyond Midlife: Reaping the Rewards

249 *Our research shows*: Eric S. Cerino et al., "Perceived Control Across the Adult Lifespan: Longitudinal Changes in Global Control and Daily Stressor Control," *Developmental Psychology* 60, no. 1 (2024): 45–58, https://doi.org/10.1037/dev0001618.

249 *In contrast, perceived control*: Margie E. Lachman and Kimberly M. Prenda Firth, "The Adaptive Value of Feeling in Control During Midlife," in *How Healthy Are We? A National Study of Well-Being at Midlife*, ed. O. G. Brim, C. D. Ryff, and R. C. Kessler (University of Chicago Press, 2004), 320–49.

249 *research shows life satisfaction*: Margie E. Lachman, Salom Teshale, and Stefan Agrigoroaei, "Midlife as a Pivotal Period in the Life Course: Balancing Growth and Decline at the Crossroads of Youth and Old Age," *International Journal of Behavioral Development* 39, no. 1 (2014): 20–31, https://doi.org/10.1177/0165025414533223.

250 *"I just generally felt"*: Jancee Dunn, "Julia Louis-Dreyfus Thinks Youth Is Overrated," *The New York Times*, March 30, 2024, https://www.nytimes.com/2024/03/30/well/wiser-than-me-podcast.html.

250 *The Third Act has also been called*: Jonathan Rauch, "America Needs to Radically Rethink What It Means to Be Old," *The Atlantic*, December 10, 2024, https://www.theatlantic.com/magazine/archive/2025/01/james-chappel-golden-years-andrew-j-scott-longevity-imperative/680762/.

250 *Since the turn of the last (twentieth) century*: Maggie Scarf, "The Bonus Years of Adult Life," *Psychology Today*, November 15, 2008, https://www.psychologytoday.com/us/blog/the-remarriage-blueprint/200811/the-bonus-years-of-adult-life.

251 *In one of the MIDUS study questionnaires*: "Subjective Aging: Importance of How Old You Feel," *Midlife in the United States (MIDUS)*, https://midus.wisc.edu/newsletter/A-2%20Subjective%20Aging%20Brochure.pdf.

251 *And studies have found that*: Markus Wettstein et al., "Postponing Old Age: Evidence for Historical Change Toward a Later Perceived Onset of Old Age," *Psychology and Aging* 39, no. 5 (2024): 526–41, https://doi.org/10.1037/pag0000812.

251 Subjective age is an important indicator: Jennifer A. Bellingtier et al., "Daily Experiences of Subjective Age Discordance and Well-Being," *Psychology and Aging* 36, no. 6 (2021): 744–51, https://doi.org/10.1037/pag0000621.

252 *Ultimately, subjective age*: Jennifer A. Bellingtier and Shevaun D. Neupert, "Feeling Young and in Control: Daily Control Beliefs Are Associated with Younger Subjective Ages," *The Journals of Gerontology: Series B* 75, no. 5 (2020): e13–e17, https://doi.org/10.1093/geronb/gbz015.

Notes

252 *Manfred Diehl, emeritus professor of human development*: Roman Kaspar et al., "Differences in Self-Perceptions of Aging Across the Adult Lifespan: The Sample Case of Awareness of Age-Related Gains and Losses," *Psychology and Aging* 38, no. 8 (2023): 824–36, https://doi.org/10.1037/pag0000783.

252 *Diehl*: Gerben J. Westerhof et al., "Longitudinal Effects of Subjective Aging on Health and Longevity: An Updated Meta-Analysis," *Psychology and Aging* 38, no. 3 (2023): 147–66, https://doi.org/10.1037/pag0000737.

252 *and Shevaun Neupert*: Shevaun Neupert and Reyyan Can, "Daily Emotional and Physical Well-Being Predicted by Personal and Other Views of Aging," *Innovation in Aging* 6, Suppl. 1 (2022): 226, https://doi.org/10.1093/geroni/igac059.901.

253 *Of the 69% of Americans with children*: Megan Brenan, "Americans' Preference for Larger Families Highest Since 1971," Gallup, September 25, 2023, https://news.gallup.com/poll/511238/americans-preference-larger-families-highest-1971.aspx.

254 *Children with intellectual or developmental disabilities*: Marsha Mailick Seltzer, "Family Caregiving Across the Full Life Span," in *Mental Retardation in the Year 2000*, ed. Louis Rowitz (Springer, 1992), 85–100.

255 *In fact, there is a growing trend*: Susan L. Brown and I-Fen Lin, "The Graying of Divorce: A Half Century of Change," *The Journals of Gerontology: Series B* 77, no. 9 (2022): 1710–20, https://doi.org/10.1093/geronb/gbac057.

255 *This is increasing with one in ten divorces today*: Renee Stepler, "Led by Baby Boomers, Divorce Rates Climb for America's 50+ Population," Pew Research Center, March 9, 2017, https://www.pewresearch.org/short-reads/2017/03/09/led-by-baby-boomers-divorce-rates-climb-for-americas-50-population/.

256 *"the dessert course of life"*: Lesley Stahl, *Becoming Grandma: The Joys and Science of the New Grandparenting* (Blue Rider Press, 2016).

257 *Sometimes the grandchild lives*: Bert Hayslip, Christine A. Fruhauf, and Joshua Fish, "Should I Do This? Factors Influencing the Decision to Raise Grandchildren Among Custodial Grandparents," *The Gerontologist* 61, no. 5 (2021): 735–45, https://doi.org/10.1093/geront/gnaa202.

257 *For some this is fine, for others*: Catherine Pearson, "The Unspoken Grief of Never Becoming a Grandparent," *The New York Times*, November 11, 2024, https://www.nytimes.com/2024/11/11/well/family/grandparent-grandchild-childfree.html.

258 *Maybe your job for the last two decades*: Beth Almeida and Isabela Salas-Betsch, "Fact Sheet: The State of Women in the Labor Market in 2023," Center for American Progress, February 6, 2023, https://www.americanprogress.org/article/fact-sheet-the-state-of-women-in-the-labor-market-in-2023/.

260 *Fifty-seven percent of American workers*: Lane Gillespie, "Survey: More Than Half of American Workers Feel Behind on Their Retirement Savings," *Bankrate*, September 25, 2024, https://www.bankrate.com/retirement/retirement-savings -survey/?tpt=a.

260 *According to recent data*: Richard Fry and Dana Braga, "The Growth of the Older Workforce," Pew Research Center, December 14, 2023, https://www.pewresearch .org/social-trends/2023/12/14/the-growth-of-the-older-workforce/.

260 *"the fastest-growing age demographic"*: Richard Fry and Dana Braga, "The Growth of the Older Workforce," Pew Research Center, December 14, 2023, https:// www.pewresearch.org/social-trends/2023/12/14/the-growth-of-the-older -workforce/.

261 *Those who saw an image of their future*: Hal E. Hershfield et al., "Increasing Saving Behavior Through Age-Progressed Renderings of the Future Self," *Journal of Marketing Research* 48, no. SPL (2019): S23–S37, https://doi.org/10.1509 /jmkr.48.SPL.S23.

262 *For instance, what does the actual retirement*: Teresa M. Amabile et al., *Retiring: Creating a Life That Works for You* (Taylor and Francis, 2024); and Christine Benz, *How to Retire: 20 Lessons for a Happy, Successful, and Wealthy Retirement* (Harriman House, 2024).

263 *back-and-forth transition*: Yulie Zhan et al., "Bridge Employment and Retirees' Health: A Longitudinal Investigation," *Journal of Occupational Health Psychology* 14, no. 4 (2009): 374–89, https://doi.org/10.1037/a0015285.

264 *There is a famous intervention study*: Linda P. Fried et al., "Experience Corps: A Dual Trial to Promote the Health of Older Adults and Children's Academic Success," *Contemporary Clinical Trials* 36, no. 1 (2013): 1–13, doi: 10.1016/j .cct.2013.05.003.

265 *The intergenerational program*: Michelle Carlson et al., "Impact of the Baltimore Experience Corps Trial on Cortical and Hippocampal Volumes," *Alzheimer's and Dementia* 11, no. 11 (2015): 1340–48, https://doi.org/10.1016 /j.jalz.2014.12.005.

266 *Inflammation and sleep in midlife*: Rachel R. Jin et al., "Sleep Quality Mediates the Relationship Between Systemic Inflammation and Neurocognitive Performance," *Brain, Behavior, and Immunity - Health* 5, no. 30 (2023): 100634, https://pmc.ncbi.nlm.nih.gov/articles/PMC10209676/.

266 *Poor physical fitness in middle*: Nicole L. Spartano et al., "Midlife Exercise Blood Pressure, Heart Rate, and Fitness Relate to Brain Volume 2 Decades Later," *Neurology* 86, no. 14 (2016): 1313–19, https://doi.org/10.1212 /WNL.0000000000002415.

267 *Those most satisfied with their life*: Robert Waldinger and Marc Schulz, *The Good Life: Lessons from the World's Longest Scientific Study of Happiness* (Simon & Schuster, 2023).

267 *Those who had higher reports*: Miharu Nakanishi et al., "Midlife Psychological Well-Being and Its Impact on Cognitive Functioning Later in Life: An Observational Study Using a Female British Birth Cohort," *Journal of Alzheimer's Disease* 72, no. 3 (2019): 835–43, https://doi.org/10.3233/JAD-190590.

267 *A higher BMI and waist size*: Shreeshti Uchai et al., "Body Mass Index, Waist Circumference and Pre-Frailty/Frailty: The Tromsø Study 1994–2016," *BMJ Open* 13, no. 2 (2023): e065707, https://doi.org/10.1136/bmjopen-2022-065707.

267 *Pulmonary function in midlife*: Brian T. Joyce et al., "Pulmonary Function in Midlife as a Predictor of Later-Life Cognition: The Coronary Artery Risk Development in Adults (CARDIA) Study," *The Journals of Gerontology: Series A* 77, no. 12 (2022): 2517–23, https://doi.org/10.1093/gerona/glac026.

267 *Participating in leisure-time physical activity*: Barbara Bendlin et al., "Midlife Predictors of Alzheimer's Disease," *Maturitas* 65, no. 2 (2010): 131–37, https://doi.org/10.1016/j.maturitas.2009.12.014.

267 *Blood pressure in midlife*: Menghui Liu et al., "Association of Mid- to Late-Life Blood Pressure Patterns with Risk of Subsequent Coronary Heart Disease and Death," *Frontiers in Cardiovascular Medicine* 8 (2021): 632514, https://doi.org/10.3389/fcvm.2021.632514.

267 *Midlife hypertension*: Arjun Kumar Ghosh et al., "Midlife Blood Pressure Predicts Future Diastolic Dysfunction Independently of Blood Pressure," *Heart* 102, no. 17 (2016): 1380–87, https://pmc.ncbi.nlm.nih.gov/articles/PMC4998951/; Keenan Walker et al., "Association of Midlife to Late-Life Blood Pressure Patterns with Incident Dementia," *JAMA* 322, no. 6 (2019): 535–45, https://jamanetwork.com/journals/jama/fullarticle/2747672#google_vignette; Leonore J. Launer et al., "The Association Between Midlife Blood Pressure Levels and Late-Life Cognitive Function. The Honolulu-Asia Aging Study," *JAMA* 274, no. 23 (1995): 1846–51, https://pubmed.ncbi.nlm.nih.gov/7500533/; and Karolina Agnieszka Wartolowska and Alastair John Stewart Webb, "Midlife Blood Pressure Is Associated with the Severity of White Matter Hyperintensities: Analysis of the UK Biobank Cohort Study," *European Heart Journal* 42, no. 7 (2021): 750–57, https://doi.org/10.1093/eurheartj/ehaa756.

267 *Being overweight in midlife*: Bendlin et al., "Midlife Predictors of Alzheimer's Disease."

267 *Midlife obesity*: Bendlin et al., "Midlife Predictors of Alzheimer's Disease."

268 *What he has learned*: Ruairi Robertson, "Why People in 'Blue Zones' Live Longer Than the Rest of the World," *Healthline*, December 3, 2024, https://www .healthline.com/nutrition/blue-zones; and Dan Buettner, *Live to 100: Secrets of the Blue Zones* (Netflix, 2023), https://danbuettner.com/.

269 *And we know from research on sarcopenia*: "How to Maintain Muscle Mass as You Age," Henry Ford Health, January 30, 2023, https://www.henryford.com/blog /2023/01/how-to-maintain-muscle-mass-as-you-age; and Rebecca Seguin and Miriam Nelson, "The Benefits of Strength Training for Older Adults," *American Journal of Preventive Medicine* 25, no. 3 Suppl 2 (2003): 141–49, https://doi .org/10.1016/s0749-3797(03)00177-6.

269 *If you sit more than seven to ten hours a day*: Jung Ha Park et al., "Sedentary Lifestyle: Overview of Updated Evidence of Potential Health Risks," *Korean Journal of Family Medicine* 41, no. 6 (2020): 365–73, https://doi.org/10.4082 /kjfm.20.0165.

269 *A study with the MIDUS participants*: Emily Urban-Wojcik et al., "Diversity of Daily Activities Is Associated with Greater Hippocampal Volume," *Cognitive, Affective, & Behavioral Neuroscience* 22 (2022): 75–87, https://doi.org/10.3758 /s13415-021-00942-5.

270 *Denise Park, a professor at the University of Texas*: Ian M. McDonough et al., "The Synapse Project: Engagement in Mentally Challenging Activities Enhances Neural Efficiency," *Restorative Neurology and Neuroscience* 33, no. 6 (2015): 865–82, https://pmc.ncbi.nlm.nih.gov/articles/PMC4927925/.

270 *Volunteer work are other great ways*: Road Scholar, https://www.roadscholar.org/.

270 *Seniors Helping Seniors*: Seniors Helping Seniors, https://seniorshelpingseniors .com/.

271 *AARP*: "Volunteer Opportunities with AARP Foundation," AARP, https://www .aarp.org/aarp-foundation/get-involved/.

271 *Ageism, which is based on stereotypes*: Becca Levy, *Breaking the Age Code: How Your Beliefs About Aging Determine How Long and Well You Live* (William Morrow, 2022).

272 *You might remember*: Becca R. Levy, Martin D. Slade, Suzanne R. Kunkel, and Stanislav V. Kasl, "Longevity Increased by Positive Self-Perceptions of Aging," *Journal of Personality and Social Psychology* 83, no. 2 (2002): 261–70, https:// doi.org/10.1037/0022-3514.83.2.261.

272 *"We need to revise how we think of aging"*: Jenna Goudreau, "Jane Fonda Reveals Her Top 10 Secrets for Aging Gracefully," *Forbes*, September 13, 2011, https:// www.forbes.com/sites/jennagoudreau/2011/09/13/jane-fonda-secrets-for -aging-gracefully/.

Bibliography

AARP. "Experience Corps Volunteer Locations." https://www.aarp.org/experience -corps/locations/.

AARP. "Volunteer Opportunities with AARP Foundation." Accessed July 3, 2025. https://www.aarp.org/aarp-foundation/get-involved/.

"Adverse Childhood Experience Questionnaire for Adults." California Surgeon General's Clinical Advisory Committee. May 5, 2020. Revised July 26, 2022. https:// www.acesaware.org/wp-content/uploads/2022/07/ACE-Questionnaire-for-Adults -Identified-English-rev.7.26.22.pdf.

Agarwal, Sumit, John C. Driscoll, Xavier Gabaix, and David Laibson. "The Age of Reason: Financial Decisions Over the Lifecycle." National Bureau of Economic Research. June 2007. https://doi.org/10.3386/w13191.

Agrigoroaei, Stefan, Angela Lee-Attardo, and Margie E. Lachman. "Stress and Subjective Age: Those with Greater Financial Stress Look Older." *Research on Aging* 39, no. 10 (2017): 1075–99. https://doi.org/10.1177/0164027516658502.

Aldwin, Carolyn M., Karen J. Sutton, and Margie E. Lachman. "The Development of Coping Resources in Adulthood." *Journal of Personality* 64, no. 4 (1996): 837–71. https://doi.org/10.1111/j.1467-6494.1996.tb00946.x.

Allen, Jennifer T. "Effective Menopause Education Methods: Addressing the Needs of Current Medical Trainees." *Menopause* 31, no. 2 (2024): 89-90. https://doi .org/10.1097/GME.0000000000002308.

Almeida, Beth, and Isabela Salas-Betsch. "Fact Sheet: The State of Women in the Labor Market in 2023." The Center for American Progress, February 6, 2023. https://www .americanprogress.org/article/fact-sheet-the-state-of-women-in-the-labor-market-in-2023/.

Almeida, David M., Susan T. Charles, Jacqueline Mogle, et al. "Charting Adult Development Through (Historically Changing) Daily Stress Processes." *American Psychologist* 75, no. 4 (2020): 511–24. https://doi.org/10.1037/amp0000597.

Alter, Adam L., and Hal E. Hershfield. n.d. "People Search for Meaning When They Approach a New Decade in Chronological Age." openICPSR. https://doi.org /10.3886/E18882V2.

Amabile, Teresa, Lotte Bailyn, Marcy Crary, Douglas Hall, and Kathy Kram. *Retiring: Creating a Life That Works for You*. Taylor and Francis, 2024.

Angelou, Maya. *I Know Why the Caged Bird Sings*. Random House, 2002.

Antonucci, Toni C., Hiroko Akiyama, and Keiko Takahashi. "Attachment and Close Relationships Across the Life Span." *Attachment and Human Development* 6, no. 4 (2004): 353–70. https://doi.org/10.1080/1461673042000303136.

Antonucci, Toni C., Kristine J. Ajrouch, and Kira S. Birditt. "The Convoy Model: Explaining Social Relations from a Multidisciplinary Perspective." *The Gerontologist* 54, no. 1 (2014): 82–92. https://doi.org/10.1093/geront/gnt118.

Baltes, Paul B. "Theoretical Propositions of Life-Span Developmental Psychology: On the Dynamics Between Growth and Decline." *Developmental Psychology* 23, no. 5 (1987): 611–26. https://doi.org/10.1037/0012-1649.23.5.611.

Baltes, Paul B., and Margret M. Baltes. "Psychological Perspectives on Successful Aging: The Model of Selective Optimization with Compensation." In *Successful Aging: Perspectives from the Behavioral Sciences*, edited by Paul Baltes and Margret Baltes. Cambridge University Press, 1990. https://doi.org/DOI:10.1017/CBO97805 11665684.003.

Baltes, Paul B., Hayne W. Reese, and Lewis P. Lipsitt. "Life-Span Developmental Psychology." *Annual Review of Psychology* 31 (1980): 65–110. https://doi.org /10.1146/annurev.ps.31.020180.000433.

Baltes, Paul B., Ursula M. Staudinger, and Ulman Lindenberger. "Lifespan Psychology: Theory and Application to Intellectual Functioning." *Annual Review of Psychology* 50 (1999): 471–507. https://doi.org/10.1146/annurev.psych.50.1.471.

Bandura, Albert. "The Psychology of Chance Encounters and Life Paths." *American Psychologist* 37, no. 7 (1982): 747–55. https://doi.org/10.1037/0003-066X .37.7.747.

Barry, Kristin, Kate D. Houter, and Karen Guggenheim. "More Than a Program: A Culture of Women's Wellbeing at Work." Gallup, December 4, 2024. https://www .gallup.com/workplace/653843/program-culture-women-wellbeing-work.aspx.

Bellingtier, Jennifer A., and Shevaun D. Neupert. "Feeling Young and in Control: Daily Control Beliefs Are Associated with Younger Subjective Ages." *The Journals of Gerontology: Series B* 75, no. 5 (2020): e13–17. https://doi.org/10.1093/geronb/gbz015.

Bellingtier, Jennifer A., Fiona S. Rupprecht, Shevaun D. Neupert, and Frieder R. Lang. "Daily Experiences of Subjective Age Discordance and Well-Being." *Psychology and Aging* 36, no. 6 (2021): 744–51. https://doi.org/10.1037/pag0000621.

Bendlin, B. B., C. M. Carlsson, C. E. Gleason, et al. "Midlife Predictors of Alzheimer's Disease." *Maturitas* 65, no. 2 (2010): 131–37. https://doi.org/10.1016/j.maturitas.2009.12.014.

Benz, Christine. *How to Retire: 20 Lessons for a Happy, Successful, and Wealthy Retirement.* Harriman House, 2024.

Berkman, Lisa F., and S. Leonard Syme. "Social Networks, Host Resistance, and Mortality: A Nine-Year Follow-Up Study of Alameda County Residents." *American Journal of Epidemiology* 109, no. 2 (1979): 186–204. https://doi.org/10.1093/oxfordjournals.aje.a112674.

"Big 5 Personality Traits." n.d. *Psychology Today.* https://www.psychologytoday.com/us/basics/big-5-personality-traits.

Bisson, Alycia N., Victoria Sorrentino, and Margie E. Lachman. "Walking and Daily Affect Among Sedentary Older Adults Measured Using the StepMATE App: Pilot Randomized Controlled Trial." *JMIR mHealth and uHealth* 9, no. 12 (2021): e27208. https://doi.org/10.2196/27208.

Blanchflower, David G., Alex Bryson, and Xiaowei Xu. 2024. "The Declining Mental Health of the Young and the Global Disappearance of the Hump Shape in Age in Unhappiness." National Bureau of Economic Research. April 2024. https://doi.org/10.3386/w32337.

Blanchflower, David G., and Carol L. Graham. "The Mid-Life Dip in Well-Being: A Critique." *Social Indicators Research* 161 (2022): 287–344. https://doi.org/10.1007/s11205-021-02773-w.

Blanchflower, David G., Carol Graham, and Alan Piper. "Happiness and Age—Resolving the Debate." *National Institute Economic Review* 263 (2023): 76–93. https://doi.org/10.1017/nie.2023.1.

Blanchflower, David G., and Andrew J. Oswald. "Is Well-Being U-Shaped over the Life Cycle?" *Social Science & Medicine* 66, no. 8 (2008): 1733–49. https://doi.org/10.1016/j.socscimed.2008.01.030.

Blieszner, Rosemary, Aaron M. Ogletree, and Rebecca G. Adams. "Friendship in Later Life: A Research Agenda." *Innovation in Aging* 3, no. 1 (2019): igz005. https://doi.org/10.1093/geroni/igz005.

Boyce, Christopher J., Alex M. Wood, and Nattavudh Powdthavee. "Is Personality Fixed? Personality Changes as Much as 'Variable' Economic Factors and More Strongly Predicts Changes to Life Satisfaction." *Social Indicators Research* 111 (2013): 287–305. https://doi.org/10.1007/s11205-012-0006-z.

Bibliography

Brenan, Megan. "Americans' Preference for Larger Families Highest Since 1971." Gallup, September 25, 2023. https://news.gallup.com/poll/511238/americans -preference-larger-families-highest-1971.aspx.

Brim, Gilbert. *Ambition: How We Manage Success and Failure Throughout Our Lives.* Basic Books, 1992.

Brim, Orville Gilbert, Carol D. Ryff, and Ronald C. Kessler. *How Healthy Are We? A National Study of Well-Being at Midlife.* University of Chicago Press, 2004.

Brooks, Arthur C. *From Strength to Strength: Finding Success, Happiness and Deep Purpose in the Second Half of Life.* Portfolio, 2022.

Brown, Stephanie L., Randolph M. Nesse, Amiram D. Vinokur, and Dylan M. Smith. "Providing Social Support May Be More Beneficial Than Receiving It." *Psychological Science* 14, no. 4 (2003): 320–27. https://doi.org/10.1111/1467-9280.14461.

Brown, Susan L., and I-Fen Lin. "The Graying of Divorce: A Half Century of Change." *The Journals of Gerontology: Series B* 77, no. 9 (2022): 1710–20. https://doi.org /10.1093/geronb/gbac057.

Bruni, Frank. *The Beauty of Dusk: On Vision Lost and Found.* Avid Reader Press, 2022.

Burack, Orah R., and Margie E. Lachman. "The Effects of List-Making on Recall in Young and Elderly Adults." *The Journals of Gerontology: Series B* 51B, no. 4 (1996): 226–33. https://doi.org/10.1093/geronb/51B.4.P226.

Butler, Robert N. "The Life Review: An Interpretation of Reminiscence in the Aged." *Psychiatry* 26, no. 1 (1963): 65–76. https://doi.org/10.1080/00332747.1963 .11023339.

Caplan, Bryan. *Selfish Reasons to Have More Kids: Why Being a Great Parent Is Less Work and More Fun Than You Think.* Basic Books, 2011.

Carlson, Michelle C., Julie H. Kuo, Yi-Fang Chuang, et al. "Impact of the Baltimore Experience Corps Trial on Cortical and Hippocampal Volumes." *Alzheimer's and Dementia* 11, no. 11, (2015): 1340–48. https://doi.org/10.1016/j.jalz.2014.12.005.

Carrozza, Giana, and Andrew Thurston. "Is Optimism the Secret to a Long Life?" *The Brink.* Boston University. November 30, 2022. https://www.bu.edu/articles/2022 /is-optimism-the-secret-to-a-long-life/.

Carson, Shelley H. "Creativity and the Aging Brain." *Psychology Today*, March 9, 2009. https://www.psychologytoday.com/us/blog/life-as-art/200903/creativity-and -the-aging-brain.

Carstensen, Laura L. "The Influence of a Sense of Time on Human Development." *Science* 312, no. 5782 (2006): 1913–15. https://doi.org/10.1126/science.1127488.

Carstensen, Laura L. "Socioemotional Selectivity Theory: The Role of Perceived Endings in Human Motivation." *The Gerontologist* 61, no. 8 (2021): 1188–96. https://doi.org/10.1093/geront/gnab116.

Carstensen, Laura L., Derek M. Isaacowitz, and Susan T. Charles. "Taking Time Seriously: A Theory of Socioemotional Selectivity." *American Psychologist* 54, no. 3 (1999): 165–81. https://doi.org/10.1037/0003-066X.54.3.165.

Carstensen, Laura L., L. Chu, T. J. Matteson, and C. M. Growney. "What's Time Got to Do with It? Appreciation of Time Influences Social Goals and Emotional Well-Being." *Psychology and Aging* 39, no. 8 (2024): 833–53. https://doi.org/10.1037/pag0000856.

Case, Anne, and Angus Deaton. *Deaths of Despair and the Future of Capitalism.* Princeton University Press, 2020.

Cerino, Eric S., Susan T. Charles, Jacqueline Mogle, et al. "Perceived Control Across the Adult Lifespan: Longitudinal Changes in Global Control and Daily Stressor Control." *Developmental Psychology* 60, no. 1 (2024): 45–58. https://doi.org/10.1037/dev0001618.

Chan, Dennis, Meredith Shafto, Rogier Kievit, et al. "Lifestyle Activities in Mid-Life Contribute to Cognitive Reserve in Late-Life, Independent of Education, Occupation, and Late-Life Activities." *Neurobiology of Aging* 70 (October 2018): 180–83. https://doi.org/10.1016/j.neurobiolaging.2018.06.012.

Charles, Susan T., Jacqueline Mogle, Hye Won Chai, and David M. Almeida. "The Mixed Benefits of a Stressor-Free Life." *Emotion* 21, no. 5 (2021): 962–71. https://doi.org/10.1037/emo0000958.

Chen, Edith, Phoebe H. Lam, Eric D. Finegood, Nicholas A. Turiano, Daniel K. Mroczek, and Gregory E. Miller. "The Balance of Giving Versus Receiving Social Support and All-Cause Mortality in a US National Sample." *Proceedings of the National Academy of Sciences* 118, no. 24 (2021): e2024770118. https://doi.org/10.1073/pnas.2024770118.

Christakis, Nicholas, and James Fowler. *Connected: The Surprising Power of Our Social Networks and How They Shape Our Lives.* Little, Brown Spark, 2009.

Cicero, M. T. *De Senectute De Amicitia De Divinatione.* Translated by William Armistead Falconer. Harvard University Press, 1923.

Cohen, Patricia. "In Midlife, Boomers Are Happy—and Suicidal." *The New York Times,* June 12, 2010. https://www.nytimes.com/2010/06/13/weekinreview/13cohen.html.

Cohen, Sheldon. "Keynote Presentation at the Eight International Congress of Behavioral Medicine: Mainz, Germany, August 25–28, 2004." *International Journal of Behavioral Medicine* 12 (2005): 123–31. https://doi.org/10.1207/s15327558 ijbm1203_1.

Collingwood, Jane. "What's Your Time Perspective?" *PsychCentral*, May 17, 2016. https://psychcentral.com/lib/whats-your-time-perspective#1.

Coy, Peter. "The Midlife Crisis Is Very Real and Nothing to Be Laughed At." *The New York Times*, September 21, 2022. https://www.nytimes.com/2022/09/21/opinion /midlife-crisis.html.

Crimmins, Eileen, Samuel Preston, and Barney Cohen, eds., *International Differences in Mortality at Older Ages: Dimensions and Sources*. National Academies Press, 2010. https://doi.org/10.17226/12945.

Crimmins, Eileen M. "Lifespan and Healthspan: Past, Present, and Promise." *The Gerontologist* 55, no. 6 (2015): 901–11. https://doi.org/10.1093/geront/gnv130.

Damian, Rodica Ioana, Marion Spengler, Andreea Sutu, and Brent W. Roberts. "Sixteen Going on Sixty-Six: A Longitudinal Study of Personality Stability and Change Across 50 Years." *Journal of Personality and Social Psychology* 117, no. 3 (2019): 674–95. https://doi.org/10.1037/pspp0000210.

Denham, Joshua, and Maha Sellami. "Exercise Training Increases Telomerase Reverse Transcriptase Gene Expression and Telomerase Activity: A Systematic Review and Meta-Analysis." *Ageing Research Reviews* 70 (2021): 101411. https://doi.org/10 .1016/j.arr.2021.101411.

"Do Social Ties Affect Our Health? Exploring the Biology of Relationships." *News in Health*. National Institutes of Health, February 2017. https://newsinhealth.nih.gov /2017/02/do-social-ties-affect-our-health.

Ebner, Natalie C., Alexandra M. Freund, and Paul B. Baltes. "Developmental Changes in Personal Goal Orientation from Young to Late Adulthood: From Striving for Gains to Maintenance and Prevention of Losses." *Psychology and Aging* 21, no. 4 (2006): 664–78. https://doi.org/10.1037/0882-7974.21.4.664.

Edwards, Autumn. "Changing Rhythms of American Family Life." *Journal of Family Communication* 9, no. 2 (2009): 126–28. https://doi.org/10.1080/152674309 02773337.

Elder, Glen H. *Children of the Great Depression, 25th Anniversary Edition*. Routledge, 1999.

Epel, Elissa S., Elizabeth H. Blackburn, Jue Lin, et al. "Accelerated Telomere Shortening in Response to Life Stress." *Proceedings of the National Academy of Sciences* 101, no. 49 (2004): 17312–15. doi:10.1073/pnas.0407162101.

Erikson, Erik. *Childhood and Society.* 2nd edition. Norton, 1963.

Fadjukoff, Päivi, Lea Pulkkinen, and Katja Kokko. "Identity Formation in Adulthood: A Longitudinal Study from Age 27 to 50." *Identity* 16, no. 1 (2016): 8–23. https://doi.org/10.1080/15283488.2015.1121820.

Faubion, Stephanie S., Felicity Enders, Mary S. Hedges, et al. "Impact of Menopause Symptoms on Women in the Workplace." *Mayo Clinic Proceedings* 98, no. 6 (2023): 833–45. https://doi.org/10.1016/j.mayocp.2023.02.025.

FBI. "FBI Highlights Growing Number of Reported Elder Fraud Cases Ahead of World Elder Abuse Awareness Day." June 14, 2024. https://www.fbi.gov/news/press-releases/fbi-highlights-growing-number-of-reported-elder-fraud-cases-ahead-of-world-elder-abuse-awareness-day.

Fingerman, K. L., L. M. Pitzer, W. Chan, K. Birditt, M. M. Franks, and S. Zarit. "Who Gets What and Why? Help Middle-Aged Adults Provide to Parents and Grown Children." *The Journals of Gerontology: Series B* 66B, no. 1 (2011): 87–98. https://doi.org/10.1093/geronb/gbq009.

"Fluid and Crystallized Intelligence." n.d. Science Direct. https://www.sciencedirect.com/topics/neuroscience/fluid-and-crystallized-intelligence.

Folkman, Susan. "Stress: Appraisal and Coping." In *Encyclopedia of Behavioral Medicine*, edited by Marc D. Gellman and J. Rick Turner, 1913–15. Springer, 2013. https://doi.org/10.1007/978-1-4419-1005-9_215.

Folkman, Susan, and Richard S. Lazarus. "An Analysis of Coping in a Middle-Aged Community Sample." *Journal of Health and Social Behavior* 21, no. 3 (1980): 219–39. https://doi.org/10.2307/2136617.

Franceschi, Claudio, and Judith Campisi. "Chronic Inflammation (Inflammaging) and Its Potential Contribution to Age-Associated Diseases." *The Journals of Gerontology: Series A* 6 (2014): Supplement 1, S4–S9. https://doi.org/10.1093/gerona/glu057.

Frankl, Victor. *Man's Search for Meaning.* Pocket Books, 1973.

Freilich, C. D., K. E. Markon, S. W. Cole, and R. F. Krueger. "Loneliness, Epigenetic Age Acceleration, and Chronic Health Conditions." *Psychology and Aging* 39, no. 4 (2024): 337–49. https://doi.org/10.1037/pag0000822.

Freund, Alexandra M., and Natalie C. Ebner. "The Aging Self: Shifting from Promoting Gains to Balancing Losses." In *The Adaptive Self: Personal Continuity and Intentional Self-Development*, edited by W. Greve, K. Rothermund, and D. Wentura, 185–202. Hogrefe and Huber Publishers, 2005.

Freund, Alexandra M., and Johannes O. Ritter. "Midlife Crisis: A Debate." *Gerontology* 55, no. 5 (2009): 582–91. https://doi.org/10.1159/000227322.

Fried, Linda P., Michelle C. Carlson, Sylvia McGill, et al. "Experience Corps: A Dual Trial to Promote the Health of Older Adults and Children's Academic Success." *Contemporary Clinical Trials* 36, no 1 (2013): 1–13. https://doi.org/10.1016 /j.cct.2013.05.003.

Friedman, Danielle. "The Constant Work to Keep a Family Connected Has a Name." *The New York Times*, May 8, 2024. https://www.nytimes.com/2024/05/08/well /family/kinkeeping-families.html.

Friedman, Howard S., and Leslie R. Martin. *The Longevity Project: Surprising Discoveries for Health and Long Life from the Landmark Eight-Decade Study*. Hudson Street Press/Penguin, 2011.

Fry, Richard, and Dana Braga. "The Growth of the Older Workforce." Pew Research Center, December 14, 2023. https://www.pewresearch.org/social-trends/2023/12 /14/the-growth-of-the-older-workforce/.

Fuchs, Eberhard, and Gabriele Flügge. "Adult Neuroplasticity: More Than 40 Years of Research." *Neural Plasticity* 1 (2014): 541870. https://doi.org/https://doi.org /10.1155/2014/541870.

Fulop, T., A. Larbi, G. Pawelec, et al. "Immunology of Aging: The Birth of Inflammaging." *Clinical Reviews in Allergy and Immunology* 64 (2023): 109–22. https://doi.org/10.1007/s12016-021-08899-6.

Galambos, Nancy L., Harvey J. Krahn, Matthew D. Johnson, and Margie E. Lachman. "The U Shape of Happiness Across the Life Course: Expanding the Discussion." *Perspectives on Psychological Science* 15, no. 4 (2020): 898–912. https://doi.org /10.1177/1745691620902428.

Garber, Megan. "The Article That 'Struck Terror in the Hearts of Single Women.'" *The Atlantic*, June 2, 2016. https://www.theatlantic.com/entertainment/archive /2016/06/more-likely-to-be-killed-by-a-terrorist-than-to-get-married/485171/.

Ghosh, Arjun Kumar, Alun David Hughes, Darrel Francis, et al. "Midlife Blood Pressure Predicts Future Diastolic Dysfunction Independently of Blood Pressure." *Heart* 102, no. 17 (2016): 1380–87. https://doi.org/10.1136/heartjnl-2015 -308836.

Gilbert, Daniel. *Stumbling on Happiness*. Vintage Canada, 2009.

Gillespie, Lane. "Survey: More Than Half of American Workers Feel Behind on Their Retirement Savings." Bankrate, September 25, 2024. https://www.bankrate.com /retirement/retirement-savings-survey.

Gilovich, Thomas, and Victoria Husted Medvec. "The Experience of Regret: What, When, and Why." *Psychological Review* 102, no. 2 (1995): 379–95. https://doi.org /10.1037/0033-295X.102.2.379.

Gilovich, Thomas, Victoria Husted Medvec, and Daniel Kahneman. "Varieties of Regret: A Debate and Partial Resolution." *Psychological Review* 105, no. 3 (1998): 602–5. https://doi.org/10.1037/0033-295X.105.3.602.

Gollwitzer, Peter M. "Implementation Intentions: Strong Effects of Simple Plans." *The American Psychologist* 54, no. 7 (1999): 493–503. https://doi.org/10.1037/0003-066X.54.7.493.

Gollwitzer, Peter M., and Paschal Sheeran. "Implementation Intentions and Goal Achievement: A Meta-analysis of Effects and Processes." *Advances in Experimental Social Psychology* 38 (2006): 69–119. https://doi.org/10.1016/S0065-2601(06)38002-1.

Goode, Erica. "New Study Finds Middle Age Is Prime of Life." *The New York Times*, February 16, 1999. https://www.nytimes.com/1999/02/16/health/new-study-finds-middle-age-is-prime-of-life.html.

Goudreau, Jenna. "Jane Fonda Reveals Her Top 10 Secrets for Aging Gracefully." *Forbes*, September 13, 2011. https://www.forbes.com/sites/jennagoudreau/2011/09/13/jane-fonda-secrets-for-aging-gracefully/.

Gough, Margaret, and Kanya Godde. "A Multifaceted Analysis of Social Stressors and Chronic Inflammation." *SSM - Population Health* 6 (2018): 136–40. https://doi.org/10.1016/j.ssmph.2018.09.005.

Gould, R. L. *Transformations: Growth and Change in Adult Life*. Simon & Schuster, 1978.

Goulet, L. R., and Paul B. Baltes. *Life-Span Developmental Psychology*. Academic Press, 1970.

Grady, Cheryl L., and Fergus Craik. "Changes in Memory Processing with Age." *Current Opinion in Neurobiology* 10, no. 2 (2000): 224–31. https://doi.org/10.1016/S0959-4388(00)00073-8.

Graham, Eileen K., Emorie D. Beck, Kathryn Jackson, et al. "Do We Become More Lonely with Age? A Coordinated Data Analysis of Nine Longitudinal Studies." *Psychological Science* 35, no. 6 (2024): 579–96. https://doi.org/10.1177/09567976241242037.

Grilli, Matthew D., Katelyn S. McVeigh, Ziad M. Hakim, et al. "Is This Phishing? Older Age Is Associated with Greater Difficulty Discriminating Between Safe and Malicious Emails." *The Journals of Gerontology: Series B* 76, no. 9 (2021): 1711–15. https://doi.org/10.1093/geronb/gbaa228.

Guevara, Jasmin E., and Kyle Murdock. "High Social Strain and Physical Health: Examining the Roles of Anxious Arousal, Body Mass Index, and Inflammation." *Psychoneuroendocrinology* 106 (2019): 155–160. https://doi.org/10.1016/j.psyneuen.2019.04.005

Gupta, Sujata. "The 'Midlife Crisis' Is Too Simple a Story, Scientists Say." *Science News*, November 4, 2024. https://www.sciencenews.org/article/midlife-crisis-mental -health-happiness.

Haidt, Jonathan. *The Anxious Generation: How the Great Rewiring of Childhood Is Causing an Epidemic of Mental Illness*. Random House, 2024.

Hakulinen, Christian, Laura Pulkki-Råback, Marianna Virtanen, Markus Jokela, Mika Kivimäki, and Marko Elovainio. "Social Isolation and Loneliness as Risk Factors for Myocardial Infarction, Stroke and Mortality: UK Biobank Cohort Study of 479,054 Men and Women." *Heart* 104, no. 18 (2018): 1536–42. https://doi.org/10.1136 /heartjnl-2017-312663.

Hall, G. Stanley. "Senescence: The Last Half of Life. 1922." *American Journal of Public Health* 96, no.7 (2006): 1160-62. https://doi.org/10.2105/ajph.96.7.1160.

Hamilton, Audrey. "Self-Esteem Declines Sharply Among Older Adults While Middle-Aged Are Most Confident." American Psychological Association. 2010. https://www .apa.org/news/press/releases/2010/04/self-esteem.

Hämmig, Oliver. "Health and Well-Being at Work: The Key Role of Supervisor Support." *SSM - Population Health* 3 (2017): 393–402. https://doi.org/10.1016 /j.ssmph.2017.04.002.

Harvard Medical School. "What Is Cognitive Reserve?" Harvard Health Publishing. February 1, 2024. https://www.health.harvard.edu/mind-and-mood/what-is -cognitive-reserve.

Haupt, Angela. "8 Signs You're in Perimenopause." *Time*. September 17, 2024. https://time.com/7019600/perimenopause-signs-symptoms/.

Hayslip, Bert, Christine A. Fruhauf, and Joshua Fish. "Should I Do This? Factors Influencing the Decision to Raise Grandchildren Among Custodial Grandparents." *The Gerontologist* 61, no. 5 (2021): 735–45. https://doi.org/10.1093/geront/gnaa202.

Hayward, George M. "New 2021 Data Visualization Shows Parent Mortality: 44.2% Had Lost at Least One Parent." US Census Bureau, March 21, 2023. https://www .census.gov/library/stories/2023/03/losing-our-parents.html.

"The Health and Retirement Study." n.d. University of Michigan. https://hrs.isr .umich.edu/about.

Heckhausen, Jutta, Carsten Wrosch, and William Fleeson. "Developmental Regulation Before and After a Developmental Deadline: The Sample Case of 'Biological Clock' for Childbearing." *Psychology and Aging* 16, no. 3 (2001): 400–413. https://doi.org /10.1037/0882-7974.16.3.400.

Bibliography

Heckhausen, Jutta, Carsten Wrosch, and Richard Schulz. "Agency and Motivation in Adulthood and Old Age." *Annual Review of Psychology* 70 (January 2019): 191–217. https://doi.org/10.1146/annurev-psych-010418-103043.

Hershfield, Hal E., Daniel G. Goldstein, William F. Sharpe, et al. "Increasing Saving Behavior Through Age-Progressed Renderings of the Future Self." *Journal of Marketing Research* 48 (2011): S23–37. https://doi.org/10.1509/jmkr.48.SPL.S23.

Hittner, Emily F., Jacquelyn E. Stephens, Nicholas A. Turiano, Denis Gerstorf, Margie E. Lachman, and Claudia M. Haase. "Positive Affect Is Associated with Less Memory Decline: Evidence from a 9-Year Longitudinal Study." *Psychological Science* 31, no. 11 (2020): 1386–95. https://doi.org/10.1177/0956797620953883.

Holt-Lunstad, Julianne, Timothy B. Smith, Mark Baker, Tyler Harris, and David Stephenson. "Loneliness and Social Isolation as Risk Factors for Mortality: A Meta-Analytic Review." *Perspectives on Psychological Science* 10, no. 2 (2015): 227–37. https://doi.org/10.1177/1745691614568352.

Holt-Lunstad, Julianne, Timothy B. Smith, and J. Bradley Layton. "Social Relationships and Mortality Risk: A Meta-Analytic Review." *PLoS Medicine* 7, no. 7 (2010): e1000316. https://doi.org/10.1371/journal.pmed.1000316.

Holt-Lunstad, Julianne, Bert N. Uchino, Timothy W. Smith, and Angela Hicks. "On the Importance of Relationship Quality: The Impact of Ambivalence in Friendships on Cardiovascular Functioning." *Annals of Behavioral Medicine* 33, no. 3 (2007): 278–90. https://doi.org/10.1007/BF02879910.

Hong, Joanna H., Margie E. Lachman, Susan T. Charles, et al. "The Positive Influence of Sense of Control on Physical, Behavioral, and Psychosocial Health in Older Adults: An Outcome-Wide Approach." *Preventive Medicine* 149 (August 2021): 106612. https://doi.org/10.1016/j.ypmed.2021.106612.

Hoppmann, Christiane A., and Theresa Pauly. "A Lifespan Psychological Perspective on Solitude." *International Journal of Behavioral Development* 46, no. 6 (2022): 473–80. https://doi.org/10.1177/01650254221130279.

Horowitz, Juliana M. "More Than Half of Americans in Their 40s Are 'Sandwiched' Between an Aging Parent and Their Own Children." Pew Research Center, April 8, 2022. https://www.pewresearch.org/short-reads/2022/04/08/more-than-half -of-americans-in-their-40s-are-sandwiched-between-an-aging-parent-and-their-own -children/.

"How to Maintain Muscle Mass as You Age." Henry Ford Health, January 30, 2023. https://www.henryford.com/blog/2023/01/how-to-maintain-muscle-mass-as -you-age."

Inagaki, Tristen K., and Edward Orehek. "On the Benefits of Giving Social Support: When, Why, and How Support Providers Gain by Caring for Others." *Current Directions in Psychological Science* 26, no. 2 (2017): 109–13. https://doi.org/10.1177/0963721416686212.

Infurna, Frank J. "Utilizing Principles of Life-Span Developmental Psychology to Study the Complexities of Resilience Across the Adult Life Span." *The Gerontologist* 61, no. 6 (2021): 807–18. https://doi.org/10.1093/geront/gnab086.

Infurna, Frank J., Nutifafa E .Y. Dey, Tita Gonzalez Avilés, Kevin J. Grimm, Margie E. Lachman, and Denis Gerstorf. "Loneliness in Midlife: Historical Increases and Elevated Levels in the United States Compared with Europe." *American Psychologist* 80, no. 5 (2024): 744–56. https://doi.org/10.1037/amp0001322.

Infurna, Frank J., Denis Gerstorf, and Margie E. Lachman. "Midlife in the 2020s: Opportunities and Challenges." *American Psychologist* 75, no. 4 (2020): 470–85. https://doi.org/10.1037/amp0000591.

Infurna, Frank J., Omar E. Staben, Margie E. Lachman, and Denis Gerstorf. "Historical Change in Midlife Health, Well-Being, and Despair: Cross-Cultural and Socioeconomic Comparisons." *American Psychologist* 76, no. 6 (2021): 870–87. https://doi.org/10.1037/amp0000817.

Isaacowitz, Derek M. "What Do We Know About Aging and Emotion Regulation?" *Perspectives on Psychological Science* 17, no. 6 (2022): 1541–55. https://doi.org/10.1177/17456916211059819.

Jin, Rachel R., Carman Nga-Man Cheung, Clive H. Y. Wong, et al. "Sleep Quality Mediates the Relationship Between Systemic Inflammation and Neurocognitive Performance." *Brain, Behavior, and Immunity - Health* 30 (July 2023): 100634. https://doi.org/10.1016/j.bbih.2023.100634.

Jones, Dusti R., and Jennifer E. Graham-Engeland. "Positive Affect and Peripheral Inflammatory Markers Among Adults: A Narrative Review." *Psychoneuroendocrinology* 123 (January 2021): 104892. https://doi.org/10.1016/j.psyneuen.2020.104892.

Joyce, Brian T., Xuefen Chen, Kristine Yaffe, et al. "Pulmonary Function in Midlife as a Predictor of Later-Life Cognition: The Coronary Artery Risk Development in Adults (CARDIA) Study." *The Journals of Gerontology: Series A* 77, no. 12 (2022): 2517–23. https://doi.org/10.1093/gerona/glac026.

Kaltenberg, Mary, Adam B. Jaffe, and Margie E. Lachman. "Invention and the Life Course: Age Differences in Patenting." *Research Policy* 52, no. 1 (2023): 104629. https://doi.org/10.1016/j.respol.2022.104629.

Bibliography

Kamis, Christina. "The Long-Term Impact of Parental Mental Health on Children's Distress Trajectories in Adulthood." *Society and Mental Health* 11, no. 1 (2021): 54–68. https://doi.org/10.1177/2156869320912520.

Kaspar, Roman, Oliver K. Schilling, Manfred Diehl, et al. "Differences in Self-Perceptions of Aging Across the Adult Lifespan: The Sample Case of Awareness of Age-Related Gains and Losses." *Psychology and Aging* 38, no. 8 (2023): 824–36. https://doi.org/10.1037/pag0000783.

Kaufman, Scott B. "Would You Be Happier with a Different Personality?" *The Atlantic*, August 5, 2016. https://www.theatlantic.com/health/archive/2016/08/would-you-be-happier-with-a-different-personality/494720/.

Kiecolt-Glaser, Janice K., Timothy J. Loving, Jeffrey R. Stowell, et al. "Hostile Marital Interactions, Proinflammatory Cytokine Production, and Wound Healing." *Archives of General Psychiatry* 62, no. 12 (2005): 1377–84. https://doi.org/10.1001/archpsyc.62.12.1377.

Kotb, Hoda, host. *Making Space with Hoda Kotb.* Season 1, "Mitch Albom: 'What We Choose to Carry Is Actually What Ends Up Defining Us.'" *Today*, October 11, 2021. Podcast, 38 min. https://www.today.com/podcasts/hoda-kotb-making-space-podcast-mitch-albom-t233118.

Lachman, Margie E. "Development in Midlife." *Annual Review of Psychology* 55 (2004): 305–31. https://doi.org/10.1146/annurev.psych.55.090902.141521.

Lachman, Margie E. "Perceived Control over Aging-Related Declines: Adaptive Beliefs and Behaviors." *Current Directions in Psychological Science* 15, no. 6 (2006): 282–86. https://doi.org/10.1111/j.1467-8721.2006.00453.x.

Lachman, Margie E., Corinne Lewkowicz, Ari Marcus, and Ying Peng. "Images of Midlife Development Among Young, Middle-Aged, and Older Adults." *Journal of Adult Development* 1 (1994): 201–11. https://doi.org/10.1007/BF02277581.

Lachman, Margie E., and Kimberly M. P. Firth. "The Adaptive Value of Feeling in Control During Midlife." In *How Healthy Are We? A National Study of Well-Being at Midlife*, edited by O. G. Brim, C. D. Ryff, and R. C. Kessler. University of Chicago Press, 2004.

Lachman, Margie E., Shevaun D. Neupert, and Stefan Agrigoroaei. "The Relevance of Control Beliefs for Health and Aging." In *Handbook of the Psychology of Aging*, edited by K. Warner Shaie and Sherry Willis. Elsevier, 2011. https://doi.org/10.1016/B978-0-12-380882-0.00011-5.

Lachman, Margie E., Lewis Lipsitz, James Lubben, Carmen Castaneda-Sceppa, and Alan M. Jette. "When Adults Don't Exercise: Behavioral Strategies to Increase Physical Activity in Sedentary Middle-Aged and Older Adults." *Innovation in Aging* 2, no. 1 (2018): igy007. https://doi.org/10.1093/geroni/igy007.

Lachman, Margie E., and Shevaun D. Neupert. "Chapter 13. Psychosocial Factors and Health: Toward a Psychosocial Prescription for Healthy Aging." In *APA Handbook of Adult Development and Aging*, edited by Margie E. Lachman and Avron S. Spiro. American Psychological Association, 2026. Forthcoming.

Lachman, Margie E., and Kylie A. Schiloski. "The Psychosocial Anti-Inflammatories: Sense of Control, Purpose in Life, and Social Support in Relation to Inflammation, Functional Health and Chronic Conditions in Adulthood." *Journal of Psychosomatic Research* 187 (December 2024): 11957. https://doi.org/10.1016/j.jpsychores.2024.111957.

Lachman, Margie E., Salom Teshale, and Stefan Agrigoroaei. "Midlife as a Pivotal Period in the Life Course: Balancing Growth and Decline at the Crossroads of Youth and Old Age." *International Journal of Behavioral Development* 39, no. 1 (2015): 20–31. https://doi.org/10.1177/0165025414533223.

Lamb, Susan. "Neuroplasticity: A Century-Old Idea Championed by Adolf Meyer." *CMAJ: Canadian Medical Association Journal* 191, no. 49 (2019): E1359–61. https://doi.org/10.1503/cmaj.191099.

Lang, Frieder R., and Laura L. Carstensen. "Time Counts: Future Time Perspective, Goals, and Social Relationships." *Psychology and Aging* 17, no. 1 (2002): 125–39. https://doi.org/10.1037/0882-7974.17.1.125.

Langer, Ellen J. *The Mindful Body: Thinking Our Way to Chronic Health*. Ballantine Books, 2023.

Langer, Ellen J. *Mindfulness*. Balance/Hachette, 2014.

Launer, Lenore J., Kamal Masaki, Helen Petrovitch, et al. "The Association Between Midlife Blood Pressure Levels and Late-Life Cognitive Function: The Honolulu-Asia Aging Study." *Journal of the American Medical Association* 274, no. 23 (1995): 1846–51. https://doi.org/10.1001/jama.1995.03530230032026.

Leahy, Robert L. "Is Regret Ever Useful?" *Psychology Today*, June 7, 2022. https://www.psychologytoday.com/us/blog/anxiety-files/202206/is-regret-ever-useful.

Lee, Lewina O., Carolyn M. Aldwin, Laura. D. Kubzansky, Daniel K. Mroczek, and Avron Spiro III. "The Long Arm of Childhood Experiences on Longevity: Testing Midlife Vulnerability and Resilience Pathways." *Psychology and Aging* 34, no. 7 (2019): 884–99. https://doi.org/10.1037/pag0000394.

Lee, Lewina O., Peter James, Emily S. Zevon, et al. "Optimism Is Associated with Exceptional Longevity in 2 Epidemiologic Cohorts of Men and Women." *Proceedings of the National Academy of Sciences* 116, no. 27 (2019): 18357–62. https://doi.org/10.1073/pnas.1900712116.

Lei, Lianlian, Amanda N. Leggett, and Donovan T. Maust. "A National Profile of Sandwich Generation Caregivers Providing Care to Both Older Adults and Children." *Journal of the American Geriatrics Society* 71, no. 3 (2023): 799–809. https://doi.org/10.1111/jgs.18138.

"Let's Talk Menopause." n.d. Let's Talk Menopause! https://www.letstalkmenopause.org.

Levinson, Daniel J. "A Conception of Adult Development." *American Psychologist* 41, no. 1 (1986): 3–13. https://doi.org/10.1037/0003-066X.41.1.3

Levinson, Daniel J. *The Seasons of a Man's Life: The Groundbreaking 10-Year Study That Was the Basis for Passages!* Ballantine Books, 1986.

Levinson, Daniel J. *The Seasons of a Woman's Life: A Fascinating Exploration of the Events, Thoughts, and Life Experiences That All Women Share.* Ballantine Books, 2011.

Levy, Becca. *Breaking the Age Code: How Your Beliefs About Aging Determine How Long and Well You Live.* William Morrow, 2022.

Levy, Becca R., Martin D. Slade, Suzanne R. Kunkel, and Stanislav V. Kasl. "Longevity Increased by Positive Self-Perceptions of Aging." *Journal of Personality and Social Psychology* 83, no. 2 (2002): 261–70. https://doi.org/10.1037/0022-3514.83.2.261.

Li, Tianyuan. "In Control of Future Time: Sense of Control Weakens the Negative Association Between Age and Future Time Perspective." *Current Psychology* 41 (2022): 5127–33. https://doi.org/10.1007/s12144-020-01019-1.

Liao, Hsiao-Wen, and Laura L. Carstensen. "Future Time Perspective: Time Horizons and Beyond. *GeroPsych: The Journal of Gerontopsychology and Geriatric Psychiatry*, 31, no. 3 (2018): 163–67. https://doi.org/10.1024/1662-9647/a000194.

Lincoln, Karen D., Donald A. Lloyd, and Ann W. Nguyen. "Social Relationships and Salivary Telomere Length Among Middle-Aged and Older African American and White Adults." *The Journals of Gerontology: Series B* 74, no. 6 (2019): 1053–61. https://doi.org/10.1093/geronb/gbx049.

Liu, Menghui, Shaozhao Zhang, Xiaohong Chen, et al. "Association of Mid- to Late-Life Blood Pressure Patterns with Risk of Subsequent Coronary Heart Disease and Death." *Frontiers in Cardiovascular Medicine* 8 (2021): 632514. https://doi.org/10.3389/fcvm.2021.632514.

Livingston, Gretchen. "They're Waiting Longer, but U.S. Women Today More Likely to Have Children Than a Decade Ago." Pew Research Center, January 18, 2018. https://www.pewresearch.org/social-trends/2018/01/18/theyre-waiting-longer-but -u-s-women-today-more-likely-to-have-children-than-a-decade-ago/.

Marcia, James E. "Identity and Psychosocial Development in Adulthood." *Identity* 2, no. 1 (2002): 7–28. https://doi.org/10.1207/s1532706xid0201_02.

Martinez, Gladys M., and Kimberly Daniels. "Fertility of Men and Women Aged 15–49 in the United States: National Survey of Family Growth, 2015–2019." *National Health Statistics Reports*, January 10, 2023. https://www.cdc.gov/nchs/data/nhsr/nhsr179.pdf.

McAdams, Dan P., Ed de St. Aubin. "A Theory of Generativity and Its Assessment Through Self-Report, Behavioral Acts, and Narrative Themes in Autobiography." *Journal of Personality and Social Psychology* 62, no. 6 (1992): 1003–15. https://doi.org /10.1037/0022-3514.62.6.1003.

McAdams, Dan P., and Jen Guo. "Narrating the Generative Life." *Psychological Science* 26, no. 4 (2015): 475–83. https://doi.org/10.1177/0956797614568318.

McAdams, Dan P., Ed de St. Aubin, and R. L. Logan. "Generativity Among Young, Midlife, and Older Adults." *Psychology and Aging* 8, no. 2 (1993): 221–30. https:// doi.org/10.1037/0882-7974.8.2.221.

McDonough, Ian M., Sara Haber, Gérard N. Bischof, and Denise C. Park. "The Synapse Project: Engagement in Mentally Challenging Activities Enhances Neural Efficiency." *Restorative Neurology and Neuroscience* 33, no. 6 (2015): 865–82. https:// pmc.ncbi.nlm.nih.gov/articles/PMC4927925/.

Medaris, Anna. "Gen Z Adults and Younger Millennials Are 'Completely Overwhelmed' by Stress." American Psychological Association, November 1, 2023. https://www.apa.org/topics/stress/generation-z-millennials-young-adults-worries.

"Menopause Basics." n.d. U.S. Department of Health and Human Services Office on Women's Health. https://www.womenshealth.gov/menopause/menopause-basics.

"Menopause in the Workplace." n.d. Carrot. https://content.get-carrot.com/rs/418 -PQJ-171/images/Carrot%20-%20Menopause%20in%20the%20workplace.pdf.

"MIDUS – Midlife in the United States: A National Longitudinal Study of Health and Well-Being." n.d. https://midus.wisc.edu.

Mikulic, Matej. "Anti-Aging: Statistics and Facts." Statista, November 14, 2024. https://www.statista.com/topics/10423/anti-aging/#topicOverview.

Milkman, Katy. *How to Change: The Science of Getting from Where You Are to Where You Want to Be.* Portfolio/Penguin, 2021.

Bibliography

"Millennials in Crisis: Survey Finds 81% Can't Afford a Midlife Crisis." Thriving Center of Psychology, April 16, 2024. https://thrivingcenterofpsych.com/blog/millennial -midlife-crisis/.

Miller, Gregory E., Edith Chen, and Karen J. Parker. "Psychological Stress in Childhood and Susceptibility to the Chronic Diseases of Aging: Moving Toward a Model of Behavioral and Biological Mechanisms." *Psychological Bulletin* 137, no. 6 (2011): 959–97. https://doi.org/10.1037/a0024768.

Miller, Gregory E., Margie E. Lachman, Edith Chen, Tara Gruenewald, Arun Karlamangla, and T. E. Seeman. "Pathways to Resilience: Maternal Nurturance as a Buffer Against the Effects of Childhood Poverty on Metabolic Syndrome at Midlife." *Psychological Science* 22, no. 12 (2011): 1591–1599. https://doi.org/10.1177/09 56797611419170.

Moersdorf, Lea, Moritz M. Daum, and Alexandra M. Freund. "For Whom Is the Path the Goal? A Lifespan Perspective on the Development of Goal Focus." *Collabra: Psychology* 8, no. 1 (2022): 31603. https://doi.org/10.1525/collabra.31603.

Morse, Anne. "Fertility Rates: Declined for Younger Women, Increased for Older Women." United States Census Bureau, April 6, 2022. https://www.census.gov /library/stories/2022/04/fertility-rates-declined-for-younger-women-increased-for -older-women.html.

Nakanishi, Miharu, Syudo Yamasaki, Atsushi Nishida, and Marcus Richards. "Midlife Psychological Well-Being and Its Impact on Cognitive Functioning Later in Life: An Observational Study Using a Female British Birth Cohort." *Journal of Alzheimer's Disease* 72, no. 3 (2019): 835–43. https://doi.org/10.3233 /JAD-190590.

Nash, Ogden. *The Private Dining Room and Other New Verses*. Little Brown, 1953.

"National Survey of Families and Households." May 25, 2018. https://www.ssc.wisc .edu/nsfh/.

Nelson, Niccole A., and Cindy S. Bergeman. "Development of Generative Concern Across Mid- to Later Life." *The Gerontologist* 61, no. 3 (2021): 430–38. https://doi .org/10.1093/geront/gnaa115.

Neugarten, Bernice L., ed., *Middle Age and Aging*. University of Chicago Press, 1968.

Neupert, Shevaun D., Margie E. Lachman, and Stacey B. Whitbourne. "Exercise Self-Efficacy and Control Beliefs: Effects on Exercise Behavior After an Exercise Intervention for Older Adults." *Journal of Aging and Physical Activity* 17, no. 1 (2009): 1–16. https://doi.org/10.1123/japa.17.1.1.

Neupert, Shevaun, and Reyyan Can. "Daily Emotional and Physical Well-Being Predicted by Personal and Other Views of Aging." *Innovation in Aging* 6, Suppl. 1 (2022): 226. https://doi.org/10.1093/geroni/igac059.901.

Newman, Catherine. *Sandwich*. HarperCollins, 2024.

"Nicholson McBride Resilience Questionnaire." n.d. BlockSurvey. https://blocksurvey .io/templates/resilience-scales/nicholson-mcbride-resilience-questionnaire.

Nielsen, Lisbeth, Melissa Riddle, Jonathan W. King, et al. "The NIH Science of Behavior Change Program: Transforming the Science Through a Focus on Mechanisms of Change." *Behaviour Research and Therapy* 101 (February 2018): 3–11. https://doi .org/10.1016/j.brat.2017.07.002.

O'Connor, Eimear, Teresa McCormack, and Aidan Feeney. "Do Children Who Experience Regret Make Better Decisions? A Developmental Study of the Behavioral Consequences of Regret." *Child Development* 85, no. 5 (2014): 1995–2010. https:// doi.org/10.1111/cdev.12253.

Olshansky, S. Jay. "From Lifespan to Healthspan." *JAMA* 320, no. 13 (2018): 1323–24. https://doi.org/10.1001/jama.2018.12621.

Orenstein, Gabriel A., and Lindsay Lewis. "Erikson's Stages of Psychosocial Development." StatPearls, November 7, 2022. https://www.ncbi.nlm.nih.gov/books /NBK556096/.

Ouellette, Nadine, and Thomas Perls. "Race and Ethnicity Dynamics in Survival to 100 Years in the United States." *Journal of Internal Medicine* 297, no. 1 (2024): 2–21. https://doi.org/10.1111/joim.20031.

"Oxidative Stress." Cleveland Clinic, February 29, 2024. https://my.clevelandclinic .org/health/articles/oxidative-stress.

Pahwa, Roma, Amandeep Goyal, and Ishwarlal Jialal. "Chronic Inflammation." StatPearls, August 7, 2023. https://www.ncbi.nlm.nih.gov/books/NBK493173.

Park, Jung Ha, Ji Hyun Moon, Hyeon Ju Kim, Mi Hee Kong, and Yun Hwan Oh. "Sedentary Lifestyle: Overview of Updated Evidence of Potential Health Risks." *Korean Journal of Family Medicine* 41, no. 6 (2020): 365–73. https://doi.org /10.4082/kjfm.20.0165.

Pearson, Catherine. "The Unspoken Grief of Never Becoming a Grandparent." *The New York Times*, November 11, 2024. https://www.nytimes.com/2024/11/11/well /family/grandparent-grandchild-childfree.html.

Pequeño, Sara. "US Plummeted in World Happiness Ranking Because of Young People Like Me. I'll Tell You Why." *USA Today*, March 25, 2024. https://www.usatoday.com /story/opinion/columnists/2024/03/25/world-happiness-report-us-millennials-gen -z-unhappy/73056887007/.

Pfund, Gabrielle N., Emily D. Bastarache, Emily C. Willroth, et al. "Lifespan Trajectories of Negative and Positive Affect: A Coordinated Analysis of 14 Longitudinal Studies." *European Journal of Personality* 39, no. 5 (2024): 747–69. https://doi.org /10.1177/08902070241293967.

Phillips, Melissa L. "The Mind at Midlife." *Monitor on Psychology* 42, no. 4 (2011): 38. https://www.apa.org/monitor/2011/04/mind-midlife.

Pink, Daniel H. "Summary of Our Mini-Survey on Regret." n.d. DanPink. https:// www.danpink.com/summary-of-our-mini-survey-on-regret/.

Pitkin, Walter B. *Life Begins at Forty*. Whittlesey House, 1932.

Poppert Cordts, Katrina M., Anna C. Wilson, and Andrew R. Riley. "More Than Mental Health: Parent Physical Health and Early Childhood Behavior Problems." *Journal of Developmental and Behavioral Pediatrics* 41, no. 4 (2020): 265–71. https:// doi.org/10.1097/DBP.0000000000000755.

Prenda, Kimberly M., and Margie E. Lachman. "Planning for the Future: A Life Management Strategy for Increasing Control and Life Satisfaction in Adulthood." *Psychology and Aging* 16, no. 2 (2001): 206. https://midus.wisc.edu/findings/pdfs /226.pdf.

"Quick Facts." n.d. United States Census Bureau. https://www.census.gov/quickfacts/.

Rauch, Jonathan. "The Real Roots of Midlife Crisis." *The Atlantic*, December 2014. https://www.theatlantic.com/magazine/archive/2014/12/the-real-roots-of-midlife -crisis/382235/.

Rauch, Jonathan. "America Needs to Radically Rethink What It Means to Be Old." *The Atlantic*, December 10, 2024. https://www.theatlantic.com/magazine/archive/2025 /01/james-chappel-golden-years-andrew-j-scott-longevity-imperative/680762/.

Reill, Amanda. "A Simple Way to Make Better Decisions." *Harvard Business Review*, December 5, 2023. https://hbr.org/2023/12/a-simple-way-to-make-better-decisions.

Reuter-Lorenz, Patricia A., and Denise C. Park. "Human Neuroscience and the Aging Mind: A New Look at Old Problems." *The Journals of Gerontology: Series B* 65B, no. 4 (2010): 405–15. https://doi.org/10.1093/geronb/gbq035.

Road Scholar. https://www.roadscholar.org.

Robbins, Alexandra, and Abby Wilner. *Quarterlife Crisis: The Unique Challenges of Life in Your Twenties*. Penguin, 2001.

Roberts, Brent W., Jing Luo, Daniel A. Briley, Philip I. Chow, Rong Su, and Patrick L. Hill. "A Systematic Review of Personality Trait Change Through Intervention." *Psychological Bulletin* 143, no. 2 (2017): 117–41. https://doi.org/10.1037/bul 0000088.

Robertson, Ruairi. "Why People in 'Blue Zones' Live Longer Than the Rest of the World." Healthline, December 3, 2024. https://www.healthline.com/nutrition /blue-zones.

Robinson, Stephanie A., Alycia N. Bisson, Matthew L. Hughes, Jane Ebert, and Margie E. Lachman. "Time for Change: Using Implementation Intentions to Promote Physical Activity in a Randomised Pilot Trial." *Psychology & Health* 34, no. 2 (2019): 232–54. https://doi.org/10.1080/08870446.2018.1539487.

Rook, Karen S. "Social Networks in Later Life: Weighing Positive and Negative Effects on Health and Well-Being." *Current Directions in Psychological Science* 24, no. 1 (2015): 45–51. https://doi.org/10.1177/0963721414551364.

Rupprecht, Fiona S., and Frieder R. Lang. "Personal Ideals of Aging and Longevity: The Role of Subjective Discordances." *Psychology and Aging* 35, no. 3 (2020): 385–96. https://doi.org/10.1037/pag0000455.

Russo, Francine. "The Best New Year's Resolution Might Be to Just Let Go of an Unfulfilled Life Goal." *Scientific American*, December 28, 2022. https://www .scientificamerican.com/article/the-best-new-years-resolution-might-be-to-just-let-go -of-an-unfulfilled-life-goal/.

Rutter, Michael. "Psychosocial Resilience and Protective Mechanisms." *American Journal of Orthopsychiatry* 57, no. 3 (1987): 316–31. https://doi.org/10.1111 /j.1939-0025.1987.tb03541.x.

Ryff, Carol D., Burton H. Singer, and Gayle Dienberg Love. "Positive Health: Connecting Well-Being with Biology." *Philosophical Transactions of the Royal Society B: Biological Sciences* 359 (2004): 1383–94. https://doi.org/10.1098/rstb.2004.1521.

Ryff, Carol, Elliot Friedman, Thomas Fuller-Rowell, et al. "Varieties of Resilience in MIDUS." *Social and Personality Psychology Compass* 6, no. 11 (2012): 792–806. https://doi.org/10.1111/j.1751-9004.2012.00462.x.

Salthouse, Timothy. "Consequences of Age-Related Cognitive Declines." *Annual Review of Psychology* 63 (2012): 201–26. https://doi.org/10.1146/annurev-psych -120710-100328.

Salthouse, Timothy. "What and When of Cognitive Aging." *Current Directions in Psychological Science* 13, no. 4 (2004): 140–44. https://doi.org/10.1111/j.0963 -7214.2004.00293.x.

Samanez-Larkin, Gregory R., and Brian Knutson. "Decision Making in the Ageing Brain: Changes in Affective and Motivational Circuits." *Nature Reviews Neuroscience* 16 (2015): 278–89. https://doi.org/10.1038/nrn3917.

Sanderson, Maureen, Charles P. Mouton, Mekeila Cook, Jianguo Liu, William J. Blot, and Margaret K. Hargreaves. "Adverse Childhood Experiences and Chronic Disease Risk in the Southern Community Cohort Study." *Journal of Health Care for the Poor and Underserved* 32, no. 3 (2021): 1384–1402. https://doi.org/10.1353 /HPU.2021.0139.

Sauer-Zavala, Shannon. "Can You Change Your Personality? Psychology Research Says Yes, by Tweaking What You Think and Do." The Conversation, September 25, 2024. https://theconversation.com/can-you-change-your-personality-psychology-research -says-yes-by-tweaking-what-you-think-and-do-237190.

Scarf, Maggie. "The Bonus Years of Adult Life." *Psychology Today*, November 15, 2008. https://www.psychologytoday.com/us/blog/the-remarriage-blueprint/200811 /the-bonus-years-of-adult-life.

Schaie, K. Warner, Sherry L. Willis, and Grace I. L. Caskie. "The Seattle Longitudinal Study: Relationship Between Personality and Cognition." *Aging, Neuropsychology, and Cognition* 11, no. 2–3 (2004): 304–24. https://doi.org/10.1080/13825580490 511134.

Schiloski, Kylie A., and Margie E. Lachman. "The Relationship Between 10-Year Changes in Cognitive Control Beliefs and Cognitive Performance in Middle and Later Adulthood." *The Journals of Gerontology Series B* 79, no. 11 (2024): gbae155. https:// doi.org/10.1093/geronb/gbae155.

Schneider, Carolin V., Kai Markus Schneider, Alexander Teumer, et al. "Association of Telomere Length with Risk of Disease and Mortality." *JAMA Internal Medicine* 182, no. 3 (2022): 291–300. https://doi.org/10.1001/jamainternmed.2021.7804.

Schutte, Nicola, and John M. Malouff. "The Association Between Optimism and Telomere Length: A Meta-Analysis." *Journal of Positive Psychology* 17, no. 1 (2022): 82–88. https://doi.org/10.1080/17439760.2020.1832249.

Schüttengruber, Victoria, Franciska Krings, and Alexandra M. Freund. "Positive and Negative Spillover Effects: Managing Multiple Goals in Middle Adulthood." In *Withstanding Vulnerability Throughout Adult Life: Dynamics of Stressors, Resources, and Reserves*, edited by Dario Spini and Eric Widmer. Springer Nature, 2023.

Seelye, Katharine Q. "Gail Sheehy, Journalist, Author and Social Observer, Dies at 83." *The New York Times*, August 25, 2020. https://www.nytimes.com/2020/08/25 /books/gail-sheehy-dead.html.

Seguin, Rebecca, and Miriam E. Nelson. "The Benefits of Strength Training for Older Adults." *American Journal of Preventive Medicine* 25, no. 3, Suppl 2 (2003): 141–49. https://doi.org/10.1016/s0749-3797(03)00177-6.

Seltzer, Marsha Mailick. "Family Caregiving Across the Full Life Span." In *Mental Retardation in the Year 2000*, edited by L. Rowitz. Springer, 1992.

Seniors Helping Seniors. https://seniorshelpingseniors.com.

Setiya, Kieran. "1. A Brief History of the Midlife Crisis." In *Midlife: A Philosophical Guide*, 6–28. Princeton University Press, 2018.

Shammas, Masood A. "Telomeres, Lifestyle, Cancer, and Aging." *Current Opinion in Clinical Nutrition and Metabolic Care* 14, no. 1 (2011): 28–34. https://doi.org /10.1097/MCO.0b013e32834121b1.

Sheehy, Gail. *Passages: Predictable Crises of Adult Life*. Dutton, 1976.

Sohn, Emily. "How Decision-Making Changes with Age." Simons Foundation, March 2, 2022. https://www.simonsfoundation.org/2022/03/02/how-decision -making-changes-with-age/.

Song, Jieun, Marsha R. Mailick, and Jan S. Greenberg. "Health of Parents of Individuals with Developmental Disorders or Mental Health Problems: Impacts of Stigma." *Social Science and Medicine* 217 (November 2018): 152–58. https://doi.org /10.1016/J.SOCSCIMED.2018.09.044.

Song, Seonghyeok, Eunsang Lee, and Hyunjoong Kim. "Does Exercise Affect Telomere Length? A Systematic Review and Meta-Analysis of Randomized Controlled Trials." *Medicina* 58, no. 2 (2022): 242. https://doi.org/10.3390/medicina58 020242.

Spartano, Nicole L., Jayandra J. Himali, Alexa S. Beiser, et al. "Midlife Exercise Blood Pressure, Heart Rate, and Fitness Relate to Brain Volume 2 Decades Later." *Neurology* 86, no. 14 (2016): 1313–19. https://doi.org/10.1212/WNL.0000000000002415.

Spiro, Avron, and Robert J. Waldinger. "Chapter 4. Studying Adult Development and Aging the Long Way: 100 Years of US Longitudinal Studies of Aging." In *APA Handbook of Adult Development and Aging*, edited by Margie E. Lachman and Avron Spiro. American Psychological Association, 2026. Forthcoming.

Stagnitti, Marie, and Doris Lefkowitz. "Trends in Hormone Replacement Therapy Drugs Utilization and Expenditures for Adult Women in the U.S. Civilian Noninstitutionalized Population, 2001–2008." Agency for Healthcare Research and Quality, November 2011. https://meps.ahrq.gov/data_files/publications/st347 /stat347.shtml.

Stahl, Lesley. *Becoming Grandma: The Joys and Science of the New Grandparenting.* Blue Rider Press, 2016.

Stefanacci, Richard G. "Changes in the Body with Aging." *Merck Manual*, April 2024. https://www.merckmanuals.com/home/older-people-s-health-issues/the-aging-body /changes-in-the-body-with-aging

Stepler, Renee. "Led by Baby Boomers, Divorce Rates Climb for America's 50+ Population." Pew Research Center, March 9, 2017. https://www.pewresearch.org /short-reads/2017/03/09/led-by-baby-boomers-divorce-rates-climb-for-americas-50 -population/.

Stewart, Abigail J., and Elizabeth A. Vandewater. "'If I Had It to Do Over Again . . .': Midlife Review, Midcourse Corrections, and Women's Well-Being in Midlife." *Journal of Personality and Social Psychology* 76, no. 2 (1999): 270–83. https://doi.org /10.1037/0022-3514.76.2.270.

Stieger, Mirjam, Mathias Allemand, and Margie E. Lachman. "Effects of a Digital Self-Control Intervention to Increase Physical Activity in Middle-Aged Adults." *Journal of Health Psychology* 28, no. 10 (2023): 984–96. https://doi.org/10.1177 /13591053231166756.

Stieger, Mirjam, Christoph Flückiger, and Mathias Allemand. "One Year Later: Longer-Term Maintenance Effects of a Digital Intervention to Change Personality Traits." *Journal of Personality* 92, no. 5 (2024): 1424–37. https://doi.org/10.1111 /jopy.12898.

Stieger, Mirjam, Christoph Flückiger, Dominik Rüegger, et al. "Changing Personality Traits with the Help of a Digital Personality Change Intervention." *PNAS* 118, no. 8 (2021): e2017548118. https://www.pnas.org/doi/full/10.1073/pnas.2017548118.

Stieger, Mirjam, Yujun Liu, Eileen K. Graham, Jenna DeFrancisco, and Margie E. Lachman. "Personality Change Profiles and Changes in Cognition Among Middle-Aged and Older Adults." *Journal of Research in Personality* 95 (2021): 104157. https://doi.org/10.1016/j.jrp.2021.104157.

Stieger, Mirjam, Stephanie A. Robinson, Alycia N. Bisson, and Margie E. Lachman. "The Relationship of Personality and Behavior Change in a Physical Activity Intervention: The Role of Conscientiousness and Healthy Neuroticism." *Personality and Individual Differences* 166 (2020): 110224. https://doi.org/10.1016 /j.paid.2020.110224.

Strough, JoNell, Corinna E. Löckenhoff, and Thomas M. Hess. "The Present, Past, and Future of Research on Aging and Decision Making." In *Aging and Decision Making*, 1–14. Elsevier, 2015. https://doi.org/10.1016/B978-0-12-417148-0.00001-7.

Sturgeon, John A., and Alex J. Zautra. "Resilience: A New Paradigm for Adaptation to Chronic Pain." *Current Pain and Headache Reports* 14 (2010): 105–12. https://doi.org/10.1007/s11916-010-0095-9.

Surachman, Agus, Elissa Hamlat, and Elissa Epel. "Chapter 10. Stress and Biological Aging." In *APA Handbook of Adult Development and Aging*, edited by Margie E. Lachman and Avron Spiro. American Psychological Association, 2026. Forthcoming.

Swan: Study of Women's Health Across the Nation. n.d. https://www.swanstudy.org.

Tedeschi, Richard G., and Lawrence G. Calhoun. "The Posttraumatic Growth Inventory: Measuring the Positive Legacy of Trauma." *Journal of Traumatic Stress* 9, no. 3 (1996): 455–71. https://doi.org/10.1002/jts.2490090305.

Teshale, Salom M., and Margie E. Lachman. "Managing Daily Happiness: The Relationship Between Selection, Optimization, and Compensation Strategies and Well-Being in Adulthood." *Psychology and Aging* 31, no. 7 (2016): 687–92. https://doi.org/10.1037/pag0000132.

"The U-Bend of Life: Why, Beyond Middle Age, People Get Happier as They Get Older." *The Economist*. December 16, 2010. https://www.economist.com/node/17722567.

Uchai, Shreeshti, Lene Frost Andersen, Laila Arnesdatter Hopstock, and Anette Hjartåker. "Body Mass Index, Waist Circumference and Pre-Frailty/Frailty: The Tromsø Study 1994–2016." *BMJ Open* 13, no. 2 (2023): e065707. https://doi.org/10.1136/bmjopen-2022-065707.

Uchino, Bert N., Ryan Trettevik, Robert G. Kent de Grey, Sierra Cronan, Jasara Hogan, and Brian R. W. Baucom. "Social Support, Social Integration, and Inflammatory Cytokines: A Meta-Analysis." *Health Psychology* 37, no. 5 (2018): 462–71. https://doi.org/10.1037/hea0000594.

Urban-Wojcik, Emily J., Soomi Lee, Daniel W. Grupe, et al. "Diversity of Daily Activities Is Associated with Greater Hippocampal Volume." *Cognitive, Affective, and Behavioral Neuroscience* 22 (2021): 75–87. https://doi.org/10.3758/s13415-021-00942-5/Published.

USAFacts. "Is the American Labor Force Getting Older?" February 8, 2024. https://usafacts.org/articles/is-the-american-labor-force-getting-older/.

U.S. Census Bureau. "Figure MS-2: Median Age at First Marriage: 1890 to Present." n.d. https://www.census.gov/content/dam/Census/library/visualizations/time-series/demo/families-and-households/ms-2.pdf.

U.S. Department of Health and Human Services. *Our Epidemic of Loneliness and Isolation: The U.S. Surgeon General's Advisory on the Healing Effects of Social Connection and Community.* 2023. https://www.hhs.gov/sites/default/files/surgeon-general-social-connection-advisory.pdf.

U.S. Department of Health and Human Services. *Parents Under Pressure: The U.S. Surgeon General's Advisory on the Mental Health and Well-Being of Parents.* 2024. https://www.hhs.gov/sites/default/files/parents-under-pressure.pdf

Waldinger, Robert, and Marc Schulz. *The Good Life: Lessons from the World's Longest Scientific Study of Happiness.* Simon and Schuster, 2023.

Walen, Heather R., and Margie E. Lachman. "Social Support and Strain from Partner, Family, and Friends: Costs and Benefits for Men and Women in Adulthood." *Journal of Social and Personal Relationships* 17, no. 1 (2000): 5–30. https://doi.org/10.1177/0265407500171.

Walker, Keenan A., A. Richey Sharrett, Aozhou Wu, et al. "Association of Midlife to Late-Life Blood Pressure Patterns with Incident Dementia." *JAMA* 322, no. 6 (2019): 535–45. https://doi.org/10.1001/jama.2019.10575.

Wang, Jun, Chen Chen, Jinhui Zhou, et al. "Healthy Lifestyle in Late-Life, Longevity Genes, and Life Expectancy Among Older Adults: A 20-Year, Population-Based, Prospective Cohort Study." *The Lancet Healthy Longevity* 4, no. 10 (2023): e535–43. https://doi.org/10.1016/S2666-7568(23)00140-X.

Wartolowska, Karolina A., and Alastair J. Webb. "Midlife Blood Pressure Is Associated with the Severity of White Matter Hyperintensities: Analysis of the UK Biobank Cohort Study." *European Heart Journal* 42, no. 7 (2021): 750–57. https://doi.org/10.1093/eurheartj/ehaa756.

Weiss, Alexander, James E. King, Miho Inoue-Murayama, Tetsuro Matsuzawa, and Andrew J. Oswald. "Evidence for a Midlife Crisis in Great Apes Consistent with the U-Shape in Human Well-Being." *Proceedings of the National Academy of Sciences* 109, no. 49 (2012): 19949–52. https://doi.org/10.1073/pnas.1212592109.

Weissman, Myrna M., Priya Wickramaratne, Marc J. Gameroff, et al. "Offspring of Depressed Parents: 30 Years Later." *American Journal of Psychiatry* 173, no. 10 (2016): 1024–32. https://doi.org/10.1176/appi.ajp.2016.15101327.

Westerhof, Gerben J., and Ernst T. Bohlmeijer. "Celebrating Fifty Years of Research and Applications in Reminiscence and Life Review: State of the Art and New Directions." *Journal of Aging Studies* 29 (April 2014): 107–14. https://doi.org/10.1016/J.JAGING.2014.02.003.

Westerhof, Gerben J., Abigail M. Nehrkorn-Bailey, Han-Yun Tseng, et al. "Longitudinal Effects of Subjective Aging on Health and Longevity: An Updated Meta-Analysis." *Psychology and Aging* 38, no. 3 (2023): 147–66. https://doi.org /10.1037/pag0000737.

Wethington, Elaine. "Expecting Stress: Americans and the 'Midlife Crisis.'" *Motivation and Emotion* 24 (2000): 85–103. https://doi.org/10.1023/A:1005611230993.

Wethington, Elaine. "Life Stories: Integrating Quantitative and Qualitative Approaches." *Motivation and Emotion* 24 (2000): 63–66. https://doi.org/10.1023 /A:1005680730084.

Wethington, Elaine, Ronald C. Kessler, and Joy E. Pixley. "Turning Points in Adulthood." In *How Healthy Are We? A National Study of Well-Being at Midlife*, edited by O. G. Brim, C. D. Ryff, and R. C. Kessler. University of Chicago Press, 2004.

Wettstein, Markus, Rinseo Park, Anna Kornadt, Susanne Wurm, Nilan Ram, and Denis Gerstorf. "Postponing Old Age: Evidence for Historical Change Toward a Later Perceived Onset of Old Age." *Psychology and Aging* 39, no. 5 (2024): 526–41. https://doi.org/10.1037/pag0000812.

Whitbourne, Susan Krauss, Joel R. Sneed, and Karyn M. Skultety. "Identity Processes in Adulthood: Theoretical and Methodological Challenges." *Identity* 2, no. 1 (2002): 29–45. https://doi.org/10.1207/S1532706XID0201_03.

Widiger, Thomas A., and Joshua R. Oltmanns. "Neuroticism Is a Fundamental Domain of Personality with Enormous Public Health Implications." *World Psychiatry* 16, no. 2 (2017): 144–45. https://doi.org/10.1002/wps.20411.

"Women in the Labor Force." U.S. Bureau of Labor Statistics. n.d. https://www.bls .gov/cps/demographics/women-labor-force.htm.

Wong, Ruth G. "Working Moms Today Spend as Much Time on Childcare as Stay-at-Home Moms 40 Years Ago." *Joyful Parenting SF*, September 7, 2023. https:// joyfulparentingsf.com/p/working-moms-today-spend-as-much.

Wrosch, Carsten, Isabelle Bauer, and Michael F. Scheier. "Regret and Quality of Life Across the Adult Life Span: The Influence of Disengagement and Available Future Goals." *Psychology and Aging* 20, no. 4 (2005): 657–70. https://doi.org/10.1037 /0882-7974.20.4.657.

Wrosch, Carsten, and Jutta Heckhausen. "Perceived Control of Life Regrets: Good for Young and Bad for Old Adults." *Psychology and Aging* 17, no. 2 (2002): 340–50. https://doi.org/10.1037/0882-7974.17.2.340.

Zautra, Alex J., Anne Arewasikporn, and Mary C. Davis. "Resilience: Promoting Well-Being Through Recovery, Sustainability, and Growth." *Research in Human Development* 7, no. 3 (2010): 221–38. https://doi.org/10.1080/15427609.2010.504431.

Zhan, Yujie, Mo Wang, Songqi Liu, and Kenneth S. Shultz. "Bridge Employment and Retirees' Health: A Longitudinal Investigation." *Journal of Occupational Health Psychology* 14, no. 4 (2009): 374–89. https://doi.org/10.1037/a0015285.

Zimbardo, Philip, and John Boyd. *The Time Paradox: The New Psychology of Time That Will Change Your Life.* Simon & Schuster, 2008.

Zwir, Igor, Javier Arnedo, Coral Del-Val, et al. "Uncovering the Complex Genetics of Human Character." *Molecular Psychiatry* 25, no. 10 (2020): 2295–2312. https://doi.org/10.1038/s41380-018-0263-6.

Index

AARP, 265, 271

action regrets, 143

acute inflammation, 121, 123

adaptive attribution, 99–101

adolescence, 15, 42, 59, 179

adult children
    caring for parent with cancer, 161–163
    caring for their children and parents, 163–164
    losing their parents during midlife, 167–168
    protecting their older parents from scams, 166–167
    returning home to visit or live, 254
    sharing responsibilities of helping parents with siblings, 165–166
    shifting roles/relationship with, 253–255

adverse childhood experiences (ACEs), 203–206

age
    at beginning and end of midlife, 9–10
    fluid intelligence declining with, 80
    at menopause, 117
    of menopause, average, 117
    for parenthood, median, 151
    at retirement, 259–260
    subjective, 251–252

age-graded influences, 20

ageism, 44, 45, 143, 271, 272

aging
    as an ever-evolving process, 248
    creativity and, 88–90
    gains and losses experienced through. *See* gains and losses
    impact of mindset about, 43–45
    inventions and, 91–92
    in Japan, 44
    memory and, 84–85, 86–88
    minimizing decline during, 19
    personality changes and identifying faulty narratives about, 67–68
    physical changes during, 114–117
    prescription for healthy, 131
    stereotypes about, 271
    stereotypes and misconceptions about, 271–272
    three common viewpoints about, 101–102
    viewpoints on, 101–102

agreeableness (personality trait), 57, 62
    being too high in, 63
    benefit of, 62–63
    changing with age, 59–60
    cognitive abilities and decrease in, 63–64
    reasons for wanting to change, 65

AI (artificial intelligence), 166

Albom, Mitch, 141–142, 146–147

alcohol abuse, 46

alcohol use, 130, 131, 175, 268

Aldwin, Carolyn, 210–211

Almeida, David, 216

Alter, Adam, 41

Alzheimer's disease
    hormone replacement therapy (HRT) and, 119
    inflammation and, 120, 121
    midlife overweight/obesity and, 267
    mindset about aging and, 44
    physical exercise and, 126

American College of Surgeons, 259

American Psychological Association, 172

amyloid deposits, 116

And Just Like That . . . (television show), 200–201

antidepressants, 108, 118
Antonucci, Toni, 170–171
anxiety, 14, 32, 36, 37, 45, 189, 217. *See also* mental health
The Anxious Generation (Haidt), 37
app, to help change parts of one's personality, 65, 66–67
Apted, Michael, 142
Asians, life expectancy and, 8
asthma, 121
The Atlantic, 33, 61
autoimmune disorders, 121
autopilot, turning off, 240–242

baby boomers, 4, 150
Baltes, Margret, 233
Baltes, Paul, 15–16, 233
Bandura, Albert, 241–242
The Beauty of Dusk (Bruni), 194
Becoming Grandma (Stahl), 256
behavior. *See also* lifestyle factors
impact of self-concept on, 63
mindset about aging impacting our, 45
personality app study and changes in, 68–69
behavior change methods, for physical activity, 126–129
Bergeman, Cindy, 182
Berkman, Lisa, 175
Berry, Anne, 89–90
Big Five personality traits, 56–57, 59–60, 64. *See also* specific traits
big-T time (historical time), 148–154
bilateral activation, 89
Bisson, Alycia, 127
Black population, life expectancy and, 8
Blanchflower, David, 33, 37
Blieszner, Rosemary, 189
blindness, 193–197
blood pressure, 44, 116, 189, 204, 214, 267
Blue Zones, 268, 269
BMI/waist circumference, 131, 267
bone loss/health, 116, 119, 198. *See also* osteoporosis
"boomerang kid," 174
Boston Roybal Center for Active Lifestyle Interventions, 126–127

brain
aging and changes in, 116
cognitive reserve in, 89–90
decision-making and the aging, 228–229
neuroplasticity and, 89
physical fitness in middle age related to later size of, 266
Brandeis University, 13. *See also* Lifespan Lab, Brandeis University
Breaking the Age Code (Levy), 43–44
Brim, Bert, 17
Bruni, Frank, 193–197, 208
Buettner, Dan, 268
Butler, Robert, 49

cancer
hormone replacement therapy (HRT) and, 119
inflammation, 122
physical exercise and, 126
telomere length of parents caring for their children with, 123
cardiovascular disease and changes, 44, 116, 119, 122, 203, 205
career. *See* work and career(s)
caregiving. *See also* parenthood and parenting
by grandparents, 256–257
of parent with cancer, 161–163
responsibilities of the sandwich generation, 163–164
telomere length and, 123
work-family balance and, 155–156
Carstensen, Laura, 139–140
cause and effect, 20
cellular aging, 122–123
centenarians, 268
Centers for Disease Control (CDC), 126, 172
Charles, Susan, 216
Chen, Edith, 204
childhood, adverse experiences in, 203–206
children. *See also* adult children; parenthood and parenting
changing relationship with their parents, 170

decision to have, 29
impact of overprotective parenting on,
    173–174
missing after they leave the house,
    73–74
parent's management of stress and,
    158–159
cholesterol, 116, 129, 130
Christakis, Nicholas, 188
chronic inflammation, 121–122, 123, 124
chronic stress, 121, 122, 205
cognitive abilities/decline. *See also*
    intelligence(s); memory and memory
    decline
    changing neurotic misconceptions and
        beliefs about, 67
    context-dependent factors related to,
        82–83
    engaging in activities for, 130
    older adults recognizing scams and, 166
    personality's impact on, 63–64
    pulmonary function in midlife and, 267
    retirement and, 263, 264
cognitive behavioral techniques, 67–68
cognitive reserve, 89–90
Cohen, Sheldon, 178
Columbine school shooting (1999), 150
compensation
    decision-making and, 21, 236, 239,
        241
    for decline in fluid intelligence, 80–84,
        89, 97
complexity paralysis, decision-making and,
    225–226
conscientiousness (personality trait), 57
    becoming more dependable and, 67
    benefits of, 62, 63
    changes in, 59–60, 61
    cognitive abilities and decrease in,
        63–64
    desire to increase, 66
    reasons for wanting to change, 65, 67
    resilience and, 212
constraints, 23, 82, 94, 95, 96, 97, 98,
    103, 128, 139, 145, 158, 230, 232,
    234, 237, 249
context, 10, 12, 20, 21, 56, 58, 83, 139,
    149, 154, 222, 225, 242

control, sense of, 94–103
    adaptive response and, 99–101
    decision-making and, 231, 235, 236
    decision-making and letting go of,
        242–243
    declining in later life, 249
    future time perspective and, 159–160
    importance of, as people age, 94–95
    major historical events and, 150
    managing regret and, 145, 147
    mitigating the effects of adverse
        childhood experiences with, 205–206
    over how you view midlife, 101–103
    perceived constraints and, 96
    personal mastery and, 95–96
    physical exercise and, 126
    planning for the future and, 97–98
    primary control, 98–99
    as psychosocial anti-inflammatory, 124,
        125
    as psychosocial prescription for healthy
        aging, 131
    secondary control, 98–99
    strength of, in midlife, 97
coping process, 214–215
cortisol, 125, 177
COVID-19 pandemic, 27, 36, 144, 150
C-reactive protein (CRP), 125
creativity, 88–90
cross-sectional studies, 16, 36, 81
crystallized intelligence, 79, 80, 81,
    82–83, 89, 92, 97
curveballs, 197, 198, 217, 279
    after a decision has been made, 236
    examples of, 199–200
    handling stress from, 213–215
    in popular culture, 200–201
    turning points through, 208–209
custodial grandparent, 257

dating, 30, 98, 135–136, 201
death(s)
    adult children losing their parents
        through, 167–168
    of author's mother, 275–276
    statistic on human behavior accounting
        for, 113
    unexpected, 200

Index

death(s) (*cont.*)
  unexpected (curveballs), 200–201,
    207–208
"deaths of despair," 14, 46
decision-making in midlife
  about a second career, 219–221
  being mindful about, 240–242
  conflict in goals and, 232, 233
  financial, 230–231
  going with the flow and, 242–243
  impact on others, 225–226
  neurological aspects of, 228–229
  in the "rush hour" of life, 226–227
  Selection, Optimization, Compensation
    (SOC) Model for, 232–239
  small, daily choices, 224–225
  time limitations and, 223–224
  turning off autopilot for, 240–242
  unique challenges during midlife,
    222–223, 228
dementia, 100, 116, 267. *See also*
  Alzheimer's disease
depression. *See also* mental health
  friendships and, 189
  myth about midlife crisis and, 46
  perimenopause and, 108, 110,
    111–112
  in younger generations, 37
developmental deadlines, 145–146
Diehl, Manfred, 252
diet, 63, 130, 201–202, 268
disease/disability, parenting a child with
  a, 172
divorce, 29–30, 40, 48, 70, 180, 208,
  211, 255–256
doctors and doctor visits, 116, 118,
  129–130
Doonesbury cartoon, 163, 171
dreams, fulfilling or giving up, 210
Dreyfus, Julia Louis, 249–250
drug overdoses, 46
Dunn, Jancee, 249

The Economist, 33
Elder, Glen, 149
Elderhostel, 270
emotional regulation, 144, 198, 212–213
emotional support, 185–186

emotion-focused approach to coping,
  214–215
emotions. *See also* happiness; regrets
  about aging, memory decline and, 45
  about turning 60, 245–246
  adverse childhood experiences and,
    203, 204–205
  coping process and, 214–215
  decision-making and, 224
  neuroticism and, 62
  social support and, 186
  unexpected life events and, 198
empty-nesting, 9, 73–75, 253–254
endorphins, 125
Epel, Elissa, 172
episodic memory, 85
Erikson, Erik, 15, 40–41, 179
estrogen, 110, 111, 112, 114, 117, 119,
  120
exercise. *See* physical activity/exercise
Experience Corps, 264–265
extroversion (personality trait), 57
  changing with age, 59–60
  cognitive abilities and decrease in,
    63–64
  desire to increase, 66
  impact of increasing, 61, 62
  making efforts to increase, 68
  psychotherapy changing, 65

family. *See also* parenthood and parenting
  caregiving by sandwich generation for,
    161–166
  empty-nesting, 73–75, 253–254
  grandparenthood, 256–258, 268
  kinkeepers in, 169–170
  loss of one's parents, 167–168
  regrets about not spending more time
    with, 142
  roles in, during midlife, 9
fatigue, 107–110
fatty liver disease, 121–122
fertility rate, 151
finances and financial difficulties
  decision-making and, 230
  impact on people living during the
    Great Depression, 149
  retirement and, 260–262

scams against older adults and, 166–167
flexibility, 19, 62, 98, 212
fluid intelligence, 79–82, 89, 90, 97, 231
Folkman, Susan, 213–214
Fonda, Jane, 272, 280
Franceschi, Claudio, 121
Freud, Sigmund, 15
Freund, Alexandra, 101
Fried, Linda, 265
friends(hips), 27–30, 155, 169, 184, 188–189, 209
future, planning for the, 97–98
future time perspective, 139–140, 159–160

gains and losses. *See also* cognitive abilities/decline; health and well-being; relationships
   with aging, 6, 7
   on the arc of the human lifespan, 5, 18
   cognitive restructuring techniques identifying faulty narratives about, 67–68
   dealing with work-related, 264–265
   individual differences in, 102
   in later adulthood, 252
   during midlife, 75–80, 101–103
   sense of control and, 94–95, 97, 101–103
   subjective age and, 252
   tradeoffs with, 76
   two intelligences and, 77–82
gain viewpoint on aging, 101
Galambos, Nancy, 35
Gallup poll, 155
gender
   kinkeeping and, 170
   life expectancy and, 8
generativity, 178
   about, 11–12, 168, 179
   impact of, 182–183
   opportunity for, in midlife, 168
   qualities of, 179–180
   through mentoring, 180–182
   through volunteering, 190–191
genetics, personality and, 57
Gen X, 4, 150, 173

Gen Z
   anxiety and depression among, 37, 159
   happiness of, 36
   parenting style of parents of, 173–174
Gerontological Society of America, 197
Gerstorf, Denis, 149–150
goals
   decision-making and conflicting, 232–233
   decision-making and facilitating, 233–234
   decision-making and modifying, 234
   optimizing what you have to achieve, 235
   "shelving," 147–148, 233, 238, 278
The Good Life (Waldinger), 177
Gould, Roger, 41
Graham, Eileen, 176
grandparenthood, 256–258, 268
"gray divorce," 255–256
Great Depression, 149
The Guardian, 33

Haidt, Jonathan, 37
happiness
   declining in one's late forties and early fifties, 33
   healthy relationships and, 177–178
   hedonic adaptation and, 38–39
   World Happiness Report (2024) on, 36
Have Faith Haiti Mission & Orphanage, 141
Haver, Mary Claire, 113
Health and Retirement Study, 78
health and well-being, 107–134. *See also* physical activity/exercise
   adverse childhood experiences and, 203, 204–205
   belief you can influence your, 129
   as determinant to conceptions on when old age begins, 251
   emotional support and, 186
   hallmarks of aging influencing, 114–117
   hormone replacement therapy (HRT) and, 118–120
   impact of myths about aging on, 43–45
   impact of not dealing with regret on, 144
   impact of who you spend time with on, 188–189
   importance of a sense of control for, 94–95

health and well-being (*cont.*)
  inflammation, 120, 121–123
  menopause, 117–120
  midlife changes and, 112–113
  negative viewpoint of middle age
    affecting, 4
  payoff of healthy habits in midlife for, 250
  perimenopause, 107–112
  personality/personality changes and,
    62, 69
  preventing problems in, 21
  psychosocial anti-inflammatories for,
    124–125
  retirement and, 263
  social isolation/weak social
    relationships and, 175–176
  social support and, 178
  steps for improving one's, 129–132
  super activities for, 269–270
  taking care of, 246–247
  unexpected life events related to,
    193–198
  variations in, after age sixty-five, 248
  views about gains and losses in later
    adulthood related to, 252
  wake-up call related to, 201–202
health span, 43–44, 124
hearing loss, 115
heart disease, 116, 126, 177, 204. *See also*
  cardiovascular disease and changes
Heckhausen, Jutta, 98, 145–146
hedonic adaptation, 38–39
Hershfield, Hal, 41, 261
Hispanics, life expectancy and, 8
historical influences, 20
historical time, 8, 148–154
Holt-Lunstad, Julianne, 176
hormonal changes, 114–115, 117, 119–120
hormone replacement therapy (HRT),
  111, 118–120, 246–247
hot flashes, 115, 117
HRT. *See* hormone replacement therapy
  (HRT)
human lifespan. *See also* late adulthood;
  midlife/middle age
  average happiness across, 38–39
  changes among friends in, 27–30
  gains and losses throughout, 5–6, 18

  impact of mindset about aging on, 43–44
  loneliness in, 176
  psychosocial struggles for stages during
    the, 179
  years added to, 250
hypertension, 205, 267

identity. *See also* self-concept
  about, 58
  changes in, 53, 60–61, 70
  exploration of, 59
  importance of reflecting on, 62
  matching the people and places in our
    lives, 69–71
  in midlife, 56
Ikaria, Greece, 268
implementation intentions, 127–129,
  132–134
inaction regrets, 143
infertility, 29, 70
infidelity, 195, 198, 256
inflammation
  acute, 121
  chronic, 121–122, 124
  estrogen and, 120
  health conditions related to, 121–122
  as predictor of later-life health, 266
  psychosocial inflammatories for, 123,
    124–125
  social support and, 178
  strained relationships and, 177
  stress and, 122–123
informational support, 185
Infurna, Frank, 149–150
innovative work (inventions), 90–92
instrumental support, 186
intelligence(s). *See also* cognitive abilities/
  decline; memory and memory decline
  crystallized, 79, 80, 81, 82–83, 89, 97
  fluid, 79–81, 89, 90, 97, 231
  how to leverage all of your, 93–94
intelligence tests, 80–82
interleukin 6 (IL-6), 125
introversion, 57, 68
inventors/inventions, 90–92

Jaffe, Adam, 90
Jagger, Mick, 271–272

Japan, 8, 44, 268
Jaques, Elliott, 32–33
John D. and Catherine T. MacArthur
  Foundation, 17
Johnson, Matthew, 35
Journal of Neuroinflammation, 120
Jung, Carl, 15

Kaltenberg, Mary, 90
Kiecolt, Glaser, Janice, 177
kinkeepers, 169–170
Kotb, Hoda, 141
Krahn, Harvey, 35

Laibson, David, 230
Langer, Ellen, 240–241
late adulthood. *See also* older adults
  conceptions on when you enter, 251
  concerns and questions about,
    247–248
  how we live midlife years impacting,
    250, 266–269
  importance of mindset about, 271–273
  life satisfaction in, 249–250
  new pursuits in, 250
  super activities during, 269–271
  transition into, 245–249
Lazarus, Richard, 213–214
Lee, Lewina, 206
Levinson, Daniel, 41, 50
Levy, Becca, 43–45, 272
libido, 114
Life Begins at Forty (Pitkin), 275
life expectancy, changes in average, 8
life reviews, 49–51
lifespan. *See* human lifespan
lifespan developmental perspective, 13
Life-span Developmental Psychology
  (Baltes), 15
Lifespan Lab, Brandeis University, 13, 64
  intergenerational team at, 92–93
  study of innovative work/inventions,
    90–92
lifespan perspective, 15–20, 248
lifestyle factors. *See also* physical activity/
    exercise
  in Blue Zones, 268
  having a sense of control about, 129

health/longevity and, 113
  for healthy aging, 129–131
  payoff of investing in healthy, 250
  super activities in late adulthood,
    269–271
locus of control, 96. *See also* control,
    sense of
Loma Linda, California, 268
loneliness, 14, 32, 36
  retirement and, 263
  sense of control and, 95
  solitude *vs.*, 189
  strained/poor relationships and, 177
  throughout the life course, 176
longitudinal studies. *See also* MIDUS
    (Midlife in the United States) study
  about, 16
  on Big Five personality traits, 59–60
  on cognitive abilities, 81
  on generativity, 182
  on happiness, 177–178
  on regret, 142
  on social isolation, 175–176
  Up film series, 142
  U-shaped study on happiness and, 39
losses. *See* gains and losses
loss viewpoint on aging, 101

MacArthur Foundation, 17, 278
maintenance viewpoint on aging, 101–102
Marco Polo (video-messaging app), 27–28
marriage(s). *See also* divorce
  after children leave the house, 255
  delay in, 139
  median age of, 151
  never too late for, 135–137
  taking time for evening walks in a,
    184–185
mastery, 23, 95–97, 125, 128, 174, 198,
    212, 216, 241, 249
Mayo Clinic, 120
McAdams, Dan, 179, 180
memory and memory decline
  adaptive response and, 100–101
  aging and, 84–85, 86–88
  concerns about, 77–78
  decline in, in the fifties into the sixties,
    83

memory and memory decline (*cont.*)
  different kinds of, 85–86
  episodic, 85
  factors impacting, 84
  fluid intelligence and working, 79
  MIDUS study on how people perceive,
    78
  for names, 84
  outlook about aging and, 45
  personality and self-rating of, 63
  working memory, 6, 79, 85, 87
menopause, 75. *See also* hormone
    replacement therapy (HRT)
  average age of, 117
  inflammation and, 120
  need for a renewed conversation about,
    120
  perimenopause, 107–112, 114–115,
    117, 120, 132
  symptoms of, 114, 117–118
Menopause, 118
mental health. *See also* control, sense of;
    depression
  adverse childhood experiences and, 204
  caregiving/parenting and, 172–173
  of more recent generations, 36–37
  myth of the midlife crisis and, 46
  of parents, importance of, 158–159,
    190
  social support in the workplace and,
    187
  of working women, 155
mentoring, 180–182, 187
metabolic disorders, 121–122
metamemory, 85–86
"middle"
  as desirable, 3–4
  negative connotations of, 3
midlife crisis, 12
  challenge and growth in, 40–41
  harm from myth of, 43–45
  importance of debunking myth on,
    45–47
  misunderstanding of, 31–32
  neuroticism and, 62
  as one of many transition periods,
    41–42
  origin of, 32–33

studies finding prevalence of, 34–35
  U-shape of happiness survey, 33–34,
    35–36
Midlife in the United States (MIDUS)
    study. *See* MIDUS (Midlife in the
    United States) study
midlife/middle age
  advantages of, 5–7
  age at beginning and end of, 7–10
  ascending the stairs into, 280
  author's research on, 277–278 .*See
    also* MIDUS (Midlife in the United
    States) study
  benefits of researching, 277
  both highs and lows experienced in, 38
  changing your personality and identity
    during, 64–69
  competing demands during, 12
  correcting the negative bias against,
    4–5, 7
  dismantling negative beliefs about,
    47–50
  gains and losses during. *See* gains and
    losses
  getting a handle of health and well-
    being during, 266–269
  health during. *See* health and well-being
  importance of mindset about,
    278–280
  individual different experiences in,
    28–30
  lasting for twenty to twenty-five years,
    249
  link to older and younger generations
    in, 11–12
  making connections between past and
    future in, 10–11
  on map of growth and decline in the
    human lifespan, 5–6
  negative viewpoint of, 3, 4, 7, 30–31
  people's sense of control over their life
    in, 97
  as a privilege, 276
  relationships in. *See* relationships
  research on, 16–17 .*See also* MIDUS
    (Midlife in the United States) study;
    research; studies
  rewriting the story of, 103–104

role of adults in, 9–10
saving for retirement in, 261
science of, 13–14
unexpected events and situations in. *See* unexpected life events
variations in when people conceive the end of, 251
your opportunities during, 22–23
midlife review, 49, 50–51
MIDMAC (Research Network on Successful Midlife Development), 17, 34
MIDUS (Midlife in the United States) study, 17–22, 142
on cognition, 83
on generativity, 179–180
on growing up in low socioeconomic circumstances, 204–205
on happiness during midlife, 39
of how people perceive their memory, 78
on memory decline and mindset about aging, 45
on midlife crisis, 34
on people's sense of control, 97
on personality and cognitive decline, 63–64
on turning points, 209–210
on value of physical activity, 269–270
on when people thought midlife ended, 251
Milkman, Katy, 157
millennials
characteristics of today's, 151–152
happiness of, 36
"helicopter parenting" and, 173
survey on midlife crisis by, 43
timing of major events for, 150, 151
Miller, Greg, 204
mindfulness, 240–241
mindset about aging and midlife. *See also* control, sense of
about late adulthood, 271–273
impact on health, 43–44
power of, 103, 278–279
when life throws you curveballs, 198–199, 213
Monitor on Psychology, 87

mood swings, 75, 108, 110, 117
mortality
hormone replacement therapy (HRT) and, 119
physical activity and, 126
sedentary lifestyle and, 269
social ties and, 175–176
telomere length and, 122
multigenerational connections, 268
muscle mass, 116, 122, 240, 269
musculoskeletal changes and disorders, 114, 122
Myers-Briggs personality test, 61
myths
about the midlife crisis, 31–39
of midlife stability, 49–50, 53–55, 60–61

National Research Council, 113
Native Americans, life expectancy and, 8
negative affect, 4
Nesselroade, John, 16
network (social), 11, 125, 130–131, 168, 170–171, 178, 207, 213, 246, 248, 268
Neugarten, Bernice, 60, 152
Neupert, Shevaun, 252
neurodegeneration, decision-making and, 229
neurodegenerative diseases, 121
Neurology, 87
neuroplasticity, 20, 89, 229–230
neuroticism (personality trait), 57
changing with age, 59–60
impact of scoring high in, 62, 63
impact on happiness by lowering, 61
as most wanted trait to decrease, 66
psychotherapy changing, 65
resilience and, 212
Newman, Catherine, 73
The New York Times, 33, 193, 249
Nicholson McBride Resilience Questionnaire, 212
night sweats, 117
NIH, MIDUS study and, 17
"9-enders," 41
nonnormative influences, 20, 200
Norway, average life expectancy in, 8

obesity, 175, 188, 205, 267
Okinawa, Japan, 268
older adults. *See also* late adulthood
  decision-making by, 229–230
  divorce among, 255–256
  financial decision-making by, 230, 231
  grandparenting by, 256–258
  looking back on midlife, 249–250
  mindset about aging, 272
  physical activity of, 269–270
  post-retirement plans, 247
  shifting roles in parenting, 253–255
  views on gains and losses, 252
Oliver, Mary, 22
openness to experience (personality trait),
    57, 60, 61, 62, 63
optimism
  mitigating the effects of adverse
    childhood experiences with, 205–206
  as psychosocial anti-inflammatory, 124
  as psychosocial prescription for healthy
    aging, 131, 273
  resilience and, 212
  telomere length and, 123
optimization, decision-making and, 21,
    235, 238–239, 241
osteoarthritis, 122, 126
osteoporosis, 119, 122, 198
Oswald, Andrew, 33
oxidative damage, 122–123
oxytocin, 125

parenthood and parenting. *See also* family
  curveball of, 29
  delay in, 139
  impact on mental health of parents,
    172–173
  investment and rewards from, 191
  median age for, 151
  overprotective parenting, 173–174
  regrets about, 141–142, 146–147
  rewards and benefits of, 191
  shifting roles in, for older adults,
    253–255
  step children, 137, 180
  stress and, 172
  support to and from children, 186
  work-family balance and, 150, 155–156

parents, adult children caring for their,
    161–163, 164
Park, Denise, 270
Parkinson's disease, 121
Passages: Predictable Crises of Adult Life
    (Sheehy), 34
patents, 90–92
perimenopause, 107–112, 114–115, 117,
    120, 132
personality. *See also* self-concept
  app helping people change their, 65,
    66–67
  behavior and, 57–58
  behavior changes driven by changes in,
    68–69
  BIG Five traits comprising, 56–57
  changing in midlife, 59–60
  definition, 56
  genetic and environmental factors
    related to, 57
  impact on health and longevity, 63–64
  impact on life satisfaction, 61–63
  importance of reflecting on, 62
  matching the people and places in our
    lives, 69–71
  in midlife, 56
  psychotherapy and changes in, 64–65
  reasons for wanting to change, 65
  self-concept and, 55, 56
  volitional personality change, 67
person-environment fit, 69–71
Pew Research, 163, 260
Phillips, Melissa Lee, 87
physical activity/exercise
  behavior change methods for, 126–
    129, 132–134
  benefits of, 126
  dementia and, 267
  diversity of, for older adults, 269–270
  during midlife, dementia related to,
    267
  mindset about aging and, 45
  personality shifts driving changes in,
    68–69
  as prescription for healthy aging, 131
  recommendations for, 126, 130
  retirement and, 264
  sense of agency/control and, 129

physical appearance, aging and changes in, 114
Piaget, Jean, 15
pilot study, 87–88
Pink, Dan, 143
Pitkin, Walter, 275
pivotal, 7, 72, 178, 196, 277
plasticity, 19, 20. *See also* neuroplasticity
Port-au-Prince orphanage, 141
positive affect
  helping people deal with adversity, 212
  in middle years, 4
  protecting against inflammation, 124, 125
  as psychosocial prescription for healthy aging, 273
  when achieving walking goals, 128
positive attitude
  as psychosocial anti-inflammatory, 125
  as psychosocial prescription for healthy aging, 131
positive images of aging, 43–44
positivity effect, 140
post-traumatic stress disorder, 217
The Power of Regret (Pink), 143
prediabetes diagnosis, 201–202
prefrontal cortex, 89, 229
pregnancy, 29. *See also* infertility
presbyopia, 115
primary control, 98–99
Primetime, 6. *See also* midlife/middle age
principle of historical time and place, 149
problem-focused approach to coping, 214
procedural memory, 85
prospective memory, 85
psychosocial anti-inflammatories, 123, 124–125
psychosocial factors for healthy aging, 131, 272–273
psychotherapy, personality traits changed through, 64–65
purpose and meaning
  adverse childhood experiences and, 205–206
  in life, 41, 125, 206, 265
  mitigating the effects of adverse childhood experiences with, 205–206

  as psychosocial anti-inflammatory, 124–125
  as psychosocial prescription for healthy aging, 131, 273

quarter-life crisis, 42

race, life expectancy and, 8
reaction time, 83, 115
Rebelsky, Freda, 15
recession of 2008, 150
regrets, 49
  about not having children, 141–142
  approaches to time and, 138, 139
  goal shelving and, 147–148
  historical time and, 148–154
  inaction *vs.* action, 143
  managing and dealing with, 143–147
  most common, 143
  re-visioning, 146–147
  studies on, 142–143
relationships. *See also* marriage(s); parenthood and parenting; social connections
  with both younger and older generations, 12
  breakup in, 29–30
  changes in the roles played in, 169–171
  curveballs related to, 195, 200
  friendships, 188–189
  giving and receiving support in, 183–187
  "growing apart" in, 70
  happiness and healthy, 177–178
  impact of personality on, 62
  infidelity in, 195
  loneliness and strained, 177
  loss of, through death, 200–201
  in one's "social convoy," 170–171
  with spouse after children leave the home, 74–75
  taking on new responsibilities in, 171–174
  types of, during midlife, 169
  types of support in, 185–186
reproductive system, aging and changes in, 114–115. *See also* menopause

research. *See also* studies; urveys
 on decision-making, 228–229
 on fluid intelligence, 80–81
 on midlife, 16–17, 277–278
 midlife crisis, 34
resilience. *See also* unexpected life events
 definition, 212
 emotional regulation and, 198
 emotion-focused approach to coping,
  214–215
 examples of, 193–197, 206–208
 examples of major life events needing,
  199–202
 post-traumatic growth and, 216
 problem-focused approach to coping,
  214
 psychosocial resources boosting,
  212–213
 when experiencing wake-up calls
  and curveballs during midlife,
  197–199
retirement, 42
 age at, 259–260
 age-based requirements for, 259
 financial considerations for, 260–261
 having a plan for, 265
 saving for, 268–269
 "super activities" in, 269–271
Road Scholar, 270
Roberts, Brent, 64–65
Robinson, Stephanie, 127
roles, 6, 8–10, 12, 56, 61, 150, 161,
  168–172, 175–177, 191,
  210, 253
Rotter, Julian, 96
Rutter, Michael, 212

Salthouse, Timothy, 82
sandwich generation, 163–164
sarcopenia, 122, 269
Sauer-Zavala, Shannon, 67
scams, 166–167
Schaie, K. Warner, 16, 81
screening tests, 129–130
secondary control, 98–99
sedentary behavior, 126–127, 260, 269
seesaw effect, 19
selection, decision-making and, 21

Selection, Optimization, Compensation
  (SOC) Model
 benefits of, 236–237
 explained, 232–236
 how to use in daily life, 237–238
self-concept, 55–56. *See also* identity;
  personality
 becoming stable in our fifties, 71–72
 in flux during midlife, 60–61
Seniors Helping Seniors, 270
sense of control. *See* control, sense of
sensory systems, 115
September 11th terrorist attack, 150
serendipitous events, 241–242
Sex and the City (television show), 200
Sheehy, Gail, 34
"shelve it," 147–148, 160, 224
shortness of breath, 115
Silent Generation, 150
skin, changes in the, 114
sleep, 108–109
 aging and changes in, 115
 for healthy aging, 131
 recommendations, 130
sleep apnea, 118, 122
smoking, 130, 131, 162, 188, 268
"snowplow parents," 173
social activity, mindset about aging and, 45
social connections
 balancing social strain with, 183–185
 having too little, 175–177
 importance of, 177–178
 multigenerational, 268
 as psychosocial anti-inflammatory,
  124–125
 as psychosocial prescription for healthy
  aging, 131, 273
 retirement and work-related losses
  related to, 264
 through volunteering, 190–191
social convoy, 170–171
social integration, 125, 190–191
social isolation, 175–177
social responsibilities
 balancing social connections with,
  183–185
 caring for a parent with cancer,
  161–163

increasing during midlife, 171–172
for the sandwich generation, 163–164
Social Security, 259, 261
social strain, 183–184, 185, 186
social support
    balance between giving and receiving
        in, 183–185, 187
    balancing social strain with, 185
    coping process and, 215
    emotional aspects of, 186
    resilience and, 212, 213
    by those who cause the most strain,
        186–187
    three types of, 185–186
    through friends, 188–189
socioeconomic status, impact of low,
    204–205
SOC (Selection, Optimization, and
    Compensation) model, 20–21
solitude, 189–190
Stability, Myth of, 54–55
Stahl, Lesley, 256
staircase, 272, 280
Stanford Center for Advanced Study in
    the Behavioral Sciences, 278
stepchildren, 137, 180
stereotypes, 12, 32, 45, 92, 253, 271
Stieger, Mirjam, 64–65
Streep, Meryl, 253
strength training, 269
stress
    adverse childhood experiences and,
        205
    decreasing psychosocial, 124–125
    inflammation and, 122–123
    managing, 158
    parenting and, 172
    post-traumatic stress disorder, 217
    reducing for healthy aging, 131
    resilience and, 213–215
    telomere length and, 122–123
    three aspects of stress process, 214
    upside of, 215–217
    work-family balance and, 155–156
stress hormones, 125, 146, 177
stress inoculation theory, 216
stressors, major life. *See* unexpected life
    events

studies. *See also* MIDUS (Midlife in
    the United States) study; research;
    surveys
    Experience Corps., 264–265
    on financial decision-making, 230–231
    on identity, 60
    on personality, 57
    on personality change using an app,
        65–66
    on regrets, 142–143
    on retirement, 263
    on sandwich generation, 164
    on social isolation, 175–176
    U-shape of happiness survey, 35–36, 39
subjective age, 251–252
subjective memory, 63
suicide, 14, 46
sunscreen, 131
surveys
    on average ages of midlife, 9
    on experience of midlife crisis, 43
    on happiness during midlife, 33, 34–35
    on regret (Dan Pink), 143
    on stress, 172
    World Happiness Report (2024), 36
Syme, S. Leonard, 175

Tale of Two Intelligences, 79–80
tau deposits, 116
telomere length, 172
    caregiving and, 123
    cellular aging and, 122
    factors related to, 123
    longevity and, 245
    parenting a sick child and, 172
    physical activity and, 126
"the Third Act," 248, 250. *See also* late
    adulthood
time
    alone, 189–190
    decision-making and limited, 223–224
    different approaches to, 138–139
    impact of historical, 148–154
    importance of parents managing,
        158–159
    managing unfortunate side effects of,
        159–160
    not having enough, 154–156

time (*cont.*)
  study on future time perspective, 139–140
  temptation bundling for managing one's, 156–158
  timing of milestones in adulthood, 152–153
tobacco products, 130. *See also* smoking
toxins and chemicals, 121
trauma, childhood, 203–206
travel, 270
T-shirt illustration, 279–280
twin studies, 57
type 2 diabetes, 119, 121

unexpected life events
  as an opportunity for growth, 198–199
  causing extreme stress or trauma, 217
  curveballs, 199–201
  dealing with, 202
  digging up adverse childhood experiences, 203–206
  examples of, 193–197, 206–208
  handling stress from, 213–215
  power of resilience for, 211–213
  turning points and, 206–211
  upside of stress from, 215–217
  wake-up calls, 201–202
United Kingdom, average life expectancy in, 8
University of Michigan, 164
University of Michigan Survey Research Center, 78
Up film series, 142
U-shape of Happiness survey, 33, 35–36, 39
U.S. Patent and Trademark Office, 90
US Surgeon General, 172, 176

vision loss, 193–197
vitamin D deficiency, 111
volitional personality change, 67
volunteering, 268
  at an orphanage, 141–142
  generativity and, 190–191
  in late adulthood, 257
  modifying your goals by, 145

  as a super activity in late adulthood, 270–271
  when dealing with work-related losses, 264–265

wake-up calls, 197, 217
  about, 201
  as a blessing in disguise, 198
  related to one's health, 201–202
Waldinger, Robert, 177
Wang, Mo, 262
The Washington Post, 33
White population, life expectancy and, 8
Winfrey, Oprah, 253
wisdom, 5–7, 11–12, 76, 80–81, 95, 171, 178, 183, 272, 279
Wiser Than Me (podcast), 249
Women's Health Initiative, 119
work and career(s)
  after age 60, 246
  balance with family, 150, 155–156
  changes in preferences for, 71
  compensation strategies for dealing with health-related issues at, 239
  decision-making and, 219–221, 223–224, 233–234
  differences among experiences with, 28–29
  goal shelving for changing, 237–238
  intergenerational cooperation for, 92–93
  menopausal symptoms and missed days at, 120
  optimizing skills for, 238–239
  retirement and, 258–265
  role in, during midlife, 9
  turning points in, 206–207, 209, 210
working memory, 6, 79, 85, 87
World Happiness Report (2024), 36
Wrosch, Carsten, 144

young adults/adulthood. *See also* Gen Z; millennials
  decision-making and, 229–230
  focus on gains *vs.* losses in their life, 101
  happiness of, 36–37
  loneliness in, 176

About the Author

Margie Lachman, PhD, is the Minnie and Harold Fierman Professor of Psychology at Brandeis University, where she directs the Lifespan Lab. She earned her AB from Boston University and her MS and PhD from The Pennsylvania State University. A leading expert on adult development and aging, Lachman is one of a small group of scholars who study midlife from a lifespan developmental perspective. Her honors include research awards from the American Psychological Association (APA) and the Gerontological Society of America. She has authored numerous scholarly articles and co-edited key volumes, including *Multiple Paths of Midlife Development* (1997), *Handbook of Midlife Development* (2001), and the forthcoming APA *Handbook on Adult Development and Aging.* Lachman was a member of the John D. and Catherine T. MacArthur Foundation Research Network on Successful Midlife Development, which launched the landmark *Midlife in the United States (MIDUS)* study. She is a co-investigator on MIDUS and several other projects exploring cognition, health, and well-being in midlife and later adulthood. At Brandeis, she teaches courses on adult development and aging and lifespan psychology.